SRI LANKA
PEACE WITHOUT PROCESS

SRI LANKA
PEACE WITHOUT PROCESS

EDITED BY B.RAMAN, N SATHIYA MOORTHY

AND

KALPANA CHITTARANJAN

WITH

AN OVERVIEW BY S. D. MUNI

SAMSKRITI

in Association with

OBSERVER RESEARCH FOUNDATION

SAṀSKṚITI

C-9020, Vasant Kunj, New Delhi - 110070

ISBN : 81-87374-47-0

Observer Research Foundation is a public policy think-tank that aims to influence formulation of policies for building a strong and prosperous India. ORF pursues these goals by providing informed and productive inputs, in-depth research and stimulating discussions. The Foundation is supported in its mission by a cross-section of India's leading public figures, academic and business leaders.

Typeset by Roma Chakraborty, D-630, Chittaranjan Park, New Delhi Printed by Bengal Book Binder, Okhla Industrial Area,, New Delhi Published by M. Sengupta for SAṀSKṚITI, New Delhi in association with the Observer Research Foundation, New Delhi.

CONTENTS

PREFACE

The Chennai Chapter of the Observer Research Foundation (ORF) organised a one-day seminar at Chennai on the 27 September 2003, on the subject of "SRI LANKA: CEASEFIRE AND AFTER". Participants at the seminar included academics, journalists, experts and others from Sri Lanka and India. The proceedings of the seminar, consisting of the papers presented and the views expressed, are compiled in this monograph, for ready reference and for providing insight into the evolving situation in the island-nation.

This was the first seminar of its kind organised by the Chennai Chapter of ORF following its inauguration on December 19, 2002. Mr.B. Raman, former Additional Secretary, Cabinet Secretariat, Government of India and Convenor, ORF, Chennai Chapter, has written the Introduction to the monograph.

The Chennai Chapter has been focussing on developments in Sri Lanka and, subsequently, in South-East Asia. It has been studying in-depth, the political, economic, military and other developments in the island-nation. The seminar was part of this effort, to focus attention on the various aspects of the Sri Lankan peace process, and their impact on the ground situation.

For this purpose, the seminar was divided into four sessions to cover

- Ground Realities
- Reconciling Various Ethnic Aspirations
- Intentions and Capabilities of the Sri Lankan Government as well as the LTTE, and
- Role of External Powers

In each session, the discussions were led by a renowned Sri Lankan scholar. This was followed by a presentation of the Indian perspective by eminent Indian analysts, and also interactive discussions with the members of the audience. Thus, each subject was analysed from the Indian as well as the Sri Lankan perspective in order to have a clearer understanding of the situation.

Vice-Admiral (retd) K.K.Nayyar, President, ORF, and Member, National Security Advisory Board, stated in his inaugural address, "Sri Lanka is not just another neighbour of India. Our culture, our history and, what is more important, our future are very deeply linked with this great neighbour of ours. Everything that happens there deeply impinges on us. To a certain extent, the other way around is also true." The problem, Admiral Nayyar said, not only in Sri Lanka but increasingly so in many parts of the world, is that "some of the instrumentalities that were shaped to fight the Cold War are now coming to affect areas in totally unexpected ways. Ethnicity is one of them. It is moving towards undoing some of the political consolidation work of the previous century."

He quoted former US President Bill Clinton's allusion to this happening in his famous Ottawa speech, on the Canadian Separatist Movement: "If we are to divide all the countries on ethnic lines, we would end up with something like 8000 political entities. This would clearly be bedlam, which is unexpected. In this day and age, where economic globalisation calls for bigger and more effective political units, anything which takes us not one step, but 10 steps backwards, and breaks the world on virtually tribal basis would be a retrograde step and an unacceptable situation."

This volume, *Sri Lanka : Peace without Process* comprises four main chapters, covering the four sessions of the seminar. Each section also comprises a brief summary of the inter-active discussions, involving the participants at the seminar. M. Rasgotra, former Foreign Secretary, who chaired the proceedings of the day, gave useful insights and comments, and these have been used at appropriate places in the volume. N. Sathiya Moorthy, Honorary Director, ORF-Chennai, and Dr Kalpana Chittaranjan, Research Fellow, ORF-Chennai, have provided additional inputs in two separate chapters.

Some of the papers presented at the seminar have been updated. We requested Prof. S.D. Muni to write an overview to update and put in perspective the dynamics of the Sri Lanka peace process. We have also included an article by B. Raman on "The Tsunami and the LTTE" in our effort to update the publication.

It is hoped that this volume will add to the existing knowledge on Sri Lanka and contribute to a better understanding of the peace process.

INTRODUCTION

The talks between the Government of Sri Lanka and the Liberation Tigers of Tamil Eelam (LTTE), which have been in a state of suspension since April 2003, have been followed with great interest and anxiety not only by the Governments of India and Tamil Nadu, but also by the public of Tamil Nadu.

The interest arises from the historic, economic and cultural links that bind India and Sri Lanka, the island's importance from the point of view of India's national security and also the anxiety from what appears to be the single-minded determination of the LTTE to achieve its objective of enforcing its effective control over the interim administration that is proposed to be set up in the Northern and Eastern Provinces of Sri Lanka even before a final settlement is reached.

The anxiety also arises from the manner in which Norway has been performing its dual role as the facilitator of the peace process and as the head of the mechanism that has been set up to monitor the implementation of the Ceasefire Agreement between the Sri Lankan Government and the LTTE. Also of concern is the unfortunate lack of a convergence of views between President Chandrika Kumaratunga and then Prime

Minister Ranil Wickremesinghe over the Government's strategy in the peace talks.

An impression was gaining ground that the Prime Minister, in his over-anxiety to keep the peace process going, was overlooking instances of alleged violations of the Ceasefire Agreement by the LTTE, particularly in the Eastern Province, and neglecting the important task of keeping the fighting capability of the Sri Lankan armed forces in order to be able to meet any eventuality. This would have been particularly so if the LTTE, frustrated by its failure to achieve its apparent objective of a virtually free "Tamil homeland", with its own army, navy and police, behind a federal facade, broke the Ceasefire Agreement, and resumed its military-cum-terrorist operations. It needs to be noted that despite its oft-proclaimed faith in the peace process, the LTTE has resisted pressure from the US and the rest of the international community to renounce its use of terrorism to achieve its political objective.

While the LTTE has not hesitated to strengthen itself by clandestinely procuring arms and ammunition abroad, and by making fresh recruitment, a similar attempt by the Government to strengthen its position has been lacking. Its reluctance to highlight and counter the LTTE's attempts to take advantage of the ceasefire to strengthen its position in the Trincomalee area of the Eastern Province has been a matter of concern not only to the Sri Lankan President and her advisers, but also to India, though this concern has not been openly articulated by New Delhi. Of equal concern are reports of a possible radicalisation of sections of the Muslim youth in the Eastern Province due to allegations of the high-handed behaviour of the LTTE cadres towards the Muslim community.

Apart from repeatedly reiterating its interest in an ultimate solution which would preserve the unity and the territorial integrity of Sri Lanka even while meeting the reasonable demands of the Sri Lankan Tamils, and encouraging Colombo to persist in its search for a political solution to the problems of the Tamils through negotiations, the Government of India has rightly refrained from too overt and active a role in matters concerning the peace process lest such a role should be misinterpreted as interventionist and prove counter-productive.

However, the lack of an overtly activist policy by the Government of India should not be misinterpreted to mean that New Delhi is disinterested in what is happening, or could happen in Sri Lanka. Any development in Sri Lanka that could weaken its unity and territorial integrity, and provide a fertile soil to elements that could create instability in that country and damage its relations with India, would be of great concern to India. New Delhi will have to have a lucid understanding of the various options available to it in the eventuality of the developments in the peace process taking a turn detrimental to India's national interests and security.

B. Raman
Distinguished Fellow, ORF,
Convenor, ORF Chennai Chapter

Peace Without Process : Sri Lanka's Dilemma

S.D.Muni

Sri Lanka's peace process to resolve the Tamil ethnic issue is passing through a critical phase. There is widespread anxiety that continuing drift in the political situation and the persistent delay in the resumption of the dialogue between the Sri Lankan Government and the LTTE may lead to renewal of hostilities and breakdown of the ceasefire. Many people fear, particularly after Liberation Tigers of Tamil Eelam (LTTE) leader Prabhakaran's Hero's Day speech on 27 November, 2004, in which he threatened to strike again, that war is imminent. Such fears have been further strengthened after the Government's strong reaction to Prabhakaran's speech that it will not accept threats and conditions for starting talks. Given this situation, so long as there are no political negotiations for resolving the ethnic conflict, Sri Lanka is likely to witness "peace without process", which may also be seen as a situation of "no peace, no war", or "negative peace".

Soon after coming to power, the United National Front government of Ranil Wickremesinghe launched the "peace process" by entering into a formal and elaborate Cease-Fire

Agreement (CFA) with the LTTE on 23 February, 2002 under Norwegian facilitation. This initiative led to six rounds of talks between the Government and the LTTE at various locations in Thailand, Norway and Japan, and continued for a period of about six months, starting in September 2002. In April 2003, the LTTE unilaterally withdrew itself from the negotiations when they suspected that substantive political issues were to come up on the table where they would have to make a commitment to a final negotiated settlement in the face of growing international pressure. The LTTE withdrew from the Sub-Committee on Humanitarian and Rehabilitation Needs in the North and the East, but kept its commitment to peace by promising to abide by the CFA. LTTE leaders described their action as a "reaction to their exclusion from the Washington Conference of donors on 15 April", a precursor to the Tokyo Conference in June 2003.

The Tokyo Conference not only promised a huge aid package, amounting to US $4.5 bn, to Sri Lanka, for relief and rehabilitation work in the conflict-affected north-eastern region, but made this assistance conditional on the continuation of peace process and its monitoring by the international community. Accordingly, the flow of international assistance for reconstruction and rehabilitation was linked to the compliance of LTTE to maintenance of peace and progress towards a final resolution of the conflict. Moreover, the US has not removed the LTTE from its list of terrorist organisations, and for good reasons, as explained by the US Deputy Secretary of State Richard Armitage when he said that the LTTE was an "organisation best known for pioneering the practice of turning its sons and daughters into human bombs".[1] The only positive move made by the LTTE since its withdrawal

1. Text of Armitage's speech at the Tokyo Conference on 10 June, 2003 http:/news.tamilnet.com/print.httml?artid-9170&catid=13

from the talks has been the presentation of its proposals on "Interim Self-Governing Authority (ISGA) in October 2003. The ISGA proposals were put forward by the LTTE after it rejected three proposals of the Sri Lankan Government on interim arrangement for the North-East, describing them as "unsatisfactory". Since then, the LTTE has refused to negotiate on anything except its ISGA proposals, saying that any further talks on a final settlement were possible only after its version of the ISGA was "instituted and made functional."

Politics of the Peace Process

In order to understand the continuing stalemate, it is necessary to look at the political dynamics behind the peace process. One obvious consideration behind the Wickremesinghe Government's desire to install a peace process was to restore peace, so keenly desired by the people of Sri Lanka, including its business community that formed a powerful part of the ruling United National Front's (UNF) political constituency. There has also been considerable international pressure as well as support for peace, and no Sri Lankan Government can afford to ignore these pressures. But in instituting the peace process, Wickremesinghe was also driven by his core political goal, of marginalizing his rival Chandrika Kumaratunga and her People's Alliance (PA). Wickremesinghe's political calculations, perhaps, were that if the peace process could be sustained for a period of three to four years, he and his party would get a formidable political advantage, both in terms of Sinhala as well as Tamil support for the next presidential elections when Chandrika Kumaratunga, having completed her two presidential terms, would not be constitutionally eligible to contest. Since there is no strong political contender in the PA to challenge him, Wickremesinghe reckoned that he and his United National Party (UNP) could have a long innings in power.

Wickremesinghe's strategy for sustaining the peace process had two dimensions: keep the LTTE in good humour and thus engaged, and mobilize international support to safeguard his regime from any undue pressures from the LTTE or PA. Considerable ground was conceded to the LTTE in accordance with the first part of the strategy. It is pertinent to note that traditionally the UNP has always depended on the Tamil votes from the North and the East in its electoral calculations. There was no doubt that the LTTE, if kept accommodated, could deliver the chunk of the northern and eastern Tamil votes to the UNP, as seemed the case during the January 2002 elections.

The Wickremesinghe government's accommodation of the LTTE was clearly evident in the structure of the CFA, in which the Government and the LTTE were treated as two equal parties and a "balance of forces" between them was recognized as a necessary condition for the maintenance of peace. Some of the CFA provisions were strongly opposed by Kumaratunga's People Alliance. Prime Minister Wickremesinghe's political motives were clearly reflected in his move to keep President Kumaratunga completely out of the CFA negotiations. The President was informed about the CFA provisions less than 24 hours before the agreement was signed. This was politically undesirable and constitutionally inappropriate in view of the constitutional position of the Executive President, particularly in the area of conflict-resolution by the State of Sri Lanka, where the President holds all the authority. The President and her party strongly objected to the manner in which the CFA was concluded, and the President in her letter to the Prime Minister within a week of signing of the agreement underlined those CFA provisions that were incompatible with Sri Lanka's constitutional requirements and security imperatives.

The CFA recognized the LTTE as the sole representative of the Tamil people and gave the LTTE legitimacy as a political force at par with the Sri Lankan Government.

Wickremesinghe's Government also accepted the rather curious formulation advanced by the LTTE of the right to "internal self-determination" by the Tamils. Inherent in this right is that while the Tamils will not form a separate State, they will also not accept any control or restraint by the Sri Lankan authorities in their affairs. The CFA also underlines a certain military balance between the Sri Lankan state and the LTTE on the ground in the north-eastern region. During the past two years, the LTTE has continued to violate this "balance of forces" principle of the CFA by enhancing it military strength through recruitments, including of child soldiers, and acquisition of arms.

According to some estimates, the military strength of the LTTE has grown from 9,000 to 19,000 fighters. The LTTE ships have brought in arms from South-East Asian and other countries. The LTTE has also fortified its position in the eastern region, with particular focus on Trincomalee harbour, the Sri Lankan navy's main base in the region, where the Tigers have the capability to launch an offensive at any time.[2] The President of Sri Lanka had alleged in October 2003 that weapons carrying ships of the LTTE (Sea Tigers) had disappeared after being spotted because the norwegian facilitators had alerted the Tigers. Wickremesinghe's Government was also pressured by the LTTE to relax the "High Security Zone" of the Sri Lankan forces created under CFA. Although some of Prime Minister Wickremesinghe's advisers appeared sympathetic to this demand of the LTTE, it was not accepted by the Government following the advice of a retired

---

[2] On the precarious security situation in Trincomalee, see, Iqbal Athas, "Situation Report: Security Alarm Over Tiger Rise in East", *The Sunday Times*, (Colombo), August 10, 2003. The Sri Lankan navy had prepared a detailed brief on this situation which was explained by the President's Adviser on International Affairs, Lakshman Kadirgamar in Sri Lanka as well as in India.

[3] Author's interviews in Prime Minister Wickramasinghe's office in Colombo, July 2003.

Indian Army General, who was contacted unofficially[3] to advise the Sri Lankan Government on this complex issue.

Wickremesinghe enjoyed considerable support from the international community, including the US, UK, EU and Japan. India was also kept well informed and in good humour by frequent official and informal consultations, as well as high-level visits. Wickremesinghe's confidant, Milind Murugoda, had frequent but low-key consultations with India's then National Security Adviser that were taken note of in the Indian media. The "international community" had formed itself into a donors' club, and after two meetings in Washington and Tokyo in April and June 2003, respectively, promised an impressive package of economic assistance to Sri Lanka as noted earlier. Of the total amount of US $4.5 bn, one-third was earmarked for the North-East areas. In all, about 90 per cent of this assistance will be in the form of loans to be extended by the World Bank. This package is clearly conditional on the continuation of the peace process and its links with the final settlement as mentioned earlier. The Tokyo Declaration of 10 June, 2003, accordingly asked for any "provisional administrative structure" for "reconstruction and development" to be linked to a "roadmap with clear milestones indicating the path towards a mutually acceptable final political solution."

The international community also undertook to 'review and monitor' such a 'peace process closely, with particular reference to' 'compliance with the cease-fire agreement', 'participation of Muslims', 'effective promotion and protection of human rights', and 'a phased, balanced, and verifiable de-escalation, de-militarization and normalization process…(for) 'arriving at a political settlement'. The international direct involvement in the peace process was considered by the Wickremesinghe Government as the 'international safety net' and made the Government confident that while it deterred the

LTTE from taking recourse to war, it would also help the Prime Minister to politically checkmate the People's Alliance.

If the Wickremesinghe Government was really sincere in seeking a lasting political settlement with the LTTE, it could not afford to ignore the opposition PA. Political and electoral dynamics as also the constitutional constraints in Sri Lanka are such that any settlement with the LTTE to be lasting should have all the mainstream Sinhala parties on board. This fact was clearly understood by President Chandrika Kumaratunga. The LTTE has also been repeatedly pointing to the fact that the divisions among the Sinhala parties are frustrating the search for legitimate rights and security in Sri Lanka. It may be recalled here that during 1999-2000, President Chandrika Kumaratunga, while trying to grant devolution of powers to the Tamil areas, had taken the then opposition party of Wickremesinghe into confidence on the devolution package.

As a result of these consultations, almost 80 per cent of the devolution package, as then proposed by President Kumaratunga's Government under the "Draft Constitution 2000", had been mutually agreed upon between the two mainstream parties. It could not be adopted as the Constitution because of differences between them on the issues relating to transfer of power and change of the system from presidential to a parliamentary one. Wickremesinghe could have displayed statesmanship by taking the President and her party into confidence on the peace process. This would have strengthened his own bargaining position *vis-à-vis* the LTTE because the Oslo Declaration of 25 November, 2002 had clearly underlined the critical role of "a national consensus on the need for a final settlement."

If Wickremesinghe's strategy was to marginalize President Chandrika Kumaratunga and her People's Alliance, the political imperative of the President was to not let this process go further. She made her political move on 4 November, 2003 by taking over the portfolios of Defence, Interior and Mass Communication under her personal charge to fulfill her constitutional obligation to safeguard the country's security and sovereignty. This disturbed the uneasy "co-habitation" between the President and the Prime Minister and led to the dissolution of Parliament and fresh elections in April 2004. This has completely altered the political context of the peace process.

Changed Political Context

While the ruling UNF of Wickremesinghe, which made the "peace process" its main election plank and claimed the sustained ceasefire as its major achievement, was defeated in the parliamentary elections of April 2004, there was no clear majority for President Chandrika Kumaratunga's People's Alliance (PA). The UNF's defeat was an indication that the way the peace process had been carried out was not acceptable to the Sinhala majority. The benefits of the peace process had not reached the people in concrete terms, in both the Sinhalese as well as the Tamil-dominated areas. The notable outcome of the elections was the consolidation of both the Sinhalese as well as the Tamil extremist positions, respectively, since the middle ground represented by the mainstream Sinhala and non-LTTE Tamil parties stood fragmented.

On the Tamil side, the Tamil National Alliance (TNA) under the domination of the LTTE emerged victorious, gaining 22 seats. Outside the LTTE's area of dominance, the Ceylon Workers Congress (CWC) of the estate sector won nine seats, and one seat in the LTTE-dominated North was won by the Eelam People's Democratic Party (EPDP). On the Sinhala side, the left-wing Janatha Vimukti Peramuna (JVP) emerged as a strong force within the PA, securing 39 seats. Outside PA, the right-wing monks' party, the Jatiya Hella Urumaya (JHU) secured nine seats. Both the JVP and the JHU have strong positions against any compromise on Sinhala domination and, therefore, are not in favour of any substantial accommodation of the Tamil demands. This is notwithstanding a small window of opportunity left by the JVP under its alliance commitment with the President's SLFP—the major partner in the PA—that the JVP will accept a compromise on the ethnic issue if all parties supported it.

After initial hiccups, the PA has managed to secure a workable majority in Parliament with the support of the CWC and a section of the Muslim parliamentarians belonging to the Sri Lanka Muslim Congress (SLMC). However, the ruling party remains far from being in a position of a two-thirds majority, required for any major constitutional change to accommodate the LTTE demands. The Wickremesinghe-led UNF, which is the main opposition party, in a tactical move promised to support any agreement reached between the Sri Lankan Government and the LTTE. However, it remains to be seen whether this promise will be kept when, and if, there is such an agreement. On the whole, therefore, the political centre in Colombo continues to remain weak and fragmented to the detriment of the peace process. Before the elections the rivalry between the mainstream Sinhalese parties, and the ruling UNF's decision to keep the PA excluded from this process, was the principle constraint. After the elections, the pressures put by the JVP within the PA and the persisting contentious politics between the PA and the UNF have kept the establishment in Colombo less confident of pushing forward the peace process.

And yet, President Kumaratunga and her party are keen on advancing the peace process by engaging the LTTE in negotiations for both an interim administration as well as a final settlement. There are various factors behind this keenness. To begin with, inspired by her father and husband, the late S.W.R.D. Bandaranaike and Vijay Kumaratunga, respectively, President Kumaratunga is perhaps the only known Sinhala leader who is sincerely committed to giving the Tamils a fair deal. This was evident throughout the Eighties when she, along with her late husband, courageously spoke for the rights of the Tamils in the midst of intense ethnic tensions. She also put forth one of the most liberal packages of devolution soon after her first presidential election in 1994. That package has subsequently been diluted under internal political pressures, but even the diluted package as formalized in the form of constitutional proposals in 2000 is more accommodating of the Tamils than any other proposals put forwarded by any Sinhala leader.

There are also international pressures and promises. The Sri Lankan economy is under a severe resource crunch. President Kumaratunga would like to utilize the aid package offered by the donors by starting peace talks with the LTTE. She would like to alter the erroneous perception of her domestic adversaries as well as the international community that she is not committed to peace and ethnic conflict resolution. This perception is the legacy of her war with the LTTE during 1995-2000, which in a way was thrust upon her by the LTTE at a time when she was naively hopeful of starting serious negotiations with the LTTE.

Chandrika's stakes in advancing the peace process may also not be bereft of her own political considerations for the future. She will be completing two presidential terms in 2006. The Constitution does not permit her a third term. The only way she can remain in active politics is through the transformation of Sri Lanka's political system, from executive presidency to parliamentary governance. This major constitutional change would allow her to contest for a parliamentary majority of her party and prime ministership for herself. It may, therefore, not be unreasonable to assume that by starting the peace process she could secure the support of the Tamils and the greater goodwill of the Sinhala masses to be able to strengthen her political position to initiate a major constitutional change, through a parliamentary process as well as a referendum. "It could be a quasi-constitutional possibility of changing the Constitution," as she put in her own words.[4]

In view of these stakes, President Kumaratunga and her PA have diluted their known stance towards the LTTE. She was opposed to the CFA, but has accepted it. She also had strong reservations in accepting the LTTE as the sole representatives of Tamils but even accepted this position, ignoring the reservations of her Tamil ally in the Government, the EPDP. She also had strong reservations on ISGA and her initial position was to talk to the LTTE not on the basis of ISGA alone, but along with a parallel proposal by her Government on an "interim administration for the North-East". Her reservations on this count have also been softened as she may be willing to start the talks on ISGA alone if the LTTE agrees to include her Government's proposals for consideration at the second round or even later stages. President Kumaratunga has also avoided bruising the LTTE's sensitivities in other areas.

One of the important pointers in this respect has been the response of the Sri Lankan Government towards 'Colonel' Karuna, the LTTE rebel leader who posed a challenge to Prabhakaran. After the initial confusion regarding the alleged support provided to Karuna by the Sri Lankan army, it has become clear that this internal conflict within the LTTE has

[4] See President Kumaratunga's interview, *The Hindu*, 11 November, 2004.

not been exploited, lest it should mar the prospects of talks. The LTTE, however, is sore on this front and has also accused the Sri Lankan Government of duplicity on the Karuna issue, but public posturing notwithstanding, the LTTE seems to accept that by and large, the Sri Lankan Government has kept itself away from Karuna. President Kumaratunga in her public statements has also been soft on LTTE. In her recent interview to an Indian daily, she said: "Nothing moves along unilateral lines. The LTTE also has changed a lot, as you know…they have opened up to the world. For the first time, they have gone on with a ceasefire agreement, with violations. But at least it is adhered to, I would say 70 per cent for a long period of time…the LTTE has also become sensitive to its people's needs to some extent, though they were not till now. The LTTE kept refusing all my offers for development of the North-East all the time, but now they don't."[5]

Despite these overtures, the prospects of talks do not appear to be promising, particularly after Prabhakaran's 'Hero's Day' speech, in which he refused to budge from his position on the peace talks.

The LTTE is also feeling the pressure in favour of talks. The persisting stalemate of 'no war no, peace' does not suit the LTTE politically. Nearly three years of ceasefire have not given any material advantage either to the LTTE leadership or to the people under their control. The LTTE cadres as well as the ordinary people in the North and Eastern regions are becoming restless. The LTTE's credibility is getting eroded and they have no adequate answers to the questions of rehabilitation and resettlement of the Tamil people. President Kumaratunga had hinted at this in the statement above. Reflecting his agony in this respect, Prabhakaran said in his speech of 27 November 2004: "Today we are faced with a

---

5 Ibid.

critical and complex situation, unprecedented in the history of our liberation struggle. We are living in a political void, without war, without a stable peace, without the condition of normalcy, without an interim or permanent solution to the ethnic conflict. Our liberation struggle will be seriously undermined if this political vacuum continues indefinitely… though we have entered into a ceasefire agreement and observed peace for three years and participated in the peace talks for six months, our people have not yet received any peace dividends. The intolerable burden of day-to-day problems is suffocating our people. Our people are desperately anticipating relief and reconstruction to put an end to their urgent existential problems. For these reasons we want the immediate resumption of peace talks, based on our proposal, so that an interim administrative authority can be established as early as possible to address the grievances of our people. If some elements of our proposals are deemed problematic or controversial, these issues can be resolved through discussion at the negotiating table …"

Prabhakaran's desperation for talks is clearly underlined in this statement. There is also constant international pressure on the LTTE to start the peace talks. To soften these international pressures, explain their predicament and mobilize international support, LTTE leader S.P. Tamilchelvan undertook a month-long visit to Europe during October-November 2004. Perhaps, as a result of this visit and consultations with the European leaders, some of whom refused to see the LTTE representative, the LTTE has underlined its keenness for talks but without diluting its stand on "only ISGA based talks".

What is coming in the way of starting these talks is the LTTE's insistence on its position and its refusal to link the talks to a "permanent settlement to the ethnic problem", until "interim administrative authority is institutionalized and becomes functional". This would ensure LTTE's access to and control over the "international assistance" which will not only provide the LTTE with legitimacy *vis-à-vis* its people and cadres, but also resources to reinforce its fighting capabilities. That is why Prabhakaran has threatened a war of separation and secession. He said in his 'Hero's Day' speech that he had reached the "borderline" of his patience and that "if the Government of Sri Lanka rejects our urgent appeal and adopts delaying tactics, perpetuating the sufferings of our people, we have no alternative other than to advance the freedom struggle of our nation." Prabhakaran's close associate Anton Balasingam has also disclosed in his latest book that the LTTE has not completely given up on its goal of a 'separate Tamil state' and if the Sri Lankan Government does not accept their IGSA proposals they may be forced to go back to war.[6]

As things stand, the Sri Lankan Government cannot resume talks with the LTTE on the latter's terms. Both the Oslo and the Tokyo Declarations and the international community as a whole, including India, endorse the Sri Lankan Government's position that the talks for interim authority should be linked to the "contours" of a final settlement. Without this link, the LTTE would keep its option for 'Eelam' open, and the interim authority may become no more than yet another step towards eventual separation. The Kumaratunga Government cannot sustain internal political pressures against conceding the LTTE demand as noted earlier. Following Prabhakaran's 'Hero's Day' speech and his threat to go to war if talks are not started on his conditions, the JVP and JHU are asking government to be prepared for another round of Eelam war.

---

[6] Anton Balasingham, *War and Peace: Armed Struggle And Peace Efforts of Liberation Tigers*, Fairmax Publishing Ltd. London, UK. 2004.

War Seems Unlikely

Prabhakaran has threatened to revert to the war of separation if talks are not started on the LTTE's ISGA proposals. There are reports of the LTTE's recruitment and propaganda activities, as also systematic killing of its Tamil rivals and Sri Lankan soft targets like intelligence agents. This has raised public and international concerns regarding the imminence of war. However, the breakout of 'Eelam War IV', as it may be called, seems less likely than feared. The LTTE has strong constraints against breaking the ceasefire and starting a direct military confrontation with the Sri Lankan State.

To begin with, the LTTE's position in eastern Sri Lanka is weak and uncertain if not wholly vulnerable. The eastern region is ethnically diverse. While the LTTE never enjoyed support among the Sinhalese and Muslims of the East, who together constitute more than 50 per cent of the total Eastern population, the revolt by Karuna has seriously eroded the LTTE's base even among the Tamils who constitute nearly 45 per cent of the population. In recent months, there have been a number of bold attacks by unidentified groups on the LTTE's military establishments in Batticaloa and elsewhere in the east. Militarily, the LTTE may still be in a firm position due to its control over the sea-front, but it may not find it advisable to launch a major offensive in view of Karuna's challenge and the fragile social base. The LTTE has started accusing the Sri Lankan armed forces for attacks on its establishments, refuting the contention that Karuna's men may be behind them. A major precondition for the LTTE to launch a full-scale military offensive would be reinforcing its position in the East and make it sure that there are no chinks in its armour on this front.

The LTTE is also concerned about the growing understanding between the Sri Lankan establishment and the new Government in India. Prabhakaran must be recalling his very tense relationship in the late Eighties with the former Indian High Commissioner in Colombo, Mr. J.N. Dixit who, until his death recently, was India's National Security Adviser to the Prime Minister. The assurances of support to the Colombo regime from India are clearly reflected in the proposed Defence Cooperation Agreement (DCA) that may soon be signed between the two countries, though without much public fanfare. Under this agreement, India will not only provide training to the Sri Lankan forces but also supply equipment and share intelligence in a regular and formal manner, which has not been done so far. There have been political and technical hitches regarding the provisions of DCA, both from the Sri Lankan and Indian sides. But these difficulties are expected to be sorted out in the next few weeks. India has also committed itself to upgrading and reinforcing the Sri Lankan military's Palaly air base in Jaffna that is vulnerable to heavy shelling by the LTTE.

Both the DCA and the support for Palaly airbase constitute a powerful Indian deterrent to the LTTE's war option. This is why the LTTE has been strongly and publicly opposing these measures, and asked India to desist from taking them. Ignoring the LTTE's displeasure, India reiterated its assurances of political and military support to President Chandrika Kumaratunga on her visit to India during 3-7 November 2004. The joint Press statement issued to mark this visit stated, "India maintains an abiding interest in the security of Sri Lanka and remains committed to its unity, sovereignty and territorial integrity. India favours the early resumption of negotiations pertaining to the peace process. Any interim arrangement on administration should be an integral part of an enduring final settlement that maintains the unity and territorial integrity of Sri Lanka and ensures the safety, well-being and prosperity of the people."

Besides being deterred by the unfavourable situation in the Eastern Province and India's promise of support to Sri Lankan establishment, the LTTE is also worried about the mood of the international community that will not tolerate breakdown of the peace process. The US has clearly driven home this point to the LTTE leadership. US concern for LTTE-led terrorism is both deep and direct, particularly in the aftermath of 9/11. There have been reports of the LTTE's links with Al-Qaeda since the late 1990's when investigations into the attack on 'USS Cole' came to light. The US is also worried that the festering ethnic conflict in Sri Lanka, and the persisting LTTE intransigence towards the Muslims of the eastern region may drive the Muslim youth towards *jihadi* extremism. Japan and the peace facilitator Norway have also been following the US lead in cautioning the LTTE to desist from reverting to conflict. The LTTE knows that it cannot afford to alienate the international community beyond a point. It is not only a question of the promised package of assistance for resettlement and rehabilitation under the Tokyo Declaration, but also the continuous flow of contributions to LTTE coffers from the Sri Lankan Tamil diaspora, settled particularly in America, Europe and Australia. There were reports in December 2004 that LTTE activists were caught in Europe with huge amounts of cash, meant to be carried to the headquarters in Jaffna. LTTE leader S.P. Tamichelvan's month-long visit to European capitals was aimed at nursing its European constituency — both the European Governments as well as the Tamil diaspora. He was received sympathetically except in some European countries.

The noise of war drums, sounded following Prabhakaran's 'Hero's Day' speech has been completely dampened by nature's fury that hit Sri Lanka, and also South-East Asian countries on Black Sunday, 26 December 2004. The death of nearly

40,000 Sri Lankans and the displacement of nearly a million more by the tsunami waves have completely changed Sri Lanka's immediate priorities and political agenda. No exact estimates are available, but there is a reasonable assumption that both the Sri Lankan security forces and the LTTE have suffered serious losses in their military capabilities. The loss is certainly greater for the LTTE as nearly 50 per cent of its 'Sea Tigers' force seems to have been washed out with their vessels and equipment. The priority before both the Sri Lankan and the LTTE leadership is to rehabilitate their people. The prospects of war in the future have certainly receded by at least six months, if not more. There are reports of Prabhakaran trying to recruit the orphaned children as young fighters, to prepare them for the eventuality of war.

The tsunami not only dampened the prospects of war but also created an opportunity for peace, in terms of the Government and the LTTE joining hands in distributing relief and undertaking reconstruction. Kumaratunga extended her hand of friendship to Prabhakaran, and a statement issued in Prabhakaran's name also expressed condolences and sympathies for the Sinhalese and Muslims who died or were displaced by the tsunami. This opportunity, however, faded out as soon as it appeared. There were incidents on the ground in aid-distribution that reflected the deep distrust between the two establishments. Following this, Kumaratunga handed over relief distribution to the Sri Lankan army, which the LTTE refused to allow into its areas. The differences also gave a reason to the LTTE to complain that the Government was not providing enough relief to the Tamil areas of the North and the East.

However, the last blow to the prospects of joint relief work was President Kumaratunga's refusal to allow Kofi Annan, the UN Secretary-General, and other international political personalities like US Secretary of State Colin Powell to visit the tsunami - affected areas under LTTE control, and talk directly to the LTTE leadership regarding relief and rehabilitation. This has marred the prospects of LTTE adding to its international profile as an independent centre of power and authority in its own right within Sri Lanka. Colombo allowed UN Special Coordinator for tsunami relief Margret Wahlstrom to visit the 'Tiger territory' on 15 January 2005, but this has not helped to heal the wounds in this respect, though the Norwegian facilitators are expected to meet Prabhakaran to explore the possibility of reviving the peace process.

The constraints and pressures identified above will keep the LTTE within the peace process, i.e. the CFA. However, once the tsunami pressures get re-utilised without improving peace prospects, growing frustration on the part of the LTTE could have the possibility of generating a trigger to a wider conflict. The LTTE has stepped up its systematic targeting of adversaries and the possibility of suicide attacks in Colombo on high visibility targets cannot be ruled out. Thus the CFA may be breached, and if that happens the Sri Lankan Army may also retaliate informally without admitting so. Accordingly, the structure of CFA could hold as long as either side is militarily confident to take on the other, or is politically resilient to redefine its position for starting the peace talks.

In the prevailing precarious stalemate, the role of the international community assumes significance for preserving the CFA and nudging the two parties towards the resumption of a more meaningful peace process. In recent months, particularly since the change of political regime in Colombo in April 2004, the international community's credibility has come under serious questioning. Norway has been particularly blamed for its 'partisan' stand of favouring the LTTE in the peace process, and sections of political opinion, including those belonging to the ruling coalition, have argued for the removal of Norway from its present role of a facilitator. There are also political sections that are asking for India to play a direct and more active role in the peace process. Any move to change the facilitator may not be practical, neither desirable, more so, as India may not be willing to assume a direct and active role.

What, however, is needed urgently on the part of the international community is to restore its credibility by being judiciously balanced between the two parties in the peace process. Norway must take the CFA violations more seriously and insist that the violating party desist from them. The international community as a whole could lean heavily on the opposition and ruling sections to evolve a true consensus on the package of accommodation for the Tamils rather than using this package as well as the contours of the peace process as an instrument in pursuing their narrow political stakes and rivalries. For instance, the opposition UNP is keeping aloof from the consensus evolving mechanism put in place by President Kumaratunga. They should be asked to join the mechanism and to support the Government. This will also help President Kumaratunga and her section in the ruling coalition to neutralise pressures from parties like the JVP. The importance of moderating the JVP is being viewed seriously by the international community as some of the community's representatives, including the US, had a meeting with President Kumaratunga on 15 December 2004 and asked for restraining the JVP (then a coalition partner) in its persistent campaign against Norway's facilitation.[7] The President, however, was confident that the LTTE and others are raising the 'JVP factor' only as an excuse. The JVP, according to her, was not a big obstacle and whatever its nuisance value, she would be able to handle it. She said in an interview: "Don't forget that the JVP has also come a long way. When they started talking with us, they were not even talking of a negotiated settlement. Now they are fully in agreement that a negotiated settlement should be the solution. They are in agreement that there should be some form of power-sharing... not to worry about the JVP matter. I will handle the matter. Believe my word for it. JVP is fully for going to talks with them."[7]

The international community should also explore ways and means to implement the aid package even without an interim administration asked for by the LTTE. People of the conflict-affected areas need urgent and adequate help, and since the promise of such help has already been made, it should be allowed to flow. In the north-eastern region, direct help to the people will result in further erosion of the LTTE's support base and may work as an additional pressure-point on the LTTE to force it to enter into negotiations. Positive activity towards rehabilitation and relief will give peace dividend to the people and restore their faith in a negotiated peace process.

India has generally kept itself somewhat distanced from the international community's role in Sri Lanka's peace process. Though not enthusiastic about Norway's facilitation, India has accepted it, making it clear that facilitation is not mediation. India has not joined the donors' group in working out the package for rehabilitation, relief and resettlement for Sri Lanka, but has stepped up its assistance to Sri Lanka through bilateral channels. It has also explored the possibility of undertaking relief and rehabilitation projects in the North-East, much to the displeasure of the LTTE.

Until the last months of the NDA Government, India had maintained an active but indirect interest in the progress of the peace process. However, in view of Norway's laxity towards the LTTE's growing reinforcement activities, India has slowly

---

[7] *The Hindu*, 16 December 2004.

moved to send signals that outbreak of conflict will not be accepted. To deter the LTTE, India has clearly stated that the 'Sea Tigers' cannot be accepted as a separate and independent naval formation on Sri Lanka's eastern and northern seaboard. To further deter the Tigers, India and Sri Lanka have streamlined intelligence - sharing to monitor the LTTE's activities. Indian and Sri Lankan navies also conducted a joint exercise around Colombo in December 2004. The speed and thrust with which both India and the US moved their navies to Sri Lanka to help in tsunami relief must have also sent a militarily deterring signal to the LTTE.

It is true that growing involvement of the international community in Sri Lanka's peace process has in effect curtailed India's strategic space in its sensitive neighbourhood. However, it may not be desirable on India's part to assume a direct participation in the peace process, notwithstanding growing pressures within Sri Lanka to do so. Two factors need to be kept in mind here. One is that any move on India's part to play a more active role will inevitably come in the way of Norwegian facilitation and will be incompatible with the overall thrust of the international community. India has a continuing dialogue with the US, the UK and Norway on the Sri Lankan situation where it can voice its concerns. Secondly, and this is more important, the peace prospects in Sri Lanka are still fraught with several complicating aspects, particularly those relating to its internal politics and power rivalries among key political forces. India's direct involvement, if not immediately, in the medium and long-term, could be dragged into such rivalries as past experience suggests. The blast carried out at a Bollywood function (Temptations 2004) in Colombo on 11 December 2004 is a clear indication that there are political forces in Sri Lanka that do not like India, and may not hesitate to exploit the 'Indian factor' in advancing their narrow political interests.

India should not risk such political controversies, particularly in view of its growing economic stakes.

The overall situation, therefore, continues to be uncertain and precarious and may remain so for some more time to come. This is notwithstanding the impatience of and the threatening noises raised from the LTTE side. Both sides are trying their best to build pressure on the other to get the talks resumed. The change will come in favour of talks only when one of the sides blinks. If not, then the prospects of yet another round of war may be unavoidable.

Ground Realities

Pitfalls and Possibilities

Paikiasothy Saravanamuttu

Ever since the cessation of hostilities and the commencement of the Sri Lanka peace process between the United National Front (UNF) Government and the LTTE, there has been persistent talk about the challenges and opportunities that make up the peace process. The challenges and opportunities grow out of the operating assumptions of the two sides at the point of commencement of the peace process. They in turn arise from their respective political aspirations and constraints, as well as from external developments.

Contributory Factors and Constituent Elements

The first point to be made is the widespread war-weariness on all sides of the ethnic divide, attested to in the general election result of December 2001 and the substantial support for direct negotiations registered in opinion polls, thereafter.[1]

[1] www.cpalanka.org

In the December 2001 election, the United National Party (UNP), the main party in the United National Front (UNF) coalition, stood on a plank of direct negotiations with the LTTE, and the establishment of an interim council for the Tamil-majority North and East of the country with their participation. This, in effect, given the situation on the ground, meant LTTE control of the interim administration. A similar proposal had been mooted by UNP leader Ranil Wickremesinghe in 1999 in his unsuccessful presidential campaign against current President Chandrika Kumaratunga. Like in 1999, in 2001 the UNP was roundly castigated by the ruling People's Alliance (PA) for proposing to hand over the North and East to the LTTE on a platter. The PA used this as its main election plank and deployed the full force of the State-controlled media to charge that there was a UNP–LTTE conspiracy to divide the country. But the polity in the South rejected the PA. This must be seen as repudiation of this charge and of the President as well. Chandrika Kumaratunga led the PA campaign and staked her personal political credibility on it.

Another key factor that contributed to war-weariness in the South was the economy. The staggering costs of the war, especially as a consequence of the rearmament that followed the LTTE capture of the strategic Elephant Pass military complex at the entrance to the Jaffna Peninsula in April 2000, and the devastating effects of the audacious LTTE attack in July 2001 on the international airport in Colombo, were clear contributory factors. In 2001, the Sri Lankan economy registered a negative growth. In the North and East, the cumulative effects of two decades of armed struggle, including the punitive sanction of embargoes on food, medicines and other essential items, took their toll. The yearning for a return to normalcy and peace could not be underestimated in 2001. Nor indeed can it be now. The Tamil polity in the North and

East voted in the main for the Tamil National Alliance (TNA), composed of four political parties who ran on the platform of direct talks with the LTTE, and recognition of the LTTE as the sole representative of the Tamils at these talks.

The second point to be made is the separate yet co-incidental recognition by both sides, that armed conflict would not further their respective political interests — the restoration of the *status quo ante* or militarily weakening of the LTTE to the point of their suing for terms favourable to the Government on the one hand, and the advancement of the secessionist project through military means on the other. Both sides felt the pressure in terms of manpower and resources, continued armed desertions on the Government side — recently estimated at a cumulative toll of 50,000 — and on the LTTE side, the continued forcible conscription of "child soldiers".

Thirdly, it's the international climate preceding and following the 9/11 Al Qaeda attack on the 'Twin Towers' in New York. For quite some time, the international community has insisted on a negotiated settlement to the Sri Lankan ethnic conflict. At the same time, a number of key international actors, including the US, the UK and India, have termed the LTTE as a 'terrorist organisation'. They have maintained that a way to the resolution of the Sri Lankan conflict lies in a negotiated political settlement within a 'united Sri Lanka', and strongly urged both sides to talk. The international community has also rallied around the Sri Lankan Government at points of military crisis, to prevent further deterioration of the military balance of power against it. In so doing, it has served notice to the LTTE on its opposition to secession by force of arms or otherwise.

The significance of 9/11 therefore lies in it being a catalyst, and as an important factor that will ensure continued LTTE participation in the peace process. It should be noted that the

LTTE indicated a willingness to talk even before 9/11, and had declared unilateral ceasefires, the last being in December 2000. The international climate post-9/11, and in particular the superpower definition of the global power configuration in terms of the war on terrorism, have impressed upon the LTTE the importance of being and appearing to be on the right side of this particular global ideological and military divide. The significance of 9/11 is, therefore, its impact on the political psyche of the LTTE and the LTTE's room for manoeuvre, internationally.

Of particular significance is the attitude of the UNF Government to the LTTE. Unlike its predecessor, it has deliberately chosen to deal with the LTTE and enlist its cooperation as a partner in the search for a political solution. In this respect, the UNF Government has recognised the reality on the ground, of effective LTTE control of sizable areas in the North and East, and acknowledged the fundamental impracticality of attempting to ignore, transcend or negate it. This reality has long been hidden from the southern polity along with the extent of the devastation of the war in the North and East. This is due to censorship and self-censorship which, in turn, is both a consequence of factors specific to the South as well as the ideological disposition of the media organisations.

The predecessor PA Government had allowed for the impression to gain ground that its far-reaching constitutional proposals — which were never formally presented to the LTTE — were aimed at cutting the political ground from under the latter's feet. These proposals, which culminated in an aborted Constitution Bill presented to Parliament in August 2000, combined with the military strategy of opening up the main supply route (A-9 Road from Colombo to Jaffna), were perceived as integral components of the Government's policy of a 'War for Peace'. The impact of the latter was to reinforce the LTTE's determination that the Government would not, as desired, militarily weaken them to the negotiating table, and negotiate from strength – or, not having to negotiate with them at all. The result of this was a stalemate in the Government's conflict-transformation strategy, and likewise in the LTTE's too, in that they could not proceed beyond securing a limited politico-military advantage.

It would appear that the peace process reactivated by the UNF and the LTTE in 2001 is based on hard-headed realism and pragmatism. The UNF Government and the LTTE realise that they cannot advance or achieve their respective political goals through military means, and that their constituencies strongly desire a return to peace and normalcy. The issue though is as to whether this phase of the peace process under the stewardship of the adversarial partnership of the UNF Government of Sri Lanka and the LTTE with Norwegian facilitation, is intended or indeed designed to yield more than an end to the ethnic war.

Current Concerns and Anxieties

Between the guns falling silent and a final settlement, there are a host of concerns, apprehensions and anxieties that have to be addressed. The current scenario is better characterised as a 'no-war-no-peace' situation rather than as one of peace, or a post-conflict situation. Admittedly, it is early days in this reactivated process. A final settlement will not come quickly, cheaply, or easily, and it will test the patience, courage, commitment and imagination of all and at all levels. The major concerns need to be flagged at the outset so that pressure and persuasion can be deployed to ensure their acknowledgement and incorporation into the process and agreements reached through it, as soon as it is practicable.

The LTTE's temporary suspension of its participation in the peace process since the third week of April 2003, ostensibly on the ground that it was not invited to a preparatory conference in Washington for the June 2003 Tokyo Donors' Conference on Sri Lanka, has stalled the process. The regular monthly sessions of negotiations between the two protagonists that were initiated in September 2002 have not taken place since. Re-activation now revolves around the issue of an interim administration in the North and East, insisted upon by the LTTE.

This is an issue which is proving to be the acid-test for the commitment of all parties to go down the road of restructuring the Sri Lankan State – the over-arching and indispensable reform for an end to the conflict. The LTTE held a meeting at the end of August 2003 in Paris to discuss the Government's suggestions regarding an interim administration and to prepare their counter-proposals. These are to be communicated to the Government by the middle of October. They will be the first official set of LTTE proposals regarding any aspect of a political settlement, and are eagerly awaited as a barometer of their commitment to a settlement through recommenced direct negotiations. In addition, the time the LTTE takes to present these counter-proposals is seen by some observers as an indication of their willingness to further deal with the UNF Government.

The six-month period following the suspension of direct talks has provided a space for reflection and reform of the modalities of the process. Were the opportunity to redesign the process missed, the prospects for success will be hampered. In such a situation, the limited use of military force to break the deadlock cannot be ruled out.

a) The Interim Administration and a Final Settlement[2]

At the commencement of the negotiations, with the emphasis on "incrementalism" as expressed through the prioritisation

[2] www.cpalanka.org/roadmap_programme.html

of relief, rehabilitation and the restoration of normalcy, the concern was that pragmatism had won the day at the expense of principle. Political issues at the heart of the conflict were to be deferred indefinitely. Trust and confidence between the two sides had to be first built up through partnership on other issues. Political issues, pivotally important though they are, could not be allowed to paralyse the process at the outset. Today, with the exclusive focus on the interim administration, the concern is that the political issues will swamp the agenda. In the eagerness to arrive at interim arrangements, the contours if not the contents, of a final settlement will be determined without greater inclusiveness and consultation with other parties.

The focus on the interim administration is yet another example of the LTTE's ability to set the agenda of the peace process. The issue brought to the forefront by them as that which will determine their participation in the process effectively pushes to the back-burner, questions of human rights, pluralism and diversity. These were flagged in the approach to the Tokyo Donors', Conference in June 2003, and found mention in the declaration following the conference. While the donors pledged an unprecedented US$4.5 billion to Sri Lanka over three years, they also made it plain that the disbursement of funds for the North and the East, beyond immediate humanitarian needs, would be linked to reactivation of the peace process through the resumption of talks. The donor-community was also keen to send a message out of Tokyo and continues to maintain this position, that certain basic standards of human rights have to be maintained in the process, though the process itself should not be held mortgage to a dogmatic position on this key issue.

Some analysts have argued that the LTTE's temporary suspension of talks and non-attendance at Tokyo were motivated less by their not being invited to the preparatory meeting in Washington, and more by their unwillingness to agree to human rights linkages to the disbursement of donor-assistance. This argument cannot be dismissed out of hand. Nor can that which points to the LTTE's emphasis on equality and partnership in the process and the particular point that the largesse obtained at Tokyo was largely attributable to their participation in the process. Indeed, without the LTTE there would be no process at all. Their decision was probably motivated by a combination of these factors. By focusing on the issue of interim administration, the LTTE has successfully brought the question of the willingness and ability of the actors in the South to go down the road of constitutional reform to effect conflict-transformation.

The LTTE's objective in the establishment of an interim administration is presented through a number of arguments, all of which have merit. The first point is that it was promised by the UNF and therefore is not something new. They also point out that relief, rehabilitation and development of the North and East cannot be carried out in the way that development has been effected in the South of the country. In this context, they point to the bureaucratic delays and lack of commitment by the Government machinery. They cite the example of the Sub-committee on Immediate Humanitarian and Rehabilitation Needs of the North and East (SIHRN), comprising both LTTE and Government representatives, which was set up following an agreement between the two parties at the beginning of 2003. The LTTE also pointed to the dismally low-level at which donor-assistance for development was absorbed in the South, as a consequence of inefficiency and corruption.

Underlying these arguments are the real political issues which relate to the institutional expression of partnership in the peace process and most fundamentally to legitimacy and the consolidation of political power. The LTTE understandably avers that they cannot be bystanders in the development process in the North and East. The political capital that will accrue from this process must accrue to them, and they believe that they have earned it. Furthermore, they have through their quasi-State apparatus, the putative institutional infrastructure to manage such a process.

These fundamental political considerations became apparent in the LTTE's initial responses to the UNF Government's proposals on an interim administration. They made the key point that what they had in mind was not the administrative and development agency that the UNF Government was proposing, but a political body with decision-making authority. The UNF Government responded with a discussion paper that the LTTE took up in Paris with its legal and constitutional experts drawn from the Tamil diaspora.

A major concern in the South, and one voiced by President Chandrika Kumaratunga and the Opposition PA, is that the LTTE seeks to define the final settlement through an interim arrangement, without explicitly committing itself to the basic principles of federalism and national unity, beyond the one-paragraph 'Oslo Declaration' of December 2002. The latter, agreed upon by the two parties, pledged that they would "explore a settlement based on internal self-determination for the Tamil-speaking peoples of the North and East in their areas of historic habitation within a federal structure and within an united Sri Lanka". In this respect the question of 'interim to what ?' – the notion of an interim administration as a bridge to a final settlement – lies at the heart of these concerns.

Indeed, as to whether the LTTE and UNF Government share a common understanding of the terms, "internal self-determination" and "federal" is open to question. To the extent that there has been any indication of the LTTE thinking below their optimum goal of a separate State, it is that of a confederation – two States coming together in their common interests for common purposes. That a Sri Lankan Government would accept, or be in a political position to accept this interpretation of the 'Oslo Declaration' is unlikely. Commencing with provincial elections in early 2004, the country enters an electoral cycle that includes a presidential election and general elections by 2006.

That the LTTE's counter-proposals on an interim administration will be their first set of official proposals on any aspect of a political settlement suggests that it is likely to be a combination of a political testament on the one hand, and, a realpolitik negotiating position on the other. It may well be pitched high, though not so high as to court certain rejection from the outset. At the same time, it will also reflect the LTTE's assessment of the political position of the UNF Government – its perception of how eagerly the UNF Government wants to have the interim administration issue resolved and out of the way when it faces the electorate. It will also, of course, reflect how eagerly the LTTE wants an interim administration, and how long it is prepared to wait for it. Despite evidence of their consolidation on the ground since the ceasefire agreement, they have yet to find a legal, institutional expression for it, and with it the authority and the resources to facilitate the improvement of the lives and livelihoods of the people of the North and East. Moreover, their cadre and the civilian population need answers. The longer the current situation lasts, the more likely is that the LTTE will also be held responsible for the lack of demonstrable progress.

On the UNF Government's side, the imperative as the election cycle approaches is the economy and the tangible evidence of the peace-dividend as reflected in the cost of living and quality of life. Unrealistic expectations on this score have been allowed to persist. It is probably the case that the UNF Government would like the peace process to reach the plateau of stabilisation and normalcy, allowing it to turn its attention to the economy. The question, therefore, of whether the UNF would like to be defending a position on the interim administration at the hustings, or rather continue to be negotiating on the issue throughout the electoral cycle, is a pertinent one. The danger with the latter is not only the response of the LTTE, it is also the danger of two sets of negotiations, in effect, being conducted simultaneously — between the UNF Government and the LTTE, on the one hand, and between the UNF Government and the southern electorate on the other. This does not bode well for conflict-transformation.

It is important that the interim administration issue not be settled in haste, but be settled in full recognition of the contours of a final settlement. What is absent from the peace process, particularly the interim administration issue, and what may well go a long way in assuaging fear and doubt and in consolidating public support and legitimacy for the process, is an explicit statement of mutual understanding on the principles that will frame the process and agreements agreed therein. This will provide a compass for the process, a reference-point as well as the basis for constructive critique. Most importantly, it will give at least an indication of a shared vision and common destiny. This will assure public opinion that a separate State is not in effect being created on the ground, or that a unitary State will always be present, in spirit, if not in law. Accordingly, these principles must include democratic pluralism, self-determination, human rights, political representation and elections, and transparency and accountability.[3]

[3]www.cpalanka.org/roadmap_programme.html, www.cpalanka.org/psg/psg.html

Indeed if this cannot be done yet, it is worth waiting until it can be. In the meantime, the issue of expediting relief and rehabilitation in the North and East will have to be dealt with through a mechanism which meets the LTTE's immediate needs but is not understood to be an interim administration that could be seen as a "bridge" to a final settlement.

b. Human Rights[4]

The incorporation of human rights concerns at the outset in any agreement is of pivotal importance. Without this, there will be no popular legitimacy and support for the process. Any agreement devoid of human rights protection will not last.

The ceasefire agreement of February 2002 was an agreement between combatants, and was aimed at building confidence between them. So is the Sri Lanka Monitoring Mission (SLMM) with Scandinavian participation, which was set up under the agreement. Following reports of continuing abduction, extortion and child-conscription by the LTTE, as well as the assassination of over 40 members and supporters of political parties opposed to the LTTE, which the SLMM has not been able to halt, the crucial importance of robust human rights protection has been heightened. Fears on this score, reinforced by Tamil-Muslim clashes, have also been raised in the context of the Muslim community in the East in particular, their treatment by the LTTE and their protection through special arrangements, right through an interim administration to a permanent settlement. The international community, including non-governmental human rights organisations such as Amnesty International and Human Rights Watch, has strongly voiced concerns about LTTE's commitment to, and behaviour regarding, human rights.

[4] www.cpalanka.org/psg/psg.html

Although the two parties agreed to a Human Rights Advisor, Ian Martin, former Secretary-General of Amnesty International, the situation has deteriorated. The contribution of Ian Martin has been seriously limited by the lack of commitment on both sides, and by the deadlock in the talks. An action plan, to be implemented by UNICEF and the Tamil Rehabilitation Organisation (TRO), the development arm of the LTTE, to deal with the rehabilitation and release of children in LTTE custody has been agreed upon. Yet, recruitment of children continues.

Human rights of course is not the monopoly of one side, and cannot be treated as such. Both sides have been guilty of horrendous violations. These have included, in addition to child-conscription, abduction and extortion, rape and torture. Furthermore, human rights has a number of dimensions, from the political and civil, to the economic and social. It runs the gamut of basic freedoms to that of self-determination, the right to return to one's home, the right to food, clothing, shelter and medicine. Consequently, it has to be approached in a way which is not seen as exclusively "targeting" one party. The LTTE has consistently pointed out that the emphasis on civil and political rights is aimed at discrediting them, and that the relative lack of emphasis on the dismantling of Army-designated High Security Zones in areas to which internally - displaced persons (IDPs) want to return to their homes, reveals the bias of the discourse on human rights in the context of the peace process.

The 'High Security Zone (HSZ) issue' brings into sharp focus the human security issues on the one hand and the perceived requirements of the balance-of-power upon which the ceasefire is predicated, on the other. A report on the HSZs by retired Indian Army General Satish Nambiar has not met with agreement from both sides. One set of arguments contend that the LTTE's interest in the HSZ issue is not the right of IDPs to return to their homes but to bring its long-range artillery closer to the Sri Lankan armed forces' air base at Palaly and the port at Kankesanthurai. Another poses the question of whether these two strategic objectives of the armed forces can be secured only through the occupation of large tracts of land and their designation as HSZs. "Whose security ?' – is a question that is yet to be answered.

One approach on human rights could be as in El Salvador, where there is a separate agreement or a memorandum of understanding on human rights. Another is to incorporate human rights into every aspect of the process, and not look upon it as a luxury or optional. At the very least, the sanctity of life and the right to life irrespective of political beliefs has to be embedded into the process. Currently, there is a debate in the international community on whether human rights should be the bedrock of conditionality in its dealings with the LTTE. Or, whether human rights should be "soft-pedalled" in the interest of ensuring that the LTTE stays in the process, and by doing so would open it to "transformation". What is clear though is that the only leverage, with the LTTE and indeed the UNF Government too, on human rights could be through the international community. The task of impressing upon it the pivotal importance of this responsibility will continue to lie with the civil society. The international community will also have to assist in augmenting local efforts with regard to effective human rights monitoring.

Along with the concern for human rights is the imperative of reconciliation between and within communities after two decades of armed conflict. The emphasis on relief and rehabilitation, economic development and the return of IDPs, has to incorporate mechanisms for reconciliation. Before the establishment of formal Truth and Reconciliation Commissions, if this is the route chosen, community-based peace and reconciliation committees are an urgent need. They are of especial importance in the multi-ethnic East where tensions are high between the Tamil and Muslim communities, and between the Tamils and the police.

c. The East[5]

The East is the potential tinder-box and the area in which the peace process will continue to face severe, and conceivably even fatal, test. The tensions and divisions between and within the political formations there, and the absence of a single authority commanding credibility and respect amongst all communities makes for a pluralism, *albeit*, one laced with anarchy. There have already been clashes between the Tamil and Muslim communities, and the Tamil community and the Special Task Force of the police. Over and above the tensions on the ground manifested on a daily basis are the questions of the merger of the North and the East, claimed by the Tamils as their "homeland". There are also the special arrangements that will have to be reached to accommodate the concerns of the Muslim community, which fears a relegation of their rights under an LTTE-dominated administration in a merged North-East province. The inclusion of Rauff Hakeem at the peace talks as leader of the principal Muslim party in the East, the Sri Lanka Muslim Congress (SLMC), rather than as a Cabinet Minister, and the understanding that there will be a separate Muslim delegation at the talks once the issue of an interim administration is taken up, need to be acted upon. The earlier Memorandum of Understanding between Hakeem and LTTE leader Velupillai Prabhakaran reflect the recognition of this dimension to the peace process.

The SLMC wants arrangements for the Muslim community who are located in non-contiguous villages in the East. In the

[5] www.cpalanka.org/roadmap_programme.html

absence of this, the demand of the more 'nationalist elements' in the community for a separate 'South-East Council for the Muslims' could gain support. Hakeem's woes are compounded by the fact that his personal political constituency lies outside the East, and the consequent lack of a standard-bearer in the East for the leadership of the Muslim cause. The resolution of the leadership problem is an important factor, though by no means the only one, in facilitating the resolution of the problems of the Muslim community in the context of the peace process.

There is the danger that the Muslim community may well undergo the political experience with armed militancy that the Tamil community underwent if mainstream political parties lose credibility and are unable to provide effective leadership to the community. A number of reports alleging the arming of Muslim youth in the East have already appeared, leading politicians including President Chandrika to voice their concerns about this.

d. Cohabitation

A final settlement will require new legislation and constitutional amendment. This could be the case with regard to interim arrangements as well. Under the present Constitution, Sri Lanka is a unitary State. An amendment to this provision will necessitate a two-thirds majority-vote in Parliament, followed by an island-wide referendum. The two-thirds majority provision, in turn, highlights the perils and challenges of the current political configuration of cohabitation between an executive President from the PA, and a Prime Minister and Government, led by the UNF.

The relationship between the two has been contentious and conflictual, characterised by public accusation and even abuse. In policy terms, the President maintains that whilst she supports the peace process, she is very concerned that the UNF

Government was conceding too much to the LTTE. The UNP on the other hand is concerned that she would exercise her powers to dissolve Parliament and/or continue to destabilise, if not disrupt, the peace process by providing ammunition to those opposed to it, through her criticism. Her criticism, the President maintains, is constructive and in fulfilment of the mandate that she received from the people in two presidential elections. Her critics point out that she stands for peace as long as she wields power. The problems of cohabitation arise, not because of fundamental differences over policy — while in power both have, acknowledged the imperative of a political solution to the conflict — but because of a power-struggle involving political parties and personalities. The two main political parties subscribe to a zero-sum notion of power, which makes them both acutely susceptible to the fear that the other will run away with all the political capital that could accrue from peace, and thereby consolidate a stranglehold on government.

The over-arching concern is that the problems of cohabitation will impact adversely on the peace process — by demonstrating that the competition for power in the South will always ensure that, even if willing, a Government in Colombo will not be able to reach and (if that is possible) implement any agreements. The solution to this particular structural conundrum in the political architecture of Sri Lanka awaits resolution. It is still possible that the two sides will have to stick it out together, until the end of the President's second term in 2005. The hope is that the prevailing climate of pragmatism in the peace process will prevail amongst all protagonists to insulate the peace process from the competition for political power.

In this context, it must be noted that the President has announced that talks between her Sri Lanka Freedom Party

(SLFP) and the Janata Vimukthi Peramuna (JVP), on an official alliance between them have been abandoned. The JVP is opposed to devolution in the North and East, and wants the Norwegian facilitators thrown out. The President, on the other hand, was the first national leader to incorporate devolution proposals into a constitutional settlement, and it was she who invited the Norwegians in the first place. That she is not interested in toppling the UNF Government at any cost, and certainly not abandoning devolution and power-sharing proposals, is heartening indeed for those who feared that party-based political competition would obscure the common ground and policy convergence between the two main parties regarding a settlement.

It is early days in the peace process, and all the platitudes about patience, courage, commitment and imagination apply to stakeholders at all levels — Track One and the civil society included. The further down the road one goes in institutionalising the process, greater are the challenges and opportunities. Thorny, tricky questions such as self-determination, federalism or confederalism, the merger of the North and East, and the structure of the Sri Lankan State have not been addressed, nor has decommissioning and the status of the LTTE 'police force' and 'courts' in the territory under its control.

What has been initiated at Sattahip is no less than the formal redesigning of the Sri Lankan State, polity and society. Apart from the constitutional arrangements, the economic aspects will be crucial in achieving success both in the South of the country as well as in the North and East. Underpinning the "step-by-step" approach to a settlement is the rationale of economic determinism – economic development is what people want and it will in turn blunt the secessionist impulse. Yet, economic development in a globalised world carries with it a host of challenges too. The citizens of the North and the East have to be stake-holders and beneficiaries in the process. This means that local capacity has to be built up to ensure fullest participation and benefit from peace. In the South, the cumulative burden of a bloated and bureaucratized public sector, inefficiency and corruption has to be addressed and in a manner that does not breed alienation and animosity. Disaffection on the economic front combined with anxiety over the peace process can make for a very combustible situation indeed, with a knock on effects for a democratic peace and for democratic governance.

Sri Lanka is now presented with the best chance in the last two decades for building peace. There are those who venture that it is the last chance as well. Whatever be the prognostications, there is no denying that there is much to build. The ceasefire agreement and the first sessions of peace talks are the first of many positive steps that will have to be taken, perhaps in more challenging and less congenial circumstances.

Grand Project?

There is never an appropriate or never an inappropriate time to talk about the question of peace. There are challenges when everyone talks about it, perhaps of a different nature, given the developments on the ground.

The 'no-war-no-peace' situation helps secure a political objective. To put it very colloquially, it is 'to get the war out of the way for the time being, and hopefully indefinitely'. Conflict-transformation process in Sri Lanka, whether involving particular actors consciously or sub-consciously, fundamentally requires the transformation of the Sri Lankan State. It is in that sense, a very grand project. The ultimate objective, the outcome and the product of the whole exercise is the root and branch transformation of the Sri Lankan State. That is what the challenge is in terms of moving from the situation of 'no-war', to one of peace.

A new constitutional settlement will have to be — and the Prime Minister has said this for the first time publicly — a federal constitutional settlement, based on the principles of power-sharing, moving away from the unitary State, probably also based on principles and notions of asymmetrical power-sharing, recognition that certain groups within the country need to be recognised constitutionally as having particular rights.

The interim administration issue is extremely important because it is the first phase of any really meaningful activity towards a new constitutional dispensation. This will be the first real institutional expression of a new partnership. So far, the Government proposals have been in the nature of administrative devolution. The LTTE wants political decision-making powers. Both the United Front Government of Ranil Wickremesinghe and President Chandrika Kumaratunga, as early as 1998, talked about the need, the necessity, the inevitability of having an interim administration in place.

To express institutionally the new partnership and the putative constitutional dispensation of a new federal Sri Lanka, it may well require a constitutional amendment, which in turn requires that the United National Front and the People's Alliance do cooperate. Both recognise (they have negotiated directly with the LTTE) that one has to move away from a unitary State to a federal State. On the economic front, they are both capitalists. The PA would like to make out that it is capitalist with a human or a humane face, whatever that is supposed to mean. Nevertheless, in ideological terms, there is no fundamental difference, but the bipartisan consensus to move towards a settlement has eluded us each time, attributable to an imbedded political culture and personal political rivalry.

That is another process which has to be engaged in earnest. The questions of peace, democracy and governance cannot be excluded from each other. They are all integral elements of one general process towards a new political culture and constitutional dispensation.

At the same time, too much should not be made out of the problem of bipartisan consensus in the South. Despite the rhetoric, and criticisms, the President has not actually done anything that has prevented the Prime Minister from going ahead with the peace process. Despite this 'Sword of Damocles' situation, there is a perverse form of political cohabitation. Perhaps, that is the only kind of consensus that can be expected – performing for stereotypical constituencies in a particular way. But one has to have the sophistication and subtlety to go beyond that, to understand that really there is a consensus.

The LTTE is expected to come out with a set of proposals soon. It would be the first official LTTE document on any aspect of the political conflict in Sri Lanka. Therefore, it would in large part be a political testament. It will say things, and say them very strongly, about discrimination and associated issues. At the same time, it will probably reiterate the 'Thimpu Proposals'. It will also probably indicate a willingness of the LTTE to get back to the table, to be able to talk, to resolve the problem by negotiation. It is important to put that document, when released, in the wider context of the political imperatives, compulsions of the LTTE as well.

There is another dimension. At the end of the day, the peace process will succeed only with public-supported legitimacy. And public support and legitimacy crucially hinges on a human rights regime with robust protection standards. That is something that our peace process quite frankly lacks. It is not only the question of assassination of political rivals by the LTTE, extortion, abduction and child-recruitment. If there is to be a peace process, it must make sense and have meaning for ordinary people. They have to be able at least begin to live in something other than fear and insecurity. That is something that we need to strive for. There is no point, frankly, in our politicians getting up and talking about the removal of roadblocks in Colombo. One needs to be able to talk about the situation in the North and in the East, which were directly affected by the conflict.

Here, a number of things cry out to be done. The first one is a conceptual debate not just among the civil society, but also among the donor-community whether there should be any human rights-conditionality attached to the dealings with both the Government and the LTTE. The donor community pledged $4.5 billion over three years for Sri Lanka in June. A third or so of this was explicitly pledged as relief and rehabilitation for the North and the East. The LTTE quite rightly points out that the relief and rehabilitation in the North and East must involve them as effective and meaningful partners in that process. There is political capital to be had from relief, rehabilitation and development, and they are not going to be hapless bystanders, while the Government secures all of that capital.

Furthermore, the LTTE has made a very valid point that the Sri Lankan bureaucracy has a record of inefficiency and corruption relating to development. The absorption-capacity of Sri Lanka of donor-assistance is also abysmally low. Japan is our key donor, and the absorption rates with regard to Japanese assistance barely reach double-digit figures. The LTTE can quite rightly say that they do not want this kind of a situation in the North and the East: "We are committed to doing a better and a more efficient job. In order to be able to do that, we need the political power and authority", may be their argument.

They also claim that the international interest in Sri Lanka results from their participation in the peace process.

There are almost a million internally-displaced people in Sri Lanka. For them to return to their homes, de-mining has to take place. There are all sorts of property disputes and gender-related problems associated with their return. There are High-Security Zones set up by the Army, a point of particular contention in the North and the East, where a clash between notions of national security, State security and human security are vividly illustrated. The explosive potential of a political nature in this is also brought to light and illustrated very strongly. There is therefore a need to look at, in the second phase of the peace process, as to how one can ensure a more robust human rights protection. Quite frankly, without effective monitoring, it makes no sense at all. Such effective monitoring would require international augmentation of local efforts, and this is a must because it is breeding a great deal of cynicism on the ground.

While these processes cannot totally be transparent, it is very important for those engaged in them to have effective communication strategies with regard to what is going on, certainly as far as their co-supporters are concerned. I engage in a fair amount of work in the south of Sri Lanka, talking to community-based organisations about the peace process. There is a tremendous sense of "We don't know what is happening". There is a tremendous amount of hunger and thirst to know, to have explained to them what 'federalism' would entail, what 'power-sharing' would really mean. This is an exercise which if the Government does not engage in a fairly assertive way, particularly in the context of this electoral cycle over the next two years that I am talking about, would lead to serious problems. A government which does not consult, which does not inform, which does not include, will alienate and isolate the people, and will have to fall upon authoritarianism to be able to maintain itself in power.

An over-riding question is whether the LTTE has really given up secessionism. Are they seriously committed to the peace process? Are they not going to look for the earliest possible opportunity to revert to hostilities as soon as they are ready and convinced that they can secure military advantage? Nothing in the official pronouncements of the LTTE, and in the 'Oslo Declaration' thereafter, indicates that secessionism is completely out of the window. The LTTE's point, made repeatedly by Anton Balasingham, is that secessionism was never the first option. Secessionism therefore will still remain hopefully the last option, which will never have to be exercised, but it is never totally out.

Secondly, look at all the infractions and the violations of the Ceasefire Agreement that we have had, the incidents at sea as well the incidents where the LTTE is setting up camps in areas controlled by the Government, defying the rulings of the Monitoring Mission with regard to removing them, the whole question of rearmament, etc. I want to make the point that the Ceasefire Agreement was essentially predicated upon a military balance of power. There may be nothing in the Ceasefire Agreement that explicitly outlaws rearmament, recruitment, etc. It accepts a particular balance of power and balance of forces, recognising that that balance of forces has resulted in a particular stalemate — and building up a set of understandings and agreements upon it.

There is every argument therefore to say that that balance of forces has to be sustained for the ceasefire to last. That may well require some recruitment and rearmament. And, of course, if the LTTE gets caught sending in ships with armament into Sri Lanka then of course, tough luck, they get caught. If the Government of Sri Lanka tries to recruit soldiers, sets targets of 5000 or 10,000, and gets only 2000 or 3000, tough luck again. But the point is that the Ceasefire Agreement is based upon a balance of forces, that balance of forces needs to be stabilised for the Ceasefire Agreement to continue. Furthermore, the Ceasefire Agreement is in effect an attempt to create, based upon that balance of forces, confidence-building and trust-making between the two sides. Its utility with regard to conflict- transformation is precisely that, to build up trust and confidence between the two sides.

The LTTE had resisted the Sri Lankan State by the force of arms, and had brought it to the stalemate that we have at the present is of fundamental importance. Otherwise, this debate, this initiative for a constitutional settlement, in the context of peace and power-sharing in a new constitutional dispensation in Sri Lanka – paradoxical, ironical even surrealistic as it might be seem – cannot and would not have taken place. The only form of leverage that the Tamil community has – and I say it categorically, unfortunately and tragically – is the military strength of the LTTE *vis-a-vis* the Sri Lankan State. Therefore, questions of decommission and de-militarisation will begin to be talked about only as we approach the last lap of this process, at the very earliest. The hard reality we have to understand and accept is that the LTTE's force of arms is a catalyst and continues to be a source of leverage. Therefore, were the process to be deadlocked, were it to be indefinitely stalemated with adverse political consequences, the possibility of surgical military action for a limited objective in order to push the process, to push the political process, cannot be ruled out. There are a number of scenarios which one can envisage in this context. Not necessarily to return to wholesale hostilities as we had before the Ceasefire Agreement, but rather a limited strategic use of military force to push the process along into the future.

Finally, the question is of how long is this going to take? It is a war that took 20 years. All the platitudes and clichés about commitment and patience do apply. There is one underlying rationale that comes out. That is, both Ranil Wickremesinghe, our Prime Minister, and Velupillai Prabhakaran, the head of the LTTE, have had their own personal experiences with time. Time has served them well. In the context of this peace process too, their understanding, their perception of time, and what it will result in or deliver politically is important. The UNF Government seems to believe that the longer it can sustain a 'no-war-no-peace' situation, the greater is the likelihood that it would not have to give a political and constitutional settlement, which has effective and meaningful power-sharing and federalism. The longer it can maintain a no-war situation, the greater are the chances that it would have blunted the cutting-edge of secessionism. In such a scenario, one does not have to be worried about secession, or indeed about confederation. The ideological rationale of the UNP is, 'Let the money flow, let the goods and services flow, mainstream everyone's concerns, turn it away from discrimination to the cost of living, and then you are well on the way to peace'. This is not cynicism, but hard-headed political reality.

For the LTTE and Prabhakaran, the question of 'no-war-no-peace', with transitional arrangements in between, may well serve to present an even stronger situation on the ground. Effective political control, with *de facto* legal authority as well, which after a point has to be considered *de jure*. Call it what you like, a rose by any other name would smell as sweet. Even if one cannot sit down and face the whole question of building a new Sri Lanka, which is federal, which is meaningful, which has power-sharing, etc., you come to a point at which you cannot ignore it any more as it is the ground reality. The notions and perspectives of the two leaders of historical and political time are now in some sort of context. There is also some sort of convergence between the two as well.

The Sri Lankan situation is full of possibilities. But it also has a number of pitfalls. The challenge is for the civil society to decide whether it wants to impress upon the political leaders the importance of a new constitutional dispensation. Or, does one want to leave the resolution of the conflict to their various political strategies and tactics, which will never really go to the heart of the root of the conflict — but which will bind at all times a fairly tense peace?

Discussion

The participants hoped that the elections early next year would not put a spanner in the works of the peace process.

One participant argued that, regarding the scenario of a 'surgical strike' by the LTTE, Prime Minister Ranil seems to be banking on an 'international safety-net'. Given the international situation, it is likely that the US will condemn the surgical act. But Dr. Saravanamuttu stated that a 'surgical strike' is something he was putting forward as a conceivable possibility in the context of wanting to break a stalemate. If the Government of Sri Lanka was to rely upon the notion of some 'international safety-net' to pull its chestnuts out of the fire, that is a very weak-link to rely upon. The international situation is indeed fluid and there are many scenarios and permutations to the LTTE winning a lot of international sympathy.

On the question of the likely deepening crisis in the South of Sri Lanka, one participant suggested that both the UNP and the PA require the 'Tamil minority' vote if they want to come to power. This could act as a strain, as a restraint, on their whipping up 'Sinhala emotions'.

But other participants felt that while it may be some kind of an inhibiting factor, the issue with regard to the 'Tamil vote' in the South is whether it will come out in full measure. There are more Tamils who are entitled to vote in the South than those who actually do vote. The President's announcement about the reasons why her Sri Lanka Freedom Party broke the JVP alliance perhaps again muddies the waters in terms of who would get that vote. Before that it was quite clear that the bulk of the 'Tamil vote' would have gone to the UNF.

On the issue of whether the Tamils see the LTTE as their real representatives, Dr. Saravanamuttu stated that based on opinion poll surveys of the Centre for Policy Alternatives and resultant 'peace confidence index', the Tamils are as diverse as anyone else and, so there cannot be a single representative of the Tamil people. In the last general elections, there seemed to be a fair degree of consensus that in the context of negotiations, the LTTE was to represent the Tamils. If and when the negotiations move to wider considerations of a constitutional settlement, there may be other representatives of the Tamil people as well. It should be as inclusive as possible. The verdict of the 2001 general elections was – and that was the TNA manifesto and platform as well – that the LTTE will represent the Tamil people at the negotiating table.

Another participant suggested that it would be useful to make a distinction between 'talks' and 'negotiations'. There are talks about talks, and that is what we are dealing with now. And 'negotiations' have not started. 'Negotiations' would be towards a final settlement. Or perhaps, negotiations for an interim administration. We are not yet into the phase of 'negotiations'. Others pointed out that the design of the Sri Lankan Constitution, a compromise between the parliamentary system and the presidential system by itself, defeats any decision-making unless there is a national consensus.

NEGATIVE PEACE

N. Ram

It is an excellent idea to revisit the peace process in Sri Lanka. It is now widely recognised that what is in place in Sri Lanka, although it is very important and widely-welcomed as well, is not a peace accord, not really an enduring peace or stable peace, as Dr. Saravanamuttu has pointed out. He called it neither peace nor war. Others have called it a spell of 'non-fighting', rather prolonged and unprecedented for the last two decades. Some others have called it 'negative peace', which I think is accurate. Initially there was euphoria, but since April 2003, when the LTTE announced the unilateral suspension of its participation in the talks, that euphoria has largely evaporated. People hope against hope, and there is support for the peace process among all constituencies in Sri Lanka, to a considerable extent in India, and internationally also. Nobody has any illusions, no serious illusions at any rate, about the situation in Sri Lanka, because we are all functioning under the shadow of what may be called as the 'LTTE model' of political behaviour.

I share many assessments of Dr. Saravanamuttu, but I differ from him by putting this first at the centre of things. When you are talking about 'Ground Realities', or any kind of assessment of what is taking shape, you have got to do reality-checks. The first task, therefore, is to look at what the track-record has been, and to look at it in an analytical sense. Some of us have been playing around with the idea that there is a model here that has some predictive value. Indeed, the predictive value of this model has been very high, up to this particular peace exercise, or non-fighting exercise. The model is as follows, these are the constituents or elements of the model:

The LTTE is uncompromisingly committed to the strategic goal of 'Tamil Eelam'. It has defined that territory very precisely in a geographical sense. It has, with all the qualifications and caveats it has put forward, proclaimed the point that this can only be achieved by armed struggle, and through no other way. I have, along with various others, interviewed Prabhakaran, had conversations with him as well as others, and never have they vacillated on this particular point. This means that the organisation's basic mode of existence is war through all means. Some would call it terrorism, the term is not important, but war through all means. At the level of Prabhakaran, the organisation has never indicated, not even in the December 2002 statement in Oslo – which was hailed superficially in a somewhat uninformed way by the international media as a 'breakthrough', towards an enduring or final political settlement. I am not talking here about Balasingham's dressed-up translations and elaboration at Prabhakaran's Kilinochchi news conference. At the serious top levels, the organisation has never indicated that it will decisively settle for anything other than a separate and, shall we say a 'Pol Pot-ist State'.

This is not some derogatory term, not meant to condemn but to characterise (the LTTE's demand). It means that this organisation will not allow any other political organisation to flourish – let alone flourish, even exist. This is the reality over the last 20 years, and even in the most recent period. It clearly flows from their ideology and their whole programme: "We are the representatives of the 'liberation cause'. We are the representatives of the 'Tamil people'. The others may be ignorant, may be they compromise, and may be some or many of them are traitors. But we are the true representatives." The sole argument arises of the 'Tamil people'. In his news conference of April 2002, Prabhakaran light-heartedly confirmed that his instructions to his cadres was to shoot him dead if he reneged on the demand for 'Tamil Eelam'. He was asked about it. It was a leading question from the Press. It was replied to light-heartedly, but underlying it was a deadly seriousness: "Yes, the instruction remains", he said.

The model also goes on to say that the LTTE simply will not be persuaded or pressured to make concrete proposals for any political solution short of an 'Eelam'. I differ from Dr. Saravanamuttu that the interim administration proposal is well along the way towards a political settlement, and that it will express the content, the essence of the political settlement The exercise relating to the interim administration proposal must be completely de-linked from whatever kind of political settlement or goal the LTTE wants. It is a bit of an old story that happened during the 1980's. The LTTE agreed, maybe under pressure, partly under persuasion, and partly to keep good relations with India. They agreed on it and it was announced, but they went back on it. So, do not read too much into the shape these proposals take.

We are all speculating when we say that the LTTE will come up with comprehensive proposals relating to an interim administration. It may be a rehashing of the 'Thimpu Principles', but asking for something more practical against that background. Who knows? So, let us wait until October before we even seek to assess the content of those proposals. But the track-record thus far shows that LTTE will not make any concrete, positive, proactive proposals short of 'Tamil Eelam'. From time to time, of course, most of us see it as guided by tactical considerations for tactical purposes to demonstrate their peacefulness or peaceability. The organisation will go in for ceasefires, and talks about talks. I am still talking about the model predating the present Ceasefire Agreement.

The model, as we have claimed in the past with a lot of validity, has predictive value, high predictive value. The LTTE will express willingness to consider reasonable constitutional and political proposals. Any number of times, Prabhakaran has told us that "we are not waging war for war's sake, we are not addicted to killing, there is no other way. These guys, the TULF and the rest, tried it, some of them sincerely and some of them not so sincerely. You know what happened. You cannot trust the Sinhalas. Therefore, we have come to this conclusion, facing hard realities". Therefore, it is not difficult for the LTTE to profess reasonable goals, saying, "If you offer a concrete alternative, we are not addicted to war. We are reasonable people, we are not terrorists, and we are not extremists even". They will sound very accommodative, conciliatory, and express willingness to consider these proposals, especially if they are in the more recent period, helped along by third parties. Earlier they talked about international mediation, now they are complaining about international-meddling. Prabhakaran, in his Heroes' Day address, and recent speeches, and the LTTE in other pronouncements, have taken to complaining about 'international ganging-up' to pressure LTTE.

The LTTE is also not above going along with vague proposals, for quite a period, not just short-spells. For instance, you have President Premadasa's *'Ellam except Eelam'* slogan, or 'Everything except Eelam'. In the Oslo Declaration, the remarkable, contortionist formulation, they said, "The final solution founded on the principle of internal self-determination in areas of the historical habitation of the Tamil-speaking peoples based on a federal structure within an united Sri Lanka". We can decode that to see whether there is any change in that particular stance because, this is the model of 'LTTE political behaviour'.

The model says that the LTTE's *de facto* 'State apparatus' and military machine will go into a higher gear to stock up and expand the gains made from the temporary cessation of hostilities. The LTTE is not above singing the praise of particular Sri Lankan Sinhalese leaders, as with late President Premadasa and, of late, President Chandrika Kumaratunga. Right now praise alternates with patronising, sometimes contemptuous, references to the Ranil Wickremesinghe Government and dispensation. And nice things are being said about Constitutional Affairs Minister G.L. Peiris and company. Meanwhile, they will stock up, go into higher gear. The paper of Iqbal Athas and other writings on this question is of great interest. We also got some briefings from President Chandrika's Senior Advisor Lakshman Kadirgamar, who was here recently, on what according to them is happening in the East, including the Trinconmalee area, particularly where much of the concentration seems to be now. The attempt to build an 'LTTE navy' and so on. I leave this question to experts who are better informed than me, but we follow this and we take this on board in any attempt to assess the state of play today.

Soon enough, patience grows into impatience, and there are public expressions of frustration, increasingly bitter complaints and harsh accusations questioning the sincerity, the capability and the good faith of the other side. Have we not witnessed this in the most recent weeks? Demands, old and new, will be orchestrated in the name of the Tamil people, with the 'liberation cause' setting the stage. I am still talking about the experience pre-dating the signing of the latest accord on the cessation of hostilities. This is the model and the question is whether we can escape the play, or the effects, of this model. Is the model still valid, or will something happen to change that?

Let me balance this comment by quickly pointing out that there is no alternative to seeking a peaceful solution. I fully agree with Dr. Saravanamuttu that both the PA (and, in particular, its outstanding leader, President Kumaratunga) and the UNP (and its interesting leader Ranil Wickremesinghe) have made bold attempts. There is no question about it, whatever be our criticism of their particular approaches. They have made bold attempts, they have seen the truth and have attempted a break-through. The question is not about their sincerity or even their commitment to the peace process. In fact, President Kumaratunga deserves credit for being the first leader to put forward in a non-chauvinistic way, a something akin to a federal solution. She has proposed it repeatedly. Ranil Wickremesinghe, although he came from another place as far as the Tamil question is concerned, has built on it. We must recognise that. We must also recognise the peace dividend – the gains of peace, even non-fighting - 'negative peace'?

The Government of India has done the right thing by doing precisely what it has done: namely, not engaging in this process for obvious political and legal reasons, but wishing the experiment well within certain contours. There are many Indian concerns, which experts presumably will discuss — including concerns over what will happen if the interim administration of the type Prabhakaran talked about, or seemed to hint at and which is being discussed now, comes into place. And concerns about the possible legitimacy of a 'third navy' if the SLMC proposal goes forward and is accepted. But I don't think it can. Then there will be pretty serious implications and even repercussions, because India has a major navy, and it simply does not want an 'LTTE navy' in this vicinity. It does not want it. Period. I think India has its ways and means to prevent it. It can incrementally and actively prevent it. However, these are areas that are best left to security and defence experts.

There are political questions. The Government of India has done the right thing, all the main political parties have done the right thing, by backing the present approach. It really took shape a long time ago, almost a decade ago, after the withdrawal of the IPKF from Sri Lanka, and particularly after the assassination of Rajiv Gandhi by an LTTE squad. Most of us are with the peace process, simply because there is nothing else that we can do. You have to keep trying, and this benighted model keeps on working all the time. Or, is it going to be different this time? That is the question.

Whether there can be a bipartisan agreement in the South is an important question but, in my opinion, a less important question than the one posed by the 'LTTE model' of political behaviour at this stage, or in the recent period. Very often they point to that, and equate the obstacles raised in the South. There are important problems with the kind of intractability that the LTTE's armed, political capability and extremist goals represent. For, the interesting question is: "Does the LTTE have a real choice?" This is a million-dollar question, to quote Dr. Saravanamuttu.

The key question is whether the LTTE is free of constraints in matters of war and peace. Here again the answers can only be speculated. Some people have contended that after 9/11 the international situation and the political climate have been transformed to such an extent that even here in this part of the world this extremist organisation has no real choice. Post-September 11, recidivism, or return to the path of war, and overt terrorism can virtually be ruled out, is the contention from many sides. The proponents view that the Tigers will not return to war because the international situation forbids. They include, or have included in the past, the so-called moderate

Tamil political parties in Sri Lanka. Now they are less certain, they are less optimistic as it appears, but most of them seem to trail the LTTE in its strategy and tactics at this juncture. There are also UNF partisans, peace campaigners, very honourable people; there is a peace constituency in Sri Lanka as elsewhere, and a fluctuating band of international pundits.

An additional factor is the hardened climate for fund-raising by the LTTE in the developed countries. It is suggested that the prospects of these external sources of major fund-raising completely drying up will act as an effective deterrent to Pol Pot-ist recidivism. It is not that LTTE does not have other means, but this is a major one.

These restraining factors are real. They are not to be made light of, and are not to be brushed aside in an exercise of reality-testing. The key question is not if these restraining factors are at work but whether their weight is such as to counteract the LTTE's proven extremism and the Pol Pot-ist character, namely its commitment to 'Tamil Eelam' through war, through all means.

We have also to address the formidable military and political capabilities that this organisation has built up over the years, something almost unique in terms of capabilities. People have written various things on this, and have suggested that the LTTE has not at all revised its fundamental objectives but is only engaged in a tactical ploy, or tactical shift, as a political ploy, to quote D.B.S. Jeyaraj. I do not want to quote him out of context because he has been writing on an evolving situation, but that is one kind of view that is being heard. This kind of reading is backed by the LTTE's horrifying track-record. I think this question must be kept absolutely open. Nobody can be certain about the answer to this question, whether the LTTE is free to do something else. Much depends on how that question is answered on the ground.

Some of us thought that the donors' exercise might exert constructive pressure on the LTTE. Somewhat surprisingly, some of our expectations have been upset, including those of the Japanese envoy Akashi. I have had the benefit of several discussions with him on this question. They keep trying but the question is whether the donors' exercise, the idea of bringing in substantial funds for relief, rehabilitation and reconstruction of the North and the East would act as an incentive. The sums are huge. Please remember that Rajiv Gandhi offered very substantial sums after the signing of the Indo-Sri Lanka Agreement in the July of 1987. That did not work and that right now we are witnessing the same kind of response: "You cannot buy us, you cannot bribe us, you cannot attract us through these incentives."

Development seems to be the answer that this extremist organisation is providing at this juncture, but let's wait and see. This absolutely central question, whether the LTTE is free to do something else in the current international situation, is uncertain. Without attempting to answer this question directly, let me point out a change in the international situation compared with the early days of this war of aggression and occupation by the US, along with its ally the UK and some others. Initially, the assessment put out was that today you cannot fight this kind of war. Everybody said it, including people I know. It turned out to be superficial. The other day President Musharraf reminded us, from the UN General Assembly, that he was trying to buck the trend of international public opinion, distinguishing between militancy for legitimate causes, and pure and simple terrorism. Others have also attempted to do it.

We also know that it is now not easy to win and to occupy. The US seems to be caught in some sort of quagmire. It is pleading for contributions of troops from countries like India

— what we may call cannon-fodder. Without going into details, the question is whether you are getting the same signals from the international system as you were getting some months ago. If the answer is no, the signal is different, and the lessons are different, the implication would be that this would provide space for the organisations like the LTTE to buck the international trend. I am not seeking to answer the question if it is free to do something else, but this has to be factored into it. At the moment, we are speculating.

The next question is whether a 'Southern consensus' is possible. Again without going into details I agree with Dr. Saravanamuttu predecessor that the executive President has not done anything to inhibit the Ranil Wickremesinghe Government. They may look for excuses. President Kumaratunga, in my opinion, has been remarkably moderate and sober, notwithstanding attempts to impeach her and to bring in a constitutional amendment to clip the executive President's wings, to virtually neutralise the executive part of the presidency. Since the Supreme Court gave that a short shrift a certain rebalancing has taken place, it appears, but there has been no attempt as far as we know to obstruct, to sabotage, or to undermine this bold initiative from the UNF Government.

There are problems with the (Sinhala right) JVP, or Janatha Vimukthi Peramuna. We note with interest what Dr. Saravanamuttu said, namely that there has not been the kind of opportunism that was feared. The obvious reason is that both the main parties are convinced – you cannot but be convinced – that there is no solution through war. Therefore, they cannot make common cause with somebody who says that Sri Lanka has to be a unitary State, that you can win or tackle this only through military means, if you are to represent the JVP position accurately. There is a very interesting report, the opinion of an expert on this question: "Though the

'Southern consensus' is not an easy issue to resolve, it is a subsidiary issue in the present situation. It is more easily won than any real progress towards a final constitutional settlement in Sri Lanka." If there was a genuine indication of the LTTE going against its grain and that it will consider reasonable proposals, I fully agree with my predecessor the attempt will be a reasonable solution, a federal solution.

This solution can only be federal. The details can be discussed. I remember that the subject given to me for the first 'Amrithalingam Memorial Lecture' in Sri Lanka, which I gave at the invitation of the TULF, was 'The need for federalism in Sri Lanka'. That it has to be federal has been obvious for a long time. But is the LTTE serious about it? At times it talks of a confederacy. Are they seriously engaging with the idea of federalism, or are they serious about the quest for a 'Tamil Eelam' through armed struggle? Federalism means a range of things, there is real range here, from what you have in India, which some people would call a quasi-federal system or model, to a more genuinely federal agreement verging on confederacy in some cases. So far, the indications are not very positive on that point.

What about the 'interim administration' in this scheme of things? The LTTE has returned to the idea put forth by Prabhakaran in the news conference of April 2002. He basically said that the LTTE was going to talks in Thailand to settle the question, to discuss the question of interim administration. It proved difficult, and so they sidelined it and took the 'empowered committee' route. They have now returned to their demand for an interim administration, knowing the difficulties that this poses. The idea of an interim administration is quite old. It is to help the LTTE take charge until a final political settlement is reached. It does not indicate the nature and contours of that final settlement.

This came on the agenda with the implementation of the India-Sri Lanka Agreement of July 1987, even though the text of that agreement did not mention or provide for an interim administration. The LTTE first agreed to it, and then went back on what was an extremely liberal Indian proposal — virtually handing it over to the LTTE, overwhelming majority was what was proposed. There was some dispute about who would head it and so on, but there was no discussion about the kind of interim administration or the kind of leadership envisaged.

The widespread impression about the approach of the Ranil Wickremesinghe Government has been that it is in no hurry to find a final political solution, because you could say cynically that it knows as much as anyone else does that it is going to be very hard. It is perhaps not realistically achievable, in its assessment. If that is the assessment, it will make a lot of sense to prolong the period of non-fighting, in any conventional reckoning. Apprehensions have been expressed, of course, in India in a rather mild way (mainly through the Press) about handing over the North and the East to the LTTE — and the implications it would have for India.

In Sri Lanka more seriously, this has run into heavy political weather. It also interacts with democratic, security and human rights concerns. They have been raised and for obvious reasons the UNF Government has been unable to put in place the interim administration of the type Prabhakaran wants and it is quite willing to concede. Politically-speaking, the Supreme Court judgment, restoring the balance of power between the President and the parliamentary majority, ruled out in principle and by implication an interim administration for the North and the East. The proposal will not pass muster with President Kumaratunga, whose executive powers cannot be taken away without a constitutional amendment requiring a two-thirds majority in Parliament and approval in a referendum.

For the LTTE to say that you have to think out-of-the-box, or to think out of the Constitution is a futile demand. It puts pressure on the system, and the Government comes up with repeated proposals, different versions of what the LTTE sees as not much of an interim administration. I do not think this is achievable easily. If the LTTE, however, decides to go along with the 'sub-interim administration' solution, it is a different thing. I do not think that even the interim administration of the type that was offered even in 1987 by Indian High Commissioner J. N. Dixit – he played a very prominent part at that time – is on the agenda, let alone an interim administrative structure that would reveal the contours of the future.

What will happen to the 'parallel State' structure? It has often been said that an "armed struggle is required for getting something for the Tamils. Without the armed struggle, we are finished. Without the 'parallel State' structure run by the LTTE, we are finished".

I read in the paper of Iqbal Athas that there are various estimates, from 6000 to 18,000, of the increase in LTTE's military strength. He is better informed on it, quoting intelligence sources – from 9000 - something to nearly 20,000. Let us say that LTTE has doubled its fighting strength during this period. On the Sri Lankan side in contrast, there have been desertions, there has been a lack of vigilance, there has been a lack of shaping-up, as it appears from a layman's point of view. There are serious concerns here. Setting up a parallel State structure and seeking to legitimise it is pretty close to 'Eelam', isn't it? In effect, the LTTE says that it already runs a 'parallel State' structure, and the job now is to legitimise it in the name of federalism or confederacy or whatever. Internal self-determination, in this context, becomes a joke of the term.

What is 'internal self-determination'? Internal self-determination is what we have in India. If we go through the Constituent Assembly debates, Dr. Ambedkar talked about the principles of federalism, the division of legislative, executive and judicial powers, and also the power between the Centre and the States. That is principle number one in federalism. It is a genuine partitioning of sovereignity, in an internal sense. Secondly, all this flows from a written, compact Constitution. It has to be constitutional. Thirdly, you need an arbiter, an arbitrator, or an umpire to judge disputes that will come up all the time when there is divided sovereignity in an internal sense. And fourthly, you may add, power-sharing at the Centre. These are the principles, the building blocks, of federalism. Is this the kind of federalism that the LTTE wants, or is going to settle for? I would very much doubt it, because you are talking about a 'parallel State structure' and legitimising it. Tax-collection and kangaroo courts. At one point, there were reports of a 'chief justice of Tamil Eelam'. And, of course, the arms business. These are serious questions.

Finally, another important question: the framework for a final settlement. Let us look at the Oslo formulation. The two sides decided to explore a solution founded on the principle of 'internal self-determination in areas of historical habitation of the Tamil-speaking people based on a federal structure in a united Sri Lanka'. At that time, there was over-interpretation, and there were some ill-informed readings in the international Press, talking about a breakthrough. It was suggested that a political agenda has been brought forward, so that the fourth and the fifth round of talks in Thailand could engage with the other three major areas identified. These are :

- Consolidation of the ceasefire,
- Humanitarian and rehabilitation action, and
- Political matters.

The actual formulation was a statement of intent, a statement of endeavour. That is all what it was. The key words in the so-called breakthrough were:

a. The principle of internal self-determination,
b. A federal structure, mentioned for the first time in an LTTE official statement,
c. Areas of the historical habitation of the Tamil-speaking people, and
d. A united Sri Lanka.

How would these key words or concepts perform together? What is, for example, the relationship between the principle of 'internal self-determination' and the 'federal structure'? Are the 'areas of historical habitation of the Tamil-speaking people' a proxy for the 'homeland' that the LTTE has always claimed as the historically-determined birthright of the Sri Lankan Tamils? Can the principle of 'internal self-determination' be exercised within a united Sri Lanka, given the 'parallel State' structure which you seek to legitimise? In order to answer these questions, we have plenty of theoretical as well as practical hints from the LTTE.

You have the first three of the four 'Thimpu Principles', put forward in July and August 1985. These are:

- Recognition of the Sri Lankan Tamils as a distinct nationality,
- Recognition of the traditional Tamil homeland, that is the North and the East in toto without excising anything, and a guarantee of the integrity of this traditional homeland, and
- Recognition of the right to self-determination of the Tamil nation.

And you have Prabhakaran's notorious instruction issued in his 1999 Heroes' Day address to his cadres, to gun him down if ever he committed treachery to the ideal of 'Tamil Eelam'. That was reiterated, light-heartedly as I said, in the Press conference of April 2002.

Given these realities, it really is an uphill task to achieve anything really enduring. I return to the theme that there is no alternative to trying. Most of us would agree that nobody wants a return to war. Nobody believes that the Sri Lankan State has the capability or the will or whatever to vanquish the LTTE, to bring it to heel. You have got to live with this situation, and that is the basis of all these endeavours. However, a reality-check would tell you that the kind of optimism and the kind of support or legitimisation of the LTTE's strategy and tactics that we hear all over the place, is ill-founded, and not based on a sound and fair assessment. It is running away from realities to some extent. It is to ignore concerns that have arisen on the security and the defence-related fronts and the human rights front as well; and this is where we are. So, we cannot realistically present any kind of optimistic assessment or prognosis. I can only leave the question if the LTTE is free to do something else at this juncture.

There are serious doubts about whether the system or the process of today is capable of delivering an interim administration that would be a real constructive solution. It has to be a solution that would take you towards a final settlement. There is no question about being optimistic about a final settlement, but at least on the interim administration, is it do-able, and should it be done? On these questions, I cannot provide any positive endorsement of what is going on.

Discussion

There was some discussion about the term 'federalism'. Some of the participants pointed out that it was not necessary to call it 'federal' if you did not want to. Nowhere in the Indian Constitution is the word 'federal' mentioned, nor even in the US Constitution, but it is very much federal in content and essence. So, federalism by whatever name, incorporating the principles, is the key. Whatever is acceptable to reasonable representatives of both sides would be fine.

Some participants questioned whether the concept of 'Tamil Eelam' will survive Prabhakaran. Others pointed out that the concept has a considerable history, well beyond Prabhakaran. It had been raised earlier, and therefore the idea has been around. But the question is whether it is winnable, and whether it is right. Other than the constituency of Sri Lankan Tamils and their supporters, the overwhelming international sentiment is, "No, no secession". And 'Tamil Eelam' means secession. However, there can be accommodation for a good part of the way, through what is now called (in a very broad or loose sense) a federal solution. But the idea will not go away.

On the issue of the effect of the 'war on terrorism' and the US ban on the LTTE, it was pointed out that Deputy Prime Minister L.K. Advani was very disappointed that Pakistan and Indian problems in Kashmir did not figure in the list when US President George Bush spoke about it. These are formal things, and there is no question that these are factors. They are dampeners, deterrents or whatever. The question is if they could overwhelm or neutralise the LTTE's extremist capabilities along the lines indicated. Nobody can answer it, except speculatively. It may not rule out any return to war. It may make war more difficult.

One should also look at the length of the present spell of non-fighting, the killings, the thuggery. The fact is that the number of deaths has come down, injuries have come down, the economic burden is much less, and that is all part of the ground realities. It was mentioned that Ranil Wickremesinghe's calculation may be that even if the LTTE makes trouble and there are ups and downs, if the process simply goes on, then it becomes 'irreversible'. Everyone claims that the process they want is irreversible, like liberalisation, globalisation, etc. Is the present process in Sri Lanka irreversible? No, it is clear that it is not irreversible.

One of the participants said that the Indian position must be clearly and emphatically stated, that we do not conceive of any situation in which there can be secession. We are solidly behind a federal Sri Lanka. Secondly, we must also make it clear to all the various factions involved that there should be no attempt to rough-ride over the legitimate aspirations of the Tamil community.

Another participant said that when the ceasefire was announced in Sri Lanka it was very clearly understood that *status quo* would be maintained. The *status quo* has not been maintained, largely by the LTTE. The strength of its armed cadres has grown in this period of 18-19 months, from 7000-8000 to 19,000-20,000. It has acquired more arms. It has recruited more people. Prabhakaran has been instrumental in assassinating more Tamil leaders of a different viewpoint, some 50 or 60 attacks were mounted, some of which were unsuccessful. So the process of violence goes on, on the one hand, and on the other, the acquisition of military strength, with the obvious thought that eventually there may have to be a clash of arms once again. There is a violation of the spirit of ceasefire, if not of the ceasefire as such in formal terms. There is no peace process. There is a kind of armed truce.

Another factor is that there are too many foreign cooks getting into the act, and not doing the right thing. The Japanese are in the act now, because the Japanese want to establish their presence in the international arena, with a view of making a case for their permanent membership in the UN Security Council. Otherwise, what role does Japan have in this? There were Norwegians and others involved already and why are these meetings taking place all over the world? Why not in Colombo, or in Jaffna, or in Trincomalee? Leave out India for the time being. Now, what are they doing? The Sri Lankan Monitoring Mission (SLMM) is indulging the LTTE. They have more or less given recognition to the 'Sea Tigers'.

Then there is the expansion of the area of LTTE's occupation and influence. What is happening in Trincomalee is of very grave concern to India. Someone shoulu give a wake up call to the Government of India, though it should not get involved in the situation. We burnt our fingers, and now we should give others a chance to try their luck. Or, the two principal parties should sort matters out between themselves. However, if India's strategic and economic interests get seriously compromised by the actions of the LTTE, the Government of India will have to seriously reconsider its own role, and its present passivity. It is not disinterested, it is watchful but it is passive.

In the Eastern province of Sri Lanka, a new situation is developing, which is full of potential for trouble. There have been attacks on the Muslim community, and the Muslim community is beginning to arm itself. Pakistan is showing some interest in Sri Lanka's internal situation. It remains to be seen as to which direction this moves, and what kind of threat it holds for the future. This is something that we need to take into account.

While the LTTE has been enhancing its war-fighting capability, there has been a decline in the capability of the Sri Lankan Government forces in the form of more desertions, no worthwhile acquisitions of the arms, ammunition and so on. As regards the "irreversibility" of the peace process or the ceasefire, there was a kind of understanding or decision between India and Pakistan in 1972, about the situation in Kashmir. For 12 years the ceasefire, that armed truce, was maintained. But we are back in trouble again. The present situation may get itself transformed into permanent peace, but a more active process is needed.

The prospect of various elections will create some difficulty for the time being, and the Sri Lankan Government will not be able to act decisively in the months to come. The presidential wing and the prime ministerial wing of the Government will have to pull their act together. That is another complication in the situation. That is the ground reality, which we have to reckon with.

Reconciling Various Ethnic Aspirations

Sri Lankan Nationalism, Ethnic Identity and Community

Dr. Devanesan Nesiah

Sri Lanka got independence from the British on 4 February 1948. There were no struggles comparable to those by anti-imperialist nationalist groups in the sub-continent. Unlike other South Asian leaders, those of pre-independence Sri Lanka remained constantly in good standing with the colonial rulers. While anti-imperialist leaders in India were frequently jailed by the British for long periods, this never happened in Sri Lanka, where only a few Marxists were arrested. The "national" leaders continued to wine and dine with their imperialist masters.

On the sub-continent, notably in India, there have been a succession of serious caste, tribal, religious, linguistic and other riots from pre-independence years, but there was also a countervailing all-India nationalism that helped to overcome and quell such riots and the tensions caused by them. There were no major ethnic riots in Sri Lanka since the anti-Muslim riots of 1915, and inter-communal relations appeared to be friendly. But what passed for "Sri Lankan nationalism" was superficial, and quickly disintegrated after independence. When riots did take place, there were no major national leaders to intervene and heal, and we stumbled into 17 years of civil war, which now stands suspended but yet unresolved.

Sadly, even though there are only two indigenous national languages, except among the Muslims, Sinhala-Tamil bilingual proficiency is very low in comparison with bilingual proficiency in other countries of South and South-East Asia. There are very few schools or other institutions that teach Sinhala to Tamil-speakers, or Tamil to Sinhala-speakers. There are very few government offices that provide adequate services in both Sinhala and Tamil. Successive Governments have not seen fit to effectively promote Sinhala-Tamil bilingualism through educational and governmental policies. The negative impact of the lack of such bilingualism on national integration is incalculable.

At the time of independence, the population of 'Malaiyaha Tamils', or 'plantation Tamils' of Indian origin was comparable in number to the 'Sri Lankan Tamil' population. It is significant that the first major post-independence political development was the elimination of the citizenship and voting rights of the 'Malaiyaha Indian Tamils'. The greater part of this population was eventually 'repatriated' to India, and a minor part eventually granted citizenship and voting rights. There is yet a residual category of the State-less, but they are likely to be granted citizenship. However, these measures have permanently changed the ethnic balance of the population and of the Sri Lankan Parliament.

Successive Governments have continued with colonial style the 'divide-and-rule' ideology, but adapted to post-independence realities. The Sri Lankan Tamil, Malaiyaha Tamil and Muslim categories of the Tamil-speaking population have remained not only socially distinct but also politically divided, very much to their disadvantage. Most of the Sri Lankan Tamil and Muslim members of Parliament had found it opportune to vote for the legislation reducing 'Indian Tamils' to Stateless-ness. In doing so, they served to significantly tilt the political balance towards majority domination and to bring about a series of ethnic crises that began in the 1950's. The trauma of the 'Indian Tamils' in being reduced to Stateless-ness immediately after independence was followed a few years later by the 'Sinhala-only' policies — which most Muslim leaders were induced to support, though these measures severely affected the status and opportunities of all Tamil-speaking persons, including Muslims — and the riots of 1956 and 1958, which caused much loss of life and property, and physical insecurity among the Tamils. These events have led to profound negative political and social changes.

As in many other parts of the globe, ethnic-consciousness is rooted in myths dear to many. The Sinhala myths include the 'Vijayan legend' related to the origins of the Sinhalas, the 'Aryan' racial classification, that of being a chosen people on a chosen island and charged by the Buddha to protect and nurture Buddhism, together with the converse – that unlike other communities of Sri Lanka, the Sinhalese have no other home. This neo-Zionist, '*Bhumiputra* concept' is widely held. Tamil myths include direct descent from the population of the civilisations of Mohenjadaro and Harappa, and another even more advanced civilisation based on lands now covered by the Indian Ocean. Muslim myths include Arab racial origins, on which are based Muslim claims to be a distinct ethnic group.

There may be a small core of truth in some of these myths, but there is also much evidence that all the major communities in Sri Lanka are racially hybrid with much the same racial inputs, though there may be modest differences in the proportions of these inputs. The racial differences within each of these communities may be greater than those between the communities.

Many also subscribed to caste myths, which are no less numerous and insidious than race myths. Caste ideology should surely derive any legitimacy from religious scriptures, but only the Hindu scriptures, notably the *Manu Smriti*, upholds caste. However, caste as understood and practised in Sri Lanka is incompatible even with the *Manu Smriti*. For example, an essential feature of high caste is that the males are entitled to and must wear the sacred thread. But even the most exalted Goigama Buddhist and Tamil Vellala families do not claim this right. Only a very small number of Brahmins and certain others, mostly of relatively recent Indian origin do so. The right of these 'certain others' to wear the sacred thread is subject to dispute. The traditional Sinhala and Sri Lankan Tamil elite, including all categories of Goigamas and Vellalas, are predominantly of *Sudra* origin. There has been some admixture of 'higher' castes but, as clearly spelt out in the *Manu Smriti*, such miscegenation does not provide escape for the progeny from Sudra status.

Ethnic Classification

The last complete all-island Census in 1981 classified the population into six ethnic groups: Sinhalese, Sri Lankan Tamil, Indian-Malaiyaha Tamil, Sri Lankan Moor, Burgher and Malay. Various other very small ethnic communities were classified as 'Others'. The census found the ethnic composition of the population to be 74 per cent Sinhalese, 12.7 per cent Sri Lankan Tamil, 5.5 per cent Malaiyaha Indian Tamil, 7 per cent Sri Lankan Moor, 0.3 per cent Burgher, 0.3 per cent Malay, and 0.2 per cent 'Others'. Since then, the categories have remained unchanged.

The percentages may have changed, but only marginally, for diverse reasons. For example, emigration and birth rate may vary from group to group. There could also be some reclassifications of ethnicity in the census declarations. The process of gradual integration of the 'Sri Lankan Moor' and 'the Malay' into the 'Muslim' community is continuing, but this development has not yet received official recognition in the census classification. For the purpose of this paper, it is this Muslim category that will engage our attention rather than the separate Moor and Malay categories. The Indian Tamil community will be referred to as Malaiyaha Tamils, which is their preferred identity.

Traditionally, ethnic identity has been defined in terms of race and descent. In some societies, race has remained the most significant factor but in many, with the progressive discrediting of race theories, the emphasis has shifted to cultural features. Because the various cultural features may not be co-related, the focus frequently, but not always, settled on language. In a few, the critical feature was religion, history, territory or citizenship. The defining features of ethnicity in Sri Lanka appeared to be history and language except that these seem to be over-ridden in the case of Muslims, by religion. But in popular consciousness these features are inseparable from the ethnic myths referred to earlier.

To define an ethnic group on the basis of religious affiliation cutting across racial and linguistic boundaries, may appear anomalous, but there is a historical background to the political evolution of the Muslim identity. Till the 1880's, this was not a major issue but the most widely-recognised ethnic identity of most Muslims in Sri Lanka was 'Moor' although, as pointed out by Ameer Ali, 'a majority of them were from the sub-continent'. A speech in the Legislative Council by the Sri Lankan Tamil leader Ponnambalam Ramanathan, claiming that the Moors were really Tamils and not entitled to separate representation under the British colonial communal representation scheme, raised the stakes.

The Moors were driven to affirming their distinct Moor ethnic identity. Following the 1915 anti-Muslim riots, the issue resurfaced with a section of the Moors reaffirming their 'Ceylon Moor' identity to distance themselves from other Muslim groups. Another section, together with the Malays and other non-Moor Muslims, preferred a unifying 'Muslim' identity. Over the decades, 'Muslim' has emerged as the preferred political identity of the Moors, Malays and several other Muslim communities in Sri Lanka.

The identifying criteria for ethnic classification is often problematic. Even the non-racial definitions such as language pose difficulties. For example, many middle class Sri Lankans and a large proportion of Sri Lankan expatriates speak English even in their homes. So, in effect, their mother tongue is English. But does this redefine their ethnicity? Similarly, most Sri Lankan Muslims speak Tamil at home, and their children have their schooling in the Tamil medium. But lately increasing proportions of Muslims speak Sinhala or English at home, and their children have their schooling in the Sinhala or English medium. Does this redefine their ethnicity?

All of us have multiple identities, which is healthy. Group identities are as necessary as individual identities. So is pluralism. Without distinctive group and individual features, life would be unbearably bland. On the other hand, few would wish to belong to a society in which there is total co-relation of all features of group identity – the ultimate end product of 'ethnic-cleansing'. The most pragmatic basis of ethnic identity may be a sense of community. Do all Sri Lankans have the same ethnic identity? Are those categorised as 'Kandyan Sinhalese' and 'Low Country Sinhalese' of the same or different ethnic identity? Are those categorised as Sri Lankan Tamils, Malaiyaha Tamils and Muslims of the same or different ethnic identity? Since we all have multiple identities, there can be no definitive answers to these questions. Perhaps, it is just as well. But this is not to deny that some identities are felt to be more important than others and, in particular, politically more potent.

The civil war in Sri Lanka relates to perceptions of ethnic identity and loyalties, and felt grievances linked to these perceptions. Conflicts cannot be overcome by mere definition or re-definition of ethnicity. Nor can ethnic identities be foisted on any community or individual. We all need to decide for ourselves what our ethnic identities are, and which of these is most salient in any particular context. In national politics one identity may surface as the most salient, in local politics another, in literary matters a third, in religious life a fourth, and so on. Moreover, the weights we attach to these identities may change over time.

For example, up to the mid-20th century, the Kandyan Sinhalese sought recognition as a distinctive ethnic community, with special political and administrative structure to secure and sustain their welfare. This was accepted and special provisions were made for the socio-economic development of the Kandyan areas and the Kandyan Sinhalese population. In addition, all revenue divisions were categorised into Kandyan Sinhalese, Low Country Sinhalese and Tamil, with separate cadres of Divisional Revenue Officers serving these areas. Recruitment to each of these three cadres was exclusively from the community concerned, and postings were to Kandyan, Low Country and Tamil areas. In this classification, 'Tamil included Muslim', but the distinction between Kandyan Sinhalese and Low Country Sinhalese was strictly maintained in both recruitment and posting. In fact, in at least one instance, a person selected to the Kandyan Sinhalese cadre was subsequently excluded from recruitment when it was found that he was of Low Country Sinhalese origin.

Perhaps, Kandyan Sinhalese no longer claim a distinctive ethnic identity requiring separate political and administrative structures. It is for them to decide on this matter, and not for others to dictate them. On the other hand, Muslims who earlier subsumed within the Tamil category in respect of the DRO service, may now wish to be recognised as a distinct ethnic community. Again, it is for them to decide, and not for others to dictate them. So too in the case of Malaiyaha Tamils, although they are virtually undifferentiated from Sri Lankan Tamils in terms of language, religion and ancestry. In the Fifties and Sixties there was a move by the Federal Party under the leadership of S.J.V. Chelvanayagam to bring the Sri Lankan Tamil, Muslim and Malaiyaha Tamil groups together into a single "Tamil-speaking people" classification, but it failed. Even the electoral alliances forged with this objective were short-lived. Perhaps, in due course, the Sri Lankan Tamil and Malaiyaha Tamil identities may merge, but this can happen only through gradual changes in self-identification, and cannot be imposed from above or from outside.

Within each of the four major officially-identified ethnic groups, viz. Sinhalese, Sri Lankan Tamil, Malaiyaha Tamil and Sri Lankan Moor, there are fundamental differences in interests and aspirations, depending on factors such as class and region. Currently, caste and religious differences within the Sinhalese and within the Tamils do not seem to have a significant impact on political activities, but remain important in social relations. The rising salience of ethnicity has muted the expression of some of these features, but they may need to be taken into the account in instituting remedial measures. In particular, the geographical distribution of each of the ethnic groups is of critical importance.

Population and Geographical Distribution

On account of the civil war, no census was attempted in 1991. The 2001 Census did not cover most of the Tamil-majority North and the East. According to the 1981 Census, the Sinhalese constituted over 74 per cent of the population in every district except Nuwara Eliya in the Central Province, Badulla in the Uva Province, and the district of the North and the East. In the Central Province as a whole they constituted over 64 per cent and in the Uva Province 73 per cent. By 2001, the Sinhalese population had increased further in these two provinces to 65.3 per cent and 79.6 per cent, respectively. Table 1 gives the percentage-distribution in respect of religion by districts, 1981 and 2001. Table 2 gives the percentage distribution in respect of ethnicity by districts, 1981 and 2001.

In 1981, the Sri Lankan Tamils were 10 per cent of the population of Colombo district, 12.7 per cent in Nuwara Eliya and less than seven per cent in every other district outside the North and the East. They were a clear majority in every district in the North and in Batticaloa. In the Northern Province, Tamils were 86 per cent, the Muslims five per cent and the Sinhalese three per cent. They were the largest ethnic group in Trincomalee, which also had very substantial numbers of Muslims and Sinhalese, and the second largest in Ampara, in which the Muslims were the most numerous, and the Sinhalese were present in large numbers. In the Eastern Province as a whole, the Tamils formed 41 per cent, the Muslims 32 per cent, and the Sinhalese 25 per cent. The largest proportion of Muslims was in Ampara district, 41.6 per cent. Of the combined population of the temporarily merged North-Eastern Province, the Tamils formed 65 per cent, the Muslims 18 per cent and the Sinhalese 13 per cent.

The Malaiyaha Tamils were 42.7 per cent of the population in Nuwara Eliya district, 20.2 per cent in Badulla district, and less than 20 per cent in every other district. But in the 2001 Census which did not cover Jaffna, Mannar, Vavunia, Mullaitivu, Kilinochchi, Batticaloa and Trincomalee districts, these percentages had dropped to 21.3 per cent and 18.2 per cent, respectively. This drop could be due to migration to India, internal migration to the North and the East and, possibly, reclassification as 'Sri Lankan Tamil'.

In terms of religion, there are four major categories. Buddhists, almost entirely Sinhalese, were 69.3 per cent of the population in 1981. Hindus, overwhelmingly drawn from the Sri Lankan Tamil and Malaiyaha Tamil populations, formed 15.5 per cent of the population, Muslims Moor and Malay 7.5 per cent, and the Christians 7.6 per cent. The Christians constituted 6.2 per cent of the Sinhalese and a little over 13 per cent of the combined Tamil population. The Christians are disproportionately concentrated in the western districts and the coastal areas of the North. They constitute 42.1 per cent of Mannar, 37.9 per cent of Puttlam, 23.4 per cent of Gampaha, 15.8 per cent of Mullaitivu, 12.6 per cent of Jaffna and 11.6 per cent of Colombo. Overall, nearly 90 per cent of the Christian population is Roman Catholic. The Sinhalese constitute about three-fifths of the Christian population, and the Tamils, about a third.

The Religious Factor

The various communities that constitute the population of Sri Lanka have co-existed for many centuries. Except for intermittent localised conflicts, which mostly manifest in bursts of religious intolerance on the part of certain rulers, this co-existence has largely been peaceful and harmonious. In particular, Buddhists and Hindus, Sinhalese and Tamils, have lived together for over two millennia. Hinduism prevailed in most of the island before the advent of Buddhism and, in some regions, in subsequent centuries. Further, over these centuries, very large numbers of Hindu immigrants to the island converted to Buddhism. In turn, Buddhism prevailed among the Tamil population of South India and Sri Lanka in the early part of the first millennium. In these centuries, the various schools of Buddhism as well as eminent Buddhist scholars and missionaries flourished and spread across Asia from centres in South India.

Of the two greatest of the available Tamil epics of the early part of the first millennium, viz. the *Silappathiharam* and the *Manimehalai*, the former is Jain, and the latter Buddhist. A critical episode of the latter epic relates to a journey to Sri Lanka of the heroine, a Buddhist nun. Hinduism, Buddhism and Jainism co-existed in South India in the period covered by these two epics, but there is no hint in either epic of any inter-religious conflict or tension. In fact, the heroines of both epics continue to be revered by people of all three faiths. Buddhist-Hindu linkages continued to be close and friendly until the militant revival of Hinduism around the middle of that millennium.

Even in subsequent centuries, despite conflict in some localities, there was continued co-existence in others with porous boundaries. The bulk of the ancestors of Sri Lankans who now profess Buddhism had been Hindu for some centuries. In turn, the bulk of the ancestors of those who now profess Hinduism had been Buddhist or Jain for some centuries. It is therefore not surprising that there are ancient Buddhist and Hindu ruins spread across many parts of the island. Moreover, many Sinhalese kings were of Tamil origin and converted to Buddhism. And many of their wives remained Hindu.

Hindu gods are worshipped in the sacred places of Buddhism, and Hindu practices, traditions and festivals are incorporated into those of Buddhism. In turn, many Hindu temples have benefited from the generosity of Buddhist kings. We need to recognise and celebrate the many shared components of the beliefs, culture, traditions, festivals and practices of the Sinhalese and the Tamils, and of the Buddhists and the Hindus. Superficially, it may appear that the ethnic conflict is primarily between the pre-dominantly Buddhist-Sinhalese and pre-dominantly Hindu-Tamils, that the essential political, social and cultural divide is Buddhist-Hindu. But in fact Buddhist-Hindu relations are not only more ancient but also deeper and more durable than any other.

Islam and Christianity also entered the island many centuries ago. Muslim travellers and traders, and Christian travellers and missionaries, have entered the island since the first millennium. But it was around the middle of the second millennium that significant numbers of the population of the island came to profess Islam or Christianity. Currently, about 7.5 per cent of the population is Muslim and a similar proportion is Christian. Of these two faiths, Christian traditions and practices seem to be closer to those of the Buddhists and the Hindus. Buddhist and Christian-Sinhalese have much in common in their beliefs, culture and festivals, as do Hindu and Christian-Tamils. In contrast, those converting to Islam lose their former ethnic identity and acquire a new one, viz. Muslim.

In relation to all four faiths, there has been a substantial degree of syncretism, for example in shared sacred spaces. Kataragama is sacred to Buddhists and Hindus alike, but it also a place of pilgrimage for small numbers of Muslims and Christians. Adam's Peak is pre-dominantly a place of Buddhist pilgrimage, but also attracts Hindu, Muslim and Christian pilgrims. The different communities associate the Peak with the Buddha, Siva and Adam, respectively. Thus, Ibn Batuta, the famed Muslim visitor to the island in AD1344, was not only motivated to ascend the Peak but also went on to affirm the Muslim claims in respect of the 'Mountain of Serendib' as follows: "At the foot of the mountain, at the place of the gateway is a grotto inscribed with the name of Iskandar Alexander the Great, and a spring of water. The impression of the noble Foot, that of our Father Adam, is observed in a black and lofty rock in an open space under a pagoda-like canopy. The foot is sunk in the stone. Its length is 11 spans."

Several Christian churches and Hindu temples attract pilgrims from other faiths. Religion-related beliefs, as in astrology or in exorcism, have spread across religious boundaries, and its practitioners have believers from diverse faiths. Similarly, devotees of god-men like Sai Baba and many lesser-known cult figures are to be found among all ethnic and religious groups. What is relevant for our purpose is not the merit or de-merit of such beliefs and practices, but the fact that they are shared by those of diverse faiths and ethnic groups, and such sharing holds some potential for national unity.

Unlike Buddhism and Hinduism, both of which originated in the Indian sub-continent, Islam and Christianity have Semitic, West Asian origins, and have not meshed as smoothly as the other two. Islam in particular has remained distinct to the extent that those who profess that faith regard themselves as constituting a separate ethnic group. However, despite the rise of religious fundamentalism among some sections of Muslims and Christians, there has been very little of the kind of inter-religious conflicts that have featured in several other countries of Asia. Except for occasional localised clashes of short duration, conflict in Sri Lanka has been rooted not in religion, but in the traditional ethnic categories.

Ethnic Concerns and Aspirations

The common concerns of all citizens, cutting across ethnic and other boundaries, are the promotion of inter-communal unity and harmony, physical security, the enjoyment of equal rights and improvements in the quality of life. Another common concern is the fear that the State and/or Sinhalese/Tamil/ Muslim non-State actors may seek to impose changes in the ethnic composition of "border areas" with a view to expanding the "ethnic frontier" of one group or the other. Differences have existed, and still exist, on the kinds or constitutional and structural changes, governmental and administrative reforms, and educational, social and cultural programmes that would best achieve the objective of inter-communal unity and harmony.

Happily, in recent years, there has been a gradually-growing consensus on the need for a "Federal Constitution" though fundamental differences exist on the structural details for administrative reforms that would ensure the enjoyment of equal rights notably, in respect of education and language by people of all communities and for a range of socio-economic programmes that would promote reconciliation at all levels. In particular, under a federal arrangement with recognised secular borders, free movement of population everywhere and across all borders could take place without giving rise to fears of imposed changes in the ethnic profile of a locality, whether through colonisation schemes or through "ethnic-cleansing". However, there are some aspects of concerns and aspirations that may be co-related to ethnicity, region and other characteristics and they need to be addressed. On economic issues, there are fundamental differences not co-related to ethnicity, but outside the scope of this paper.

While the unity and integrity of Sri Lanka is a concern shared by the entire population, the Sinhalese have long entertained fears of eventual Indian/Tamil domination and, linked to these fears, of secession of the North-East. These fears have been encoded in the ancient Sinhalese chronicles and sustained over nearly two millennia. Although there has been close and friendly Sinhalese-Tamil cooperation over most of this period, the primordial fears and suspicions have re-emerged from time to time, and are not easily banished. These concerns have served to harden the Sinhalese resistance to the concepts of an autonomous, unified Tamil majority region even within a united Sri Lanka and federalism, and to promote a hegemonic tendency to subsume the Sri Lankan identity within the Sinhalese identity. This has proved to be counter-productive in terms of national unity, but the concerns need to be addressed, rather than dismissed as irrational. It may be necessary to have secure constitutional provisions against unilateral secession, perhaps supplemented by international guarantees. (For a fuller discussion of Sinhalese concerns, see Roberts 2001 A, 2001 B & 2001 C).

Within the North-East, the Sinhalese concerns would be to ensure that they are not discriminated against, in particular that their physical security, language and other rights are protected. The Sinhalese form the overwhelming majority in the Ampara electoral division. There have been ancient Sinhalese villages in the East, but the large majority of the Sinhalese in that region are colonists from the South of the first, second or, at the most, third generation. However, they are now well-established and are an integral part of the region. With the likely devolution of greater autonomy to the predominantly Tamil-speaking North-East, Ampara electoral division could continue to be a part of that region in which case, the Sinhalese would constitute a significant minority in that region, or could opt to be attached to a neighbouring predominant Sinhala-speaking district like Monaragala. This is an issue of concern to all the Sinhalese of the North-East.

Outside the North-East, the Sinhalese enjoy clear numerical dominance in every province. Their primary concern may be to avoid the fragmentation of these Provinces. There are significant pockets of Malaiyaha Tamil majority in parts of Nuwara Eliya district in Central Province and Badulla district in Uva Province, but these pockets do not adjoin the North-East, and are not large enough to constitute separate provinces. There are also smaller pockets of Malaiyaha Tamil and Muslim populations in several provinces, but none of these challenge the numerical dominance of the Sinhalese.

Though the leaders of the Sri Lankan Tamils, like those of other communities, used ethnic slogans for opportunistic reasons, deep-seated caste and regional prejudices had long hindered the development of 'Sri Lankan Tamil nationalism'. Tamils of Jaffna origin and of Vellala caste have traditionally looked down on all other Tamils, and this animosity was widely reciprocated – by those from the East, the Vanni region and the hill country, as well as from the 'lower' castes within Jaffna. The introduction of universal franchise in 1931 created conditions favourable to the promotion of 'Sri Lankan Tamil nationalism', a process which was accelerated by certain post-independence developments like "Sinhala only" that threatened collective Sri Lankan Tamil interests.

It needs to be noted that Chelvanayagam stood out from most other Sri Lankan Tamil leaders in that he vigorously opposed the move to disenfranchise the Malaiyaha Tamils, broke off from the Tamil Congress of which he was deputy leader on this issue and founded the Federal Party around the concept of Tamil-speaking people. He was successful in forging alliances with Muslim and Malaiyaha Tamil leaders, and getting several Muslims elected to Parliament on the Federal Party ticket. But the Tamil-speaking people concept did not percolate deep into the consciousness of the Tamils and the Muslims, and it was soon abandoned.

This concept has been revived from time to time. There were Muslims in the ruling EPRLF-led North-East Provincial Government in the late Eighties and early Nineties, and again in the LTTE some years ago. But successive Governments and, in particular, the armed services used Muslims in moves against Tamils, including massacres and "ethnic-cleansing". In turn, the LTTE became suspicious of the Muslims and engaged in a series of massacres and "ethnic-cleansing" of Muslims. Although there have been some expressions of regret, a full Tamil-Muslim reconciliation does not appear to be imminent. However, the violence of recent years has served to bring together different sections of the Sri Lankan Tamil population.

Thus, "Sri Lankan Tamil nationalism" is of post-independence origin. For the first three decades, this evolving nationalism expressly renounced separatism — its aspiration was internal, and not external self-determination, federalism and not secession. Even federalism came to be adopted only in 1956 in the wake of the 'Sinhala-only' policy. Up to the mid-Seventies, every candidate advocating secession suffered demoralising defeat at every election to every Parliament seat. It was the trauma of 'standardisation' in effect, linguistic quotas in relation to university admissions beginning in 1971, followed by the majoritarian Constitution of 1972 which marginalised the minorities and the Tamil language as never before, which set the stage for the gradual transition from the goal of internal to external self-determination. The statement of Federal Party leader Chelvanayagam on winning the Kankesanthurai by-election in February 1975, marks a fateful turning-point:

> "We have for the last 25 years made every effort to secure our political rights on the basis of equality with the Sinhalese in a united Ceylon. It is a regrettable fact that successive Sinhalese Governments have used the power that flows from independence to deny us our fundamental rights and reduce us to the position of a subject

> people. I wish to announce to my people and to the country that I consider the verdict at this election as a mandate that the 'Tamil Eelam' nation should exercise the sovereignty already vested in the Tamil people and become free."

Though 'Tamil nationalism' has been late in developing, it has been forged on the anvil of an extended civil war and tempered in the fire of recurrent pogroms in the context of sustained discriminatory policies. It has found expression in the 'Thimpu Principles', jointly put forward by the Tamil groups at the Thimpu negotiations brokered by India in July and August 1985. It has the rare virtue of a Sri Lankan Tamil consensus mostly elusive before and since, reinforced by its expression in language that permits multiple interpretations. The two controversial principles relate to a 'Tamil homeland' and to 'self-determination'. These concepts may superficially appear to be separatist, but could be interpreted to be fully compatible with a united, though not, unitary Sri Lanka.

This feature has served to legitimise Government-LTTE negotiations at the highest levels. In fact, the LTTE has gone on to broadly define the concepts of 'homeland' and 'self-determination' in terms on which a national consensus could be based, although there are many matters that need to be sorted out before any solution could emerge. (For a fuller discussion of Sri Lankan Tamil concerns, see Nesiah 2001 A & 2001 B, and of Peace Negotiations, see Uyangoda 2001).

An extended temporary merger of the North and the East is part of the current reality. Despite the increasing intrusion of ethnicity in political mobilisation, an autonomous East, with its unique history, culture and tri-ethnic mix, could have been a model of co-existence for Sri Lanka. Each of the ethnic groups would have been motivated to seek coalitions with one or both of the other ethnic groups so as to form the regional government, and equally motivated to avoid falling out with either of the other groups so as not to damage future prospects.

In turn, national political parties, mindful of both their current and future interests in the East, would have been motivated to avoid resorting to racist politics anywhere in the island. Sadly, much brutal violence and ethnic cleansing appear to have closed the option of an autonomous East and increased the likelihood of its break-up. In the circumstances, the continued merger of the North with all, or a part, of the East appears to be unavoidable.

The 'Sri Lankan Tamils' enjoy numerical dominance in nearly all of the North and in several parts of the East. In the East, however, the areas of Tamil numerical dominance are not contiguous. But, together with the Muslims, they form a Tamil-speaking majority in almost every division of the North-East except the Ampara electoral division. Moreover, the distribution of Tamil and Muslim populations in the East is such that if a contiguous Muslim majority province is to be demarcated, it would contain only a minor fraction of the Muslim population, and only a fraction of one district Ampara out of the 25 that constitute Sri Lanka. Approximately a third of the Muslims live in the East, and a third of that number would be within that Muslim-majority province. Nearly 90 per cent of all Muslims would be living outside that province. Moreover, significant numbers of the Sinhalese and Tamil populations of the East would be caught up in that province, particularly if it is expanded to take in major pockets of Muslim population outside Ampara district.

Perhaps, the Muslim and Tamil interests and aspirations would be best secured if they could come to a workable understanding for co-existence and power-sharing in a Tamil speaking North-East province. This arrangement will have to take into account the concerns of the Sinhalese of that region, but it is the agreement between the Tamils and Muslims that would be the most difficult to work out. As McGilvray (2001) has pointed out:

> "The Tamil-speaking Hindu and Muslim Moorish communities of the East coast have become absolutely pivotal to Sri Lanka's ethnic future. The eastern region of the island remains an ethnic crucible out of which a political link essential to resolving Sri Lanka's conflict must still be forged. Over the past century, a combination of colonially-engineered ethnic competition, opportunistic party politics, and eventually civil war pre-empted whatever goodwill might have developed between the two groups under more foresighted leadership. However, because their common geographical and historical destiny offers them little choice, the Tamils and Muslims in the Batticaloa region must eventually come to a renewed appreciation of their shared cultural roots, as well as an honest appraisal of their past prejudices. The cultural, political, and economic basis for a respectful inter-ethnic community of interest between the Tamils and the Muslims is still there, but in the wake of massacres and reprisals, expulsions, displacements, land thefts and masked betrayals, both compassion and true ethnic statesmanship on all sides will be needed to nurture it."

A distinctive feature of the Muslim population is that they are spread out across the length and breath of the island. But the nature of their presence in Mannar district and the East is fundamentally different to their presence elsewhere. In Mannar and the East, their occupational profile is not very different from that of the Tamil and Sinhalese populations. But elsewhere, they are disproportionately in certain fields of economic activity, notably trade. Moreover, the interests and concerns of the Muslims of the North-East are similar to or compatible with those of the Tamils in some respects, e.g. physical security, identity Muslim, language Tamil, territory, colonisation, and self-government.

Elsewhere in the island, apart from physical security and identity, the main Muslim concern may be economic opportunities. It is possible that devolution arrangements based on 'internal self-determination' could be worked out to satisfy Tamil and Muslim concerns in the North-East, but these could make the Muslims elsewhere feel even more isolated and vulnerable. Non-territorial safeguards would therefore be needed to meet the various concerns of the Muslims elsewhere.

The Sinhalese, Sri Lankan Tamils, Malaiyaha Tamils and Muslims everywhere have legitimate claims to equal language rights in areas in which they live in large numbers. In the case of Sri Lankan Tamils and Muslims, they have a 'homeland' in the sense of a large, contiguous Tamil-speaking majority territory in the North-East in which those of their linguistic group are numerically dominant. Perhaps with the prospective gradual fusion of the Sri Lankan Tamil and Malaiyaha Tamil communities, a process that may have already begun to the concern of some Malaiyaha Tamil leaders – in the form of assimilation of Malaiyaha Tamils settled in the North-East or in Colombo—Malaiyaha Tamils may eventually come to see the North-East as the region to which they can go if they wish to live in a Tamil-speaking region under a regional government that could be expected to promote their language, religion, culture and other concerns.

The Sri Lankan Tamils residing outside the North-East have roots in that region and feel that a regional government ought to be established on these terms. The Muslims, almost half the number, do not have their roots in the North-East and this may be why many of them are not very supportive of autonomy for the North-East. In the case of the Malaiyaha Tamils, their immediate concerns relate to the citizenship status of a small fraction that remains Stateless, and the political, economic and social marginalisation of the vast majority. With spatial mobility, their territorial base in some parts of the hill country has already begun to erode, and with the likely further diversification of their employment and greater internal migration, this process may continue. Eventually, the identification of Malaiyaha Tamils with the plantations and the plantation areas may weaken except in a few districts including, perhaps, Nuwara Eliya and Badulla. Large numbers have migrated to a few cities, notably Colombo, and to the North-East. One long-term option is gradual integration with the 'Sri Lankan Tamil' population. But immediate integration may not be in the interest of Malaiyaha Tamils, since it may degenerate into assimilation and they may lose the prospects of upward mobility through bargaining with the Government. If integration does take place, it will be a long, slow process with sustained commitment on both sides. To date, that commitment seems to be lacking.

Internal Self-determination and Federalism

In the context of developments over the last five decades, the right to internal self-determination and federalism have emerged as an essential component of 'Tamil nationalism'. A widespread misconception, shared alike by many supporters and many opponents of secessionism, is the identification of the right to self-determination with the right to unilateral secession. On the contrary, Kirgis, Jr, 1994, points out the many faces of self-determination :

- The right of limited autonomy short of secession, for groups defined territorially or by common ethnic, religious and linguistic bonds — as in autonomous areas within confederations.

- Rights of minority groups within a larger political entity, as recognised in Article 27 of the Covenant on Civil and Political Rights and in the UN General Assembly's 1992 Declaration on the Rights of Persons Belonging to National or Ethnic, Religious and Linguistic Minorities.

In international law, the right to secede is only one of the options and even that option cannot be exercised unilaterally. In fact, this question was posed by the Governor-General in Council of Canada to the Supreme Court 1998 as follows: "[Is] there a right to self-determination under international law that would give the national Assembly, legislature or government of Quebec, the right to effect the secession of Quebec from Canada unilaterally?" In response, the Supreme Court of Canada (1998) set out its opinion very clearly:

- The recognised sources of international law established that the right to self-determination of a people is normally fulfilled through internal self-determination — a people's pursuit of its political, economic, social and cultural development within the framework of an existing State. A right to external self-determination which in this case potentially takes the form of the assertion of a right to unilateral secession arises in only the most extreme of cases and, even then, under carefully defined circumstances.
- The international law, the principle of self-determination has evolved within a framework of respect for the territorial integrity of existing States.
- There is no necessary incompatibility between the maintenance of the territorial integrity of existing States, including Canada, and the right of a 'people' to achieve a full measure of self-determination. A State

whose government represents the whole of the people or peoples resident within its territory, on a basis of equality and without discrimination, and respects the principles of self-determination in its internal arrangements, is entitled to the protection under international law of its territorial integrity.

- A number of commentators have further asserted that the right of self-determination may ground a right to unilateral secession...when a people is blocked from the meaningful exercise of its right to self-determination internally... The Vienna Declaration... adds credence to the assertion that such a complete blockage may potentially give rights to a right of secession.

We note that the Canadian Supreme Court, and much of the literature on the subject (e.g. Steiner and Alston, 2000) draw a clear distinction between internal and external self-determination. Effective provision for internal self-determination, e.g., federalism combined with non-discrimination, far from paving the way for unilateral secession, de-legitimises any recourse to it. On the other hand, the denial of due internal self-determination could legitimise a right of secession.

Fundamental to the federal concept is that none of the federating units is exclusive – i.e., all citizens of the country, have free access to every federating unit. While there could be legitimate ground to oppose State-aided settlement schemes designed to alter the ethnic balance of any region, a federation of ethnically exclusive regions cannot be viable. This reality needs to be accepted by Sri Lankan Tamils and by those of all other communities in respect of all the regions of Sri Lanka. There has been much 'ethnic-cleansing' of Sinhalese, Tamils and Muslims. Effective counter-action is necessary. The entire island belongs equally to all citizens, irrespective of whether the administration is unitary or federal.

In a yet-unpublished study of federalism as a peace-building structure, Galtung (2003) draws a distinction between a 'majoritarian democracy' — in which decision-making is in terms of debate, vote and majority rule – and 'consensus democracy', in which decision-making is in terms of dialogue and consensus. He also suggests that in the context of asymmetry in the political reality of Sri Lanka, it is only the North-East that may want autonomy, but there is a need, both at the all-island and regional levels, for bicameral systems with the second chamber, at each level, being constituted of equal numbers of elected representatives from the different ethnic groups in keeping with the principles of 'consensus democracy'. For practical reasons, there could be a cut-off limit of, say, five per cent of the population for an ethnic group to qualify for such representation in the second chamber. At each level, the second chamber will have powers, within constitutionally-prescribed limits, to temporarily veto decision-making in specified areas such as the use of the national languages and the practice of religions, but this veto may be challenged in, and over-ridden by the Supreme Court.

There is merit in Galtung's proposal, but there is no need to limit the offer of autonomy. It could be offered to each Province or region, combination of provinces up to the degree of autonomy conferred on the North-East. Since the cost of administering an autonomous region will increase with the level of autonomy, and this cost will have to be met from regional taxes, not every Province or region may want autonomy in full measure in respect of every sector. This matter could be negotiated with the Centre by each Province or region. Thus there could be symmetry in the offer of autonomy but, very likely, a range of asymmetry in its acceptance.

The range of federal models to draw inspiration from is vast. Every model is unique. At one end of the spectrum are quasi-federal countries, e.g. India, in which the Centre could, and not infrequently, does suspend the functioning of State Governments and substitute itself for it. Another model would be ostensibly unitary States, e.g. the U.K, which provides for widely asymmetric devolution to Northern Ireland, Scotland and Wales. At the other end of the spectrum are countries such as the US and Switzerland which, in different forms, enjoy very advanced kinds of federalism. We in Sri Lanka need to negotiate and agree on a model of federalism to meet our special requirements.

Towards Territorial Internal Self-Determination

Recurring ethnic, religious and caste conflicts have plagued many of the regions that now constitute India, Pakistan and Bangladesh for over a century. In contrast, except for one brief period of anti-Muslim riots in 1915, we in Sri Lanka had not, until the Fifties, faced such conflict on the scale or intensity experienced in those regions. The anti-Tamil violence of 1956 and 1958 came as a rude shock. Those of 1977, 1979 and 1981 prepared the ground for the pogrom of 1983 and the civil war that followed.

At least over the last six decades, the overall trend in inter-ethnic relations in Sri Lanka has, subject to some minor fluctuations, been negative. In particular, the Sri Lankan Tamils, who were happy with a unitary Sri Lanka till five decades ago, abruptly demanded internal self-government through an autonomous North-East region. For over two decades, they strongly and consistently opposed secessionism, but, during the Seventies, there emerged a strong demand for external self-determination, or secession. After nearly two decades of civil war, it appears that there could possibly be a national settlement based on internal self-determination, as proposed five decades earlier by the Sri Lankan Tamil leadership and then resoundingly rejected by all sections of the Sinhalese leadership.

Ethnic-consciousness and aspirations have evolved in the decades since independence and, in particular, in the last two decades which have been dominated by the pogrom of 1983, 17 years of civil war, and a year of negotiations. Currently, the 'ruling elites' of the Sinhalese society have come to accept the inevitability of a political settlement to the ethnic conflict, and the validity of power-sharing arrangements in a settlement framework, [and] that the unitary State structure of Sri Lanka needs a pluralist re-orientation. Similarly, the gradual weakening of the secessionist project in the Sri Lankan Tamil society as well as the willingness on the part of radical Tamil nationalist forces to re-examine the relevance of a protracted armed struggle to achieve autonomy/secessionist objectives are profoundly significant transformations that the protracted war seems to have set in motion (Uyangoda, 2001, 2); (Uyangoda's paper is in the Marga Monograph Series of 2001, but was written and published in late 2002.)

As the Uyangoda (2001), goes on to suggest, space for negotiation was created in the context of 'conflict-ripening' (Zartman, 1995) in which there is mutual recognition that no win is possible, that the original aims cannot be achieved but, rather, the two parties are on a "hurting stalemate, a flat, unpleasant terrain stretching into the future, providing no later possibilities for decisive escalation or for graceful escape" (Zartman, 1985:268). Uyangoda further suggests that "the most feasible outcome of Sri Lanka's present peace is likely to be the de-escalation of the war, leading towards a protracted period of no-war ... with a limited agenda, a limited scope and limited trajectories ... One of the most important transformative dynamics of the present ceasefire-negotiation process in Sri Lanka is that it promises to de-link the ethnic conflict from war and violence" (Uyangoda, 2001, 20-22). But lasting peace can emerge only if the various ethnic concerns and aspirations could be reconciled. What are these, and are they reconcilable?

The question arises as to whether a settlement on the basis of internal self-determination has become necessary only on account of the conflict over the last five or six decades, or whether such a development was inevitable. In the light of the significant global increase in the salience of ethnicity in political organisation and governance, and as a focus of conflict worldwide, it seems clear that in the Sri Lankan context, any system of governance that did not provide for internal self-determination would not have remained viable. A further question then arises on the choice as between territorial and non-territorial self-determination, that is, as between language-sensitive regional autonomy, for example, as in Canada or India, and some form of non-territorial ethnic representation in the political system and in governance, for example., as in Malaysia.

It is relevant to note that internal self-determination on the basis of territory permits governance to be otherwise secular. Except in respect of the language of administration, the laws and politics of one self-governing region need not be different to those of another; nor is there a need for rights and opportunities to be defined in terms of ethnicity. In such a situation, a gradual reduction in ethnic consciousness is possible, though not inevitable.

On the other hand, if self-determination is not based on territory, ethnicity needs to be reflected explicitly in the laws and regulations, in the institutions and in the political system, ensuring the perpetuation of ethnic consciousness. Such is the situation in Malaysia, where political organisation is on the basis of ethnicity. Both the ruling party and the opposition are inter-ethnic coalitions, and *Bhumiputra* policies dictate that rights and opportunities are defined in ethnic terms.

In India, while linguistic nationalism has been largely defused by the linguistic reorganisation of States, caste and tribal-consciousness continue to be sustained by the special arrangements made for prescribed caste and tribal representation in the Union and State legislatures, and in recruitment to the public services and admission to educational institutions. The fact that India's major linguistic groups are concentrated in territories large enough to be self-governing units helps to mitigate linguistic nationalism. In contrast, the fact that Dalit 'untouchable' communities are scattered in locations too small to be self-governing makes it necessary to constitutionally provide for explicit caste quotas, rather than secular arrangements, to ensure due representation for them in the legislatures, public services and educational institutions. The tribal position is intermediate in that there are several tribal reservations with a measure of self-government, but most of these reservations are small. Moreover, many tribal communities are even more marginalised than many Dalit communities in respect of socio-economic development. Hence there are constitutional provisions of quotas for tribals too in the same manner as for the Dalits.

In this light, the residential concentration of Tamil-speakers or Tamils and Muslims in Sri Lanka's North-East is an advantage in that it permits internal self-determination through secular devolution on a territorial basis. The alternative would have been to make special ethnicity-specific arrangements such as in Malaysia, ensuring the perpetuation of heightened ethnic consciousness. It is not suggested that autonomous regions should be mono-ethnic – that would be a terrible disaster, or that past 'ethnic-cleansing' should not be reversed. In fact, it is desirable for all autonomous regions including the North-East to be ethnically diverse. However, to safeguard the rights of the regional minorities in the North-

East mostly Sinhalese and in the other regions Sri Lankan Tamils, Malaiyaha Tamils and Muslims, it may be necessary to have constitutional safeguards such as appropriately designed second chambers at both national and regional levels.

If a system of territorial internal self-determination is both desirable and inevitable, why was it not installed at the time of Sri Lanka's independence or even earlier? Clearly, there was lack of foresight. There was also a lack of inter-ethnic consultation, which has been an unfortunate feature of our political culture. The Kandyan Sinhalese had pressed such territorial internal self-determination in the twenties and thirties, but the claims were expressed in Kandyan sectarian terms and opposed by the leadership of the other communities, including the Sri Lankan Tamils. When the Malaiyaha Tamils were deprived of citizenship and voting rights, it was done with the backing of most Sri Lankan Tamil and Muslim leaders. Again, when the Sri Lankan Tamils were pushed to advocating territorial internal self-determination in the fifties and sixties, they too couched their demands in sectarian terms, provoking opposition from the others, especially the Sinhalese.

Even the Communist Party, which in line with Marxist ideology, had proposed a measure of territorial autonomy in the forties, could not find common cause with the Sri Lankan Tamil federalists. The opportunity to forge a multi-ethnic coalition to present federalism as a secular alternative to unitary governance was missed. In the event, there was a long, erratic journey covering over five decades of political conflict and nearly two decades of civil war that has led us to recognise regional autonomy as an essential component of constitutional arrangements needed to hold Sri Lanka together. Clearly, it is possible to reconcile the diverse ethnic concerns and aspirations. In fact, virtually every national leader had, at various times, identified the broad outlines of such a reconciliation structure.

At other times, the same leaders, for opportunistic reasons, had been unwilling to concede one component or the other of that structure.

There was good progress in moving towards a reconciliation in 2002, but we seem to be again caught up in a "hurting stalemate" on "a flat unpleasant terrain stretching into the future", from which the only possible exits may be back to war or, as Uyangoda suggests, a pragmatic, limited settlement. Perhaps, it is only a succession of such limited settlements that could lead, in the long run, to comprehensive and enduring peace.

Discussion

Some participants suggested that given the caste problems, the North-East region could one day split. Others suggested that but for the ethnic conflict over the last few years, there would have been no demand for the unification of the North and the East. In a sense, this is something that has developed through the civil war. Some unity within the Sri Lankan Tamil community across castes and regional barriers has been forged, and they may survive for sometime, because the ethnic conflict will not go away so quickly. If tomorrow there is perfect ethnic peace, then maybe some of those old divisions may re-emerge. It is unlikely for many years. And hopefully, those divisions will not recur in the form as 25 years ago.

It was pointed out that the divisions between the Sri Lankan Tamils and the Malaiyaha Tamils are very deep, and the Malaiyaha Tamils have a good reason to feel bitter. It was hoped that they too will ultimately go away. There is no rationale, in the long run, say 25 years from now, to have two separate ethnic communities, who are neither racially or linguistically differentiated, to be regarded as two different ethnic communities. It is a little different in the case of the Muslims, as they have a different religion. In the case of the Malaiya Tamils, even that difference is not there. So there is no rationale. However, it may not be in their immediate interest for the Malaiya to merge with the Sri Lankan Tamils, at the moment.

Some suggested that the advocacy of territorial internal self-determination to fulfil the aspirations if there is a demographic concentration of a minority. If they are spread over the entire country, non-territorial constitutional safeguards, could lead to creating a hierarchy among the minorities and emphasise the territorial nature of the solution, diverting attention from the fact that there needs to be power-sharing at the Centre.

But others pointed out that there was not much alternative. What could you do if a community is scattered? You cannot transport them to one area and put them into an autonomous region. After all, that is how India dealt with the situation. Major linguistic groups which were already concentrated in certain areas have autonomous States but other communities like the Dalits who are scattered have other forms of constitutional safeguards – which are not equal. But there is no alternative. There is no way in which you can transform or transpose one kind of minority into another, because they are scattered. You have to come to terms with the reality.

There is a need for power-sharing, both at the Centre and in the regions. One way in which it can be achieved is through a second chamber of legislature. For instance, you could have a second chamber, where you could have an equal number of representatives from each ethnic group, say seven or eight from each. They could have the veto power – subject to review by the Supreme Court – on certain issues that particularly affect that ethnic group. It is very important to have power-sharing arrangements, both constitutionally provided for as well as traditionally built up, at every level. In addition to this, within each self-governing State, there could be some areas that could be having their own form of internal self-government of a lesser level, as in India, self-governing districts within a State. It would be a complex kind of arrangement and not amenable to one simple solution.

As far as the scattered populations are concerned, it is true, their bargaining power is less. But what is the solution? There is no way in which they can be given the same rights as people living in large areas, which can be self-governing. So the only alternative is to have non-territorial safeguards, which is what India has done. There is no need for the rule to be different for India and Sri Lanka. The same factors operate. If a group occupies a large piece of territory, they can have self-government. It is healthy for the whole country if they have such a government. If they do not occupy such lands but are scattered in large areas, some other solution has to be found, and it is the same, whether it is India or Sri Lanka. We may have to think of quotas or some other ways in which those minorities are provided safeguards, but it is not possible to give them the same benefits as those people living in large territories — not because they are less important but because the ground realities do not permit it.

One participant argued that the Muslims want to identify themselves with the majority community because they are trade-oriented, and there is a big sociological, societal change. They are all studying Sinhalese in Sinhalese schools, and the LTTE's brand of alienation has only speeded up this process.

Another said that even though the mother-tongue of the Muslims is Tamil, they pretend otherwise. A few days after the Indo-Sri Lanka Agreement was signed, Tamil Muslims in a village near Trincomalee, told visiting Indian journalists that they would "vote the UNP, or SLFP", not any of the Tamil parties, in the ensuing provincial council elections. This was typical of the hedging-the-bets attitude of the Muslims, which has led to their alienation from the Tamils. Many Muslims who were earlier with Tamil groups left the militant movement because they said their business interests do not go along with the separatist cause.

Another participant pointed out that opportunism is not a vice peculiar to any particular community. So, it may be that the Muslims are so placed that they feel more vulnerable. The Tamil interests are concentrated in areas in the North-East, and are much more stable. They do not need to shift between the LTTE, TULF and the other groups all the time.

But the blame should not entirely be on one party. Right from the time of independence, the Malaiyaha Tamil people were deprived of citizenship and voting rights. The Government was able to virtually bribe, not financially but through political inducement, the Sri Lankan Tamil and the Muslim leaders to vote for disenfranchising the Malaiyaha Tamils. This was the basic divide-and-rule policy that the British were very good at, and the Sri Lankan Government continued after independence. If the Sri Lankan Muslims and Tamils had not voted to disenfranchise the Malaiyaha Tamils, 'Sinhala-only' would not have come. But having done that, it was the turn of the Sri Lankan Tamils and the Muslims to feel the ill-effects of discrimination. Here again, although the Muslims of the East particularly were as wedded to the Tamil language as the Tamils, the leadership of the Muslims was from the South, and they were again induced through the portfolios in the Government and so many things to vote for 'Sinhala-only'.

References

i. ***Galtung, Johan*** 2003: Federation as Peace Structure: The Case of Sri Lanka unpublished.

ii. ***McGilvray, Dennis*** 2001: Tamil and Muslim Identities in the East, Marga Monograph Series, Colombo.

iii. ***Nesiah, Devanesan*** 2001 A : Tamil Nationalism, Marga Monograph Series, Colombo.
2001 B: The Claims to Self-Determination: A Sri Lankan Tamil Perspective, in Contemporary South Asia, 10:1

iv. ***Roberts, Michael*** 2001 A: Sinhala-ness and Sinhala Nationalism, Marga Monograph Series, Colombo.
2001 B: Primordialist Strands in Contemporary Sinhala Nationalism in Sri Lanka:
Urumaya as Ur, Marga Monograph Series, Colombo.
2001 C: Burden of History: Obstacles to Power Sharing in Sri Lanka, Marga Monograph Series, Colombo.

v. ***Uyangoda, Jayadeva*** 2001: Beyond the Talks: Towards Transformative Peace in SriLanka, Marga Monograph Series, Colombo.

vi. ***Zartman, William I*** 1985: Ripe for Resolution: Conflict and Intervention in Africa, Oxford University Press, New York and Oxford.
1995: Dynamics and Constraints in Negotiations in Internal Conflicts, in Zartman ed, Elusive Peace, Negotiating an End to Civil Wars, The Brookings Institution, Washington DC.

Percentage Distribution of Ethnicity by Districts, 1981 and 2001 - Table 1

District	Total Population No. = 100%		Sinhalese %		Sri Lanka Tamils %		Indian Tamil %		Sri Lanka Moor %		Burgher %		Malay %		Other* %	
	1981	2001	1981	2001	1981	2001	1981	2001	1981	2001	1981	2001	1981	2001	1981	2001
Colombo	1,699,241	2,234,289	77.6	76.6	10.0	11.0	1.2	1.2	8.2	9.2	1.2	0.7	1.3	0.9	0.5	0.5
Gampaha	1,390,862	2,066,096	92.0	91.1	3.5	3.1	0.4	0.4	2.7	3.9	0.6	0.5	0.6	0.6	0.2	0.4
Kalutara	829,704	1,060,800	87.2	87.1	1.2	1.3	4.1	2.7	7.4	8.8	0.1	0.1	0.1	0.1	0.1	0.0
Kandy	1,048,317	1,272,463	74.3	74.0	5.0	3.9	9.4	8.4	10.5	13.3	0.2	0.2	0.3	0.2	0.3	0.1
Matale	357,354	442,427	80.0	80.2	5.8	5.4	7.0	5.3	7.0	8.8	0.1	0.1	0.2	0.1	0.2	0.1
Nuwara-Eliya	603,577	700,083	42.1	40.0	12.7	5.9	42.7	21.3	2.0	2.5	0.1	0.1	0.2	0.1	0.2	0.0
Galle	814,531	990,539	94.5	94.3	0.9	1.2	1.4	0.9	3.2	3.6	0.1	0.0	0.0	0.0	0.1	0.0
Matara	643,786	761,236	94.5	94.2	0.7	0.6	2.2	2.2	2.5	2.9	0.0	0.0	0.0	0.0	0.0	0.0
Hambantota	424,344	525,370	97.1	97.1	0.6	0.4	0.1	0.1	1.2	1.1	0.0	0.0	1.0	1.4	0.0	0.0
Jaffna	830,552	..	0.8	..	95.2	..	2.4	..	1.6	..	0.04	..	0.0	..	0.01	...
Mannar	106,235	..	8.2	..	51.3	..	13.0	..	26.1	..	0.03	..	0.03	..	1.3	..
Vavuniya	95,428	..	16.5	..	56.8	..	19.6	..	6.8	..	0.03	..	0.03	..	0.2	..
Mullativu	77,189	..	5.2	..	75.4	..	14.5	..	4.7	..	0.1	..	0.02	..	0.0	..
Batticaloa	330,333	..	3.4	..	70.7	..	1.2	..	23.9	..	0.7	..	0.01	..	0.4	..
Trincomalee	255,948	..	33.4	..	34.3	..	2.1	..	29.3	..	0.4	..	0.3	..	0.1	0.1
Ampara	388,970	589,344	37.8	39.3	20.0	18.7	0.4	0.1	41.5	41.6	0.2	0.2	0.1	0.0	0.1	0.0
Kurunegala	1,211,801	1,452,369	92.9	91.7	1.2	1.2	0.6	0.2	5.0	6.7	0.1	0.1	0.1	0.1	0.1	0.0
Puttalam	492,533	705,342	82.6	73.8	6.6	6.9	0.5	0.3	9.9	18.7	0.1	0.1	0.2	0.1	0.1	0.2
Anuradhapura	587,929	746,466	91.1	90.8	1.4	0.7	0.1	0.1	7.1	8.2	0.0	0.0	0.1	0.0	0.2	0.2
Polonnaruwa	261,563	359,197	91.4	90.3	2.0	2.0	0.1	0.0	6.4	7.6	0.0	0.0	0.1	0.0	0.2	0.0
Badulla	640,952	774,555	69.1	72.1	5.9	4.2	20.2	18.2	4.2	5.2	0.0	0.1	0.2	0.2	0.4	0.1
Monaragala	273,570	396,173	92.7	94.5	2.0	1.4	3.2	1.9	1.9	2.0	0.1	0.0	0.1	0.0	0.1	0.0
Ratnapura	797,087	1,008,164	85.0	86.6	2.4	3.4	10.6	7.8	1.7	2.1	0.1	0.0	0.1	0.0	0.2	0.0
Kegalle	684,944	779,774	85.9	85.6	2.2	1.8	6.7	5.9	5.0	6.6	0.0	0.0	0.1	0.0	0.1	0.0
Total	**14,846,750**	**16,864,687**	**73.9**	**81.9**	**12.7**	**4.3**	**5.5**	**5.1**	**7.0**	**8.0**	**0.3**	**..0.2**	**0.3**	**0.3**	**0.2**	**0.2**

Not available

1981 and 2001 figures are not comparable because all the districts of the North and the districts of Batticaloa and Trincomalee in the East were not covered in the 2001 census. Kilinochchi District does not figure in this table. In 1981, it was a part of Jaffna District. It became a separate District in 1984, but since then there has never been a census in that district.

Percentage Distribution of Religion by Districts, 1981 and 2001 - Table 2

District	Total Population No. = 100%		Buddhist %		Hindu %		Islam %		Roman Catholic %		Other Christian %		Other* %	
	1981	2001	1981	2001	1981	2001	1981	2001	1981	2001	1981	2001	1981	2001
Colombo	1,699,241	2,234,289	70.1	70.4	7.7	8.9	9.9	10.7	9.4	7.8	2.4	2.1	0.2	0.2
Gampaha	1,390,862	2,066,096	71.1	71.6	1.9	2.1	3.5	4.6	22.5	20.4	0.9	1.4	0.1	0.1
Kalutara	829,704	1,060,800	84.3	83.9	4.5	3.4	7.6	8.9	3.3	3.3	0.3	0.4	0.0	0.0
Kandy	1,048,317	1,272,463	73.6	73.1	12.7	10.7	11.1	13.7	1.9	1.8	0.7	0.7	0.1	0.1
Matale	357,354	442,427	78.6	79.1	11.6	9.7	7.3	9.0	2.1	1.8	0.3	0.3	0.0	0.0
Nuwara Eliya	603,577	700,083	41.6	39.5	50.3	51.3	2.5	2.9	4.7	4.7	0.9	1.5	0.0	0.1
Galle	814,531	990,539	94.2	94.1	1.9	1.6	3.2	3.6	0.4	0.4	0.2	0.3	0.1	0.0
Matara	643,786	761,236	94.6	94.0	2.4	2.4	2.6	3.0	0.3	0.4	0.1	0.3	0.0	0.0
Hambantota	424,344	525,370	97.1	96.9	0.5	0.3	2.2	2.5	0.1	0.2	0.1	0.2	0.0	0.0
Jaffna	830,552	..	0.6	..	85.0	..	1.8	..	11.5	..	1.1	..	0.01	..
Mannar	106,235	..	3.2	..	27.2	..	27.4	..	41.1	..	1.0	..	0.1	..
Vavuniya	95428	..	16.5	..	68.7	..	7.1	..	6.8	..	0.9	..	0.02	..
Mullativu	77,189	..	1.4	..	77.9	..	4.9	..	15.2	..	0.6	..	0.01	..
Batticaloa	330,333	..	2.8	..	66.2	..	23.8	..	6.0	..	1.1	..	0.02	..
Trincomalee	255,948	..	32.3	..	31.6	..	29.8	..	5.6	..	0.5	..	0.2	..
Ampara	388,970	589,344	37.5	39.2	18.7	17.2	41.7	41.6	1.5	1.4	0.6	0.5	0.1	0.0
Kurunegala	1,211,801	1,452,369	90.1	88.9	1.2	1.0	5.3	6.9	3.0	2.8	0.3	0.5	0.1	0.0
Puttalam	492,533	705,342	48.0	43.1	3.9	4.3	10.2	19.0	37.5	32.7	0.4	1.0	0.1	0.0
Anuradhapura	587,929	746,466	90.1	90.1	1.2	0.6	7.3	8.3	1.2	0.8	0.2	0.3	0.0	0.0
Polonnaruwa	261,563	359,197	90.1	89.3	1.8	1.9	6.5	7.7	1.3	1.0	0.1	0.2	0.0	0.1
Badulla	640,952	774,555	68.8	71.6	24.3	20.7	4.6	5.5	1.8	1.6	0.5	0.6	0.0	0.0
Moneragala	273,570	396,173	92.7	94.4	4.7	3.0	2.0	2.1	0.4	0.4	0.1	0.2	0.0	0.0
Ratnapura	797,087	1,008,164	84.8	86.4	11.6	9.9	2.0	2.2	1.4	1.1	0.3	0.5	0.0	0.0
Kegalle	684,944	779,774	85.2	84.7	7.9	6.8	5.2	6.8	1.2	1.1	0.5	0.6	0.0	0.0
Total	**14,846,750**	**16,864,687**	**69.3**	**76.7**	**15.5**	**7.9**	**7.5**	**8.5**	**6.9**	**6.1**	**0.7**	**0.8**	**0.1**	**0.1**

...Not available

- *1981 and 2001 figures are not comparable because all the districts of the North and the districts of Batticaloa and Trincomalee in the East were not covered in the 2001 census. Kilinochchi District does not figure in this table. In 1981, it was a part of Jaffna District. It became a separate District in 1984, but since then there has never been a census in that District.*

Prospects For Reconciliation

Dr. V. Suryanarayan

"I do not believe in a Hindu Sri Lanka, a Sinhala Sri Lanka or a Muslim Sri Lanka, but in one united Sri Lanka ... There can be no more traditional Tamil lands, nor Muslim traditional lands, nor Sinhalese traditional lands. North, South, East and West will be one traditional land henceforth for every Lankan of one family."

– former Sri Lankan President,
the late J.R. Jayewardene

"We have not abandoned the path of peace. We want to resolve the conflict through peaceful means, through civilised methods, without recourse to a blood bath and the destruction of life".

– LTTE supremo V. Prabhakaran

'Mortals, beware of words, with words we lie, can say peace when we mean war."

– W.H. Auden

The People of India, the on-going research project of the Anthropological Survey of India, attempts to provide the cultural profile of all communities in India, the impact of change, and linkages and diversities among them. One interesting conclusion needs special mention. Communities, cutting across religions, share a great many cultural traits. Thus the Hindus share a very high percentage of traits with Muslims at 97.7 per cent, Buddhists 91.9 per cent, Sikhs 88.99 per cent and Jains 77.46 per cent. Other communities that share a high percentage of traits are Muslim-Sikhs 89.95 per cent, Muslim-Buddhists 91.18 per cent and Jain-Buddhists 81.34 per cent. As K.S.Singh, former Director-General of the Anthropological Survey of India, remarks: "Diversities and linkages, freedom and tolerance, go together".

Looking at the past through the prism of the present will lead to falsification of history. Despite the diversities, the people of Sri Lanka, like their Indian counterparts, have come to share many common cultural attributes. But with the exacerbation of the ethnic conflict, the chauvinists among the Sinhalas and the Tamils, two sides of the same coin, started projecting the two communities as antagonistic identities, who were at war with each other for several centuries. Two illustrations are given below to substantiate the point that truth and objectivity are the first casualty in times of conflict.

In his book, *The National Question and The Tamil Struggle,* Satchi Ponnambalam claims that the original inhabitants of the island were Tamils – Sinhala were originally Tamils, who later on were converted to Buddhism and adopted the Sinhala language. Much of what the Sinhala consider as their great monuments were constructed by the Tamils. *The Sinhala Commission Report* provides an entirely opposite view. According to it, there is no evidence of a distinct Tamil community or a Tamil kingdom in the Jaffna peninsula before the 13th century. On the contrary, Sinhala chronicles and inscriptions indicate that there were large and extensive Sinhala settlements from very early times. The Sinhalas were the lawful rulers of, and legal heirs to, the Jaffna kingdom until 1815.

What is the reality? Prof. Stanley Tambiah, after years of painstaking research, has come to the conclusion that the Sinhalas and the Tamils share many parallel features of "traditional caste, kinship, popular religious cults, customs and so on. But they have come to be divided by their mythic charters and tendentious historical understandings of the past". The common belief in Sri Lanka is that the Sinhala are "fair Aryans", and the Tamils are "dark Dravidians". Prof. Tambiah has exploded this myth. Quoting Gananath Obeyesekere, Tambiah adds: "If it were possible to trace the present-day Sinhala population's ancestry far enough, all lines in major part lead back to South India." According to Obeyesekere, "Biologically-speaking, those whom we call Sinhala are in fact racially inter-mixed with the south Indian peoples, and with aboriginal groups like the Vedas. And the Tamils who live in the North and the East are also similarly biologically mixed."

Dr. K.S. Singh has pointed out that in India there are several communities that can be classified as having more than one religion. It is interesting to note that Sinhala religious practices also point in the same direction. The Hindu *Bhakti* cult has influenced Theravada Buddhism, and there are images of Hindu gods in Buddhist temples. The deity of Skanda Muruga in Kataragama, located near the Yala sanctuary, continues to be the "major institutional inter-section of several religious faiths. … All go to Kataragama, where the atmosphere is one of tolerance and goodwill". Buddhist pilgrims often far out-number Hindus. The Sinhalas carry the *kavady* with great devotion and fervour.

According to Buddhist chronicles, the founding-father of the first Sinhala kingdom was Prince Vijaya, a Kshatriya from north India, who came to the island with 700 followers in 544 BC. Vijaya aligned himself with an aboriginal princess named Kuveni, married her, and with her assistance became the king of the country. Later, he drove Kuveni away, and married a princess from Madurai, and made her the queen. His followers also married maidens of high birth from the Pandyan kingdom. In other words, even according to Buddhist sources, the Sinhala nation was the product of assimilation between the Sinhalas and the Tamils from the very beginning.

Given the geographical contiguity, Sri Lanka has had close cultural contacts with Tamil Nadu and Kerala. The narrow and shallow Palk Straits was not a barrier, it was a bridge through which religious leaders, merchants and ordinary people moved freely. Few Sri Lankan scholars want to subscribe to the objective truth that Buddhism was a virile religion in South India, and that the spread and efflorescence of Theravada Buddhism in the island had much to do with fruitful contacts with Buddhist centres of learning in Kancheepuram, Kaveripattinam and Madurai. Buddhaghosha of Magadha, "poet, philosopher and commentator" of Theravada Buddhism, was patronised by Sanghapala, King of Kancheepuram. It is a matter of pride for the Tamils that one of the greatest epics of Theravada Buddhism is in Tamil language. *Manimekhalai,* written in the second century AD, is one of the finest jewels of Tamil-Buddhist literature.

Kerala's relations with Sri Lanka, and interaction with the Sinhalas and the Tamils remain an unexplored area of historical research. According to Gananath Obeysekere, when Hinduism began to dominate the religious scene in Kerala from the 10th century, a large number of Buddhists migrated to Ceylon. It was easy for them to assimilate with the local people and make their impact on all aspects of the island's life. The spread of the cult of the Goddess Pattini is an illustration of benign interaction among various religious groups. It is also a pointer to the ingratiating and assimilable qualities of the peoples of South Asia.

An analysis of the ideological constructs and a review of Sinhala writings provide fascinating insights into the majority community's concept of nation-building, which had been the main stumbling block to the emergence of a tolerant, multi-ethnic society in Sri Lanka. The concepts of '*Sinha Dipa*', the 'Land of the Sinhalas' and '*Dhamma Dipa*' the 'Land of (Buddhist) Dharma', were exploited to portray the Tamils and the Muslims as non-native intruders, who had to subordinate themselves to the "sons of the soil". The popular Sinhala formulation was that the Sinhalas have only Sri Lanka while the Tamils could go back to Tamil Nadu, and the Muslims to Arabia.

The distorted vision of India and Tamil Nadu in Sinhala minds has been aptly summed up by Prof. Urmila Phadnis as follows: "While Sri Lanka continues to look upon north India as the cradle of its religion, it perceives its contacts with south India, particularly with Tamil Nadu, as having been, by their very nature, a source of perennial concern for its integrity as a nation-State." To look upon dynastic rivalries for territorial expansion as an expression of enmity between India and Sri Lanka, or between the Hindus and the Buddhists will lead to falsification of history.

Prof. Anuradha Senevitratna, Professor of Sinhala in the Peradeniya University, in his book "*The Lions and the Tigers: Religious and Cultural Background of the Sinhala-Tamil Relations*", provides certain interesting facts. "In the war between Elara and Dutugemunu, there had been Sinhala commanders fighting for Elara, while the Sinhala king Dutugemunu had commanders of south Indian origin." In times of political unrest in the island, the kings of south India "would have found it politically expedient to invade the country".

Sometimes, as part of political strategy, the Sinhala kings took the assistance of south Indian kings to strengthen their position against their rivals. Prof. Seneviratna adds, "Whenever there was trouble in Sri Lanka, whether it was political unrest or famine, the Buddhist monks made a habit of escaping to south India for safety. South Indian Dravidian monks also followed the same example. Sri Lankan kings made grants available to the Tamil monks."

The Buddhist revival, and the resultant 'Sinhala nationalism' during the colonial period gave a fillip to Sinhala chauvinism. As Kumari Jayewardene sums up, "The Sinhala-Buddhists who felt economically hemmed in, politically oppressed and culturally deprived were to find succour in racist myths and legends, and were to give vent to their frustrations in attacking ethnic and religious minorities, thereby espousing the retrograde ideology of communalism which Bipan Chandra has rightly characterised as the 'false consciousness of the historical process of the last 100 years'."

The roots of ethnic conflict lie in the manner of nation-building attempted by the Sinhala ruling elite in the post-independence period since 1948. They wanted to build the 'Sri Lankan nation' on the basis of Sinhala language and Buddhist religion, to the exclusion of minority claims. The falsification of Sri Lankan history recalls a moving narrative from Sivanandan's absorbing novel, *When Memory Dies.* Sivanandan describes a conversation between Uncle Para and Vijay. Uncle Para tells Vijay, "When memory dies, people die." Vijay asks Uncle Para, "But if we make false memories?" Uncle Para responds, "That is worse, that is murder."

Nation Building: Two Contrasting Scenarios

A journalist asked Abdul Wali Khan, son of Khan Abdul Ghaffar Khan, the Afghan-Pushtun political leader, a few years ago: "Are you a Pakistani, a Muslim or a Pathan?" Wali Khan replied that he combined all the three attributes. The journalist persisted and asked Wali Khan what his primary identity was.

Wali Khan responded: "I am a Pakistani for the past 30 years, a Muslim for 1400 years, and a Pathan for 5000 years". The multiple identities of South Asians, an intrinsic feature of the socio-political profile of the region, have made the task of nation-building an exciting and fascinating exercise.

Political scientists unfortunately use the terms 'nation' and 'State' as synonymous. This semantic confusion has done incalculable harm in understanding the politics of developing countries. Louis Halle, for example, maintained "a prime fact about the world is that it is largely composed of nation-States". The statement is not true. The world consists of States, not nation-States. A survey of the world's 132 States in 1971 found that only 12 of them, or a mere nine per cent, could justifiably be called nation-States in the sense of the boundaries of the "territorial-juridiction entity being co-terminous with the distribution of a particular national group". The comment made by Massimo d'Azeglu with special reference to Italy after unification holds true of most of the States which came into existence after the Second World War: "We have made Italy, now we must make Italians."

There are two propositions which can be considered as the yardstick for the success of nation-building in the multi-ethnic societies of South Asia. First, the political system should provide sufficient space for minorities so that they can preserve, promote and foster their separate identities, while being a part of a united country. Second, a federal polity, with entrenched provisions for sharing of powers between the Centre and the States, can lead to a softening of secessionist demands and pave the way for eventual political integration. Two illustrations, one a success story from India and second, a tragic narrative from Sri Lanka, both relating to Tamil minority groups, will make the point. What is interesting to note are the differing political developments and contrasting responses on the issue of nation-building.

In Sri Lanka, the Tamil political leaders drifted from collaboration with Sinhalese political elite, and eventually began to demand a 'separate State' of 'Tamil Eelam'. The Dravidian movement in India followed a diametrically opposite course. Scholars working on the Dravidian movement are unanimous in pointing out the important milestones – the formation of the Justice Party and the non-Brahmin movement, *Periyar* E.V. Ramaswamy Naicker's 'Self-respect Movement' and anti-Hindi agitation, the formation of the Dravida Kazhagam in the mid-Forties and the advocacy of a 'separate State' of 'Dravida Nadu', the formation of the Dravida Munnetra Kazhagam (DMK) under the late C.N. Annadurai in 1949, the coming to power of the DMK following the 1967 elections, and the domination of the DMK and its offshoot, All-India Anna Dravida Munnetra Kazhagam (AIADMK) formed in 1972, in the politics of Tamil Nadu.

The DMK got gradually domesticated because the Indian political system provides sufficient space within which Tamil identity and regional autonomy could be protected and fostered. What is more, these tendencies were evident even before Annadurai formally renounced secessionism after the Sino-Indian conflict and the Sixteenth Amendment to the Constitution, which proscribed secessionism and required all candidates seeking political office to take an oath to uphold the Constitution and unity of the country. The DMK/AIADMK stakes in the unity of the country were further strengthened when these parties started sharing power at the Centre. The AIADMK joined the Charan Singh Government in the late Seventies, and the DMK joined the V.P. Singh Government in the Eighties.

In other words, you can see a situation emerging in India beginning from secession. You can see where you have provisions in the Constitution — though not spelt out as federal — where the two identities need not be in conflict. You can be a Tamil and an Indian as well. The greatest day since the day of Independence was the day Deve Gowda became the Prime Minister. For the first time a leader from the South and not knowing Hindi was accepted as Prime Minister. Coalition politics further softens the regionalism of the regional parties, and enables them to work together.

On the contrary, an overview of Sri Lankan Tamil politics since independence clearly shows that the Tamils had been mainly "reactive" to Sinhala politics. Since their hopes and aspirations were never fulfilled by the Sinhala-dominated Governments, frustrations became intense, demands became more radical, culminating in the slogan of a 'separate State of Tamil Eelam' in Vaddukodai in 1976. From a consensual associational politics from 1948-56, when the Tamil leaders were a part of the Government, it became competitive politics, to conflictual politics to conflagrational politics.

The politics of Tamil Opposition started with the demand for balanced representation and responsive cooperation, which spanned the period of 1948-56. The demand progressed to one for a 'federal State' and non-cooperation during 1957-72, escalated to separatist slogans during 1973-76, and ended with the demand for a 'separate State' in 1976. However, while the demands changed, the mainstream of Tamil political leadership confined its strategies to peaceful agitation, parliamentary and non-parliamentary, alike. In 1977, the TULF won on a slogan of 'Tamil Eelam', and militancy crept in. From 1979, militancy began to creep in to Tamil politics. To the Tamil youth, majoritarian democracy meant the rule of the brute Sinhala majority. They were not enamoured by earlier forms of peaceful struggles.

Thus, we have two situations, both related to Tamil minority groups, one in India which is a success story and the other in Sri Lanka which is a story of failure.

By the mid-Seventies, the Sri Lankan Tamils, who were reluctant secessionists to begin with, began to define themselves as a 'separate nation', entitled to self-determination and a 'separate State'. Their stance was the consequence of the discriminatory legislative enactments and governmental policies in the spheres of language, education, land-colonisation, religion and employment opportunities. Then there was the abrogation of the Bandaranaike-Chelvanayakam Pact of 1956 and the Senanayake-Chelvanayakam Pact of 1966, which conferred limited autonomy to the Tamil areas, the competitive Sinhala politics, which marginalised the Tamils and, above all, brutal military repression. These happenings convinced the Sri Lankan Tamils that their cultural identity and legitimate rights could be guaranteed only by a 'separate State'. As is well known, the savage violence of the LTTE and the equally brutal military response of Colombo have converted Sri Lanka into one of the most notorious "killing fields" in the world.

Tigers' Negotiating Strategy

What is the LTTE's negotiating strategy? Will Prabhakaran settle for a solution within a united Sri Lanka? An understanding of LTTE's stance in earlier negotiations can help in analysing the short-term and long-term strategies of the LTTE.

Let us look at the negotiating strategy of the LTTE, the Thimpu talks, the talks of 1987 when New Delhi tried to persuade and pressurise Prabhakaran to accept the 1987 Accord, the talks with President Premadasa, the talks with President Chandrika Kumaratunga, and currently the talks with Prime Minister Ranil Wickremesinghe. The basic fact is that during those years the LTTE made tactical retreats, taking one step backward so that it could take two steps forward. They never gave up their demand for 'Tamil Eelam', nor did they have any faith that the Sinhalas would give them a fair deal.

The first negotiations in which the LTTE participated – as an integral part of the Eelam National Liberation Front (ENLF), comprising EPRLF, LTTE, TELO and EROS – were the two rounds at Thimpu, Bhutan, in July and August 1985. The People's Liberation Organisation of Tamil Eelam (PLOTE) and the Tamil United Liberation Front (TULF), which were outside the ENLF, broadly agreed with the political strategy set forth by the ENLF. The Tamil militant groups were reluctant participants. Senior officials of the Research and Analysis Wing (RAW), India's external intelligence wing, told them bluntly that if they did not go to Thimpu, "neither Indian soil, nor Indian sea, would be available to them".

It was apparent from the beginning that the talks were bound to fail. The Tamil militants, according to Ketheeswaran Loganathan, who represented the EPRLF in the talks, "subjected the Sri Lankan delegation to a series of talks on what constituted the 'ethnic question', and why the burden lay with Colombo to come out with a solution 'worthy' of our consideration." To buttress their claims, they put forward four cardinal principles, which came to be known as the 'Thimpu Principles':

- Recognition of the Tamils as a distinct nationality,
- Recognition of the traditional homeland of the Tamils, and guarantee of its territorial integrity,
- Recognition of the inalienable right of self-determination, and
- Conferment of citizenship on all Tamils who looked upon the island as their country.

The first three principles were deliberately couched in vague terms. To the Sinhala leaders, who at that time viewed even 'federalism' as a first step towards separation, the 'Thimpu Principles' were like a red-rag to the bull. The Sri Lankan delegation responded within a legal framework, and rejected the principles outright. The Thimpu talks ended in a fiasco. It must be pointed out that Prabhakaran was convinced that the Thimpu talks would not lead to a political solution. At the same time, he did not want to cross swords with New Delhi. Lawrence Thilakar and Sivakumaran represented the LTTE in the first round of talks. Yogaratnam Yogi joined the second round. They were instructed to maintain a low profile. As a result, Satyendra of the TELO and the TULF leaders performed most of the verbal acrobatics.

Prabhakaran was taken aback when he was confronted with the *fait accompli* of the India-Sri Lanka Accord of July 1987. His hopes of putting forward his demand to the Indian Prime Minister Rajiv Gandhi, and negotiating with the Sri Lankan President Jayewardene, to finalise the agreement were shattered. However, Prabhakaran made use of the opportunity to salvage his position as much as possible. In his view, the LTTE was the sole representative of the Tamils, and his survival was inextricably linked to the survival of the Tamil people. As several writers have pointed out, Prabhakaran received "financial incentives" from New Delhi. He received the assurance of majority representation in the interim administration and, above all, he was only going to make a "symbolic gesture" of surrendering arms.

The LTTE viewed the India-Sri Lanka Accord as a clever device to snatch away the fruits of their hard-won struggle. Prabhakaran made it clear that he had no faith in the Accord. J.N. Dixit, former Indian High Commissioner in Colombo, in his book, *Assignment Colombo,* with the benefit of hindsight, has made a correct assessment of Prabhakaran: "One over-arching miscalculation of India was our under-estimating Prabhakaran's passionate, even obsessive, commitment to the cause of 'Tamil Eelam', his authoritarian and single-minded nature, his tactical cleverness and his resilience in adversity.

The second miscalculation about him and his cadres was that India and Sri Lanka together could persuade other Tamil groups and the Tamil population in general to join the mainstream of democratic politics, bypassing the LTTE."

President Ranasinghe Premadasa's negotiations with the LTTE spanned the period of May 1989 to June 1990. The two hitherto antagonistic forces came together because they found a convergence of interests to get the IPKF out of Sri Lanka. Bradman Weerakoon, who was Adviser to President Premadasa on international relations, has given a rare insight into the Premadasa-LTTE negotiations. During the negotiations, Colombo made several gestures to the LTTE. According to Bradman Weerakoon, "These included the permission for the LTTE delegates who came to Colombo to have their own armed security, allocation of an entire floor of a five-star hotel in Colombo, a secret supply of money and weapons to the LTTE to fight the IPKF, arrangements for Prabhakaran's wife and children to be brought from abroad and flown to the Vanni, and Premadasa conceding the demand to publicly call for the IPKF to be withdrawn."

The honeymoon lasted until the IPKF left the island on 30 March 1990. The vacuum left by the IPKF was filled by the LTTE, and it gained complete control of the North-East of Sri Lanka. Weerakoon highlights the fact that during the 14 months of negotiations, "there is no record of any serious talks". After the IPKF left, Prabhakaran put forward two demands: the dissolution of the North-East Provincial Council, and repeal of the Sixth Amendment to the Sri Lankan Constitution. The Government rejected the two demands and the 'Second Eelam War' commenced.

The LTTE's negotiations with President Chandrika Kumaratunga from November 1994 to April 1995 show that the two parties were speaking at different wave lengths.

Following the victory in the 1994 elections, Kumaratunga had pledged that she would bring about "ethnic reconciliation" in the island. She expressed her readiness to start negotiations with the LTTE "without any pre-conditions", and held out the promise of peace with honour for the Tamils. As a first step in this direction, the Government lifted the embargo on certain items, as a gesture of goodwill.

How did Prabhakaran respond? In his book, *Politics of Duplicity – Re-visiting the Jaffna Talks,* LTTE ideologue Anton Balasingham has written: "From the outset, Mr. Prabhakaran, the leader of the LTTE, was skeptical of Chandrika's gesture. He felt it was a political gimmick to win the support of the Tamils and the Sinhalese for the forthcoming presidential elections. I advised him to respond to her positively. She is a new leader emerging on the Sri Lankan political horizon, articulating progressive politics. It would be politically prudent on our part to initiate a dialogue with her Government to find out whether or not she is genuine in resolving the problems of the Tamils." Prabhakaran concurred with Balasingham's views. As a "positive step" to the Government's "conciliatory gesture", the Tigers released 10 policemen who were in their custody as 'prisoners of war'. Simultaneously, Prabhakaran demanded the "lifting of the economic embargo completely", which would pave the way for the restoration of normalcy in the Tamil areas.

As the exchange of letters and the talks revealed, there was a basic difference in the approach of the two parties. The peace process, according to the LTTE, should proceed in two stages. The early stages of negotiations should address the restoration of normalcy and the creation of a peaceful environment. After normalcy was restored, talks could commence to find a peaceful solution. Colombo, on the other hand, maintained that there should be simultaneous talks relating to the day-to-day problems of the people and finding a political solution. Finally, the LTTE accused the Government of acting in "bad faith" and started the 'Third Eelam War' in April 1995.

Chandrika Kumaratunga explained the LTTE's behaviour to N. Ram, Editor of *Frontline,* as follows: "The LTTE will do what they have always done ... That is, drag on and on and on until they build themselves up again militarily, and then start attacking again." Is history repeating itself? Is the LTTE laying a peace-trap?

The LTTE used the interval between negotiations to carry forward its policy of annihilation of political opponents. Thus, Amirtalingam, the leader of the TULF, was killed even as talks were going on with the Premadasa Government. The LTTE also killed Gamini Dissanayake during the Kumaratunga-LTTE negotiations. Neither Premadasa, nor Chandrika, said anything against the LTTE, fearing that such statements would adversely affect the peace talks. The present interval of ceasefire is unfortunately being used by the LTTE to carry on its policy of annihilation of political opponents, belonging to other Tamil groups.

Unfortunately, the Ranil Wickremesinghe Government has failed to provide sufficient security to non-LTTE Tamil political leaders. These incidents have created doubts as to the *bona fide* of Prabhakaran in pursuing a political solution and to behave in conformity with basic concepts of democracy and pluralism. Equally alarming is the rapid military build-up of the LTTE. According to informed Sri Lankan sources, the Tigers have, during recent months, built a network of camps in order to encircle the strategically significant port of Trincomalee. Obviously, Prabhakaran believes in the dictum, "If you want peace, prepare for war".

Background to Cessation of Hostilities

The 'Third Eelam War', fought with determination and ferocity by both sides, slowly drifted into a quagmire. The belief that many entertained after the capture of Jaffna by the Sri Lankan Army, that civilian administration could be restored in the peninsula and a link could be established between Jaffna and Vavuniya through the Vanni jungles, turned out to be a mirage. The military expenditure escalated and Sri Lanka, for the first time, registered a negative growth rate in 2001-02. However, despite some daring military operations, the Tigers were in no position to militarily accomplish their objectives. It was apparent that it was extremely difficult for either side to secure an outright victory. The military stalemate compelled both sides to think in terms of a face saving formula.

The unilateral ceasefire declared by the LTTE, followed by its offer to the Norwegian emissaries that the Tigers were prepared for a just and honourable settlement, has to be viewed in the backdrop of certain important developments. Foremost was the growing international isolation of the LTTE. India, the US, the UK and Canada had banned the LTTE, and countries like Australia, members of the European Union, Malaysia and Singapore kept the LTTE under strict surveillance. The killing of innocent civilians, the attack on *Dalida Maligawa* (The Temple of the 'Sacred Tooth'), the dastardly assassination of the Neelan Tiruchelvam, the savage attack on Katunayake air base and Bandaraniake International Airport, and the recruitment of young boys and girls as cannon-fodder in the pursuit of military objectives, had created a sense of revulsion among large sections of intelligentsia in different parts of the world.

The LTTE's statements during the last five years have been aimed at winning back international support. Prabhakaran is showing the "velvet glove" to project the "soft image" of the

LTTE as a 'liberation organisation' that is an 'aggrieved party' and a 'victim of oppression', a 'peace-loving group' pitted against 'war-mongers'. As an example of his earnestness, Prabhakaran highlighted the cooperation extended by the LTTE to the Norwegian initiative to defuse the crisis and start the peace process. What is more, the inept handling of the Norwegian initiative by the Chandrika Government, and its systematic pursuance of the military option, enabled the Tigers to get sympathy and support from foreign sources.

Prabhakaran wants the international community to believe that the Tigers are not terrorists: "We are not mentally demented as to commit blind acts of violence impelled by racist and religious fanaticism. We are fighting and sacrificing our lives for the love of a noble cause, i.e. human freedom. We are freedom-fighters." Prabhakaran wants the world, especially the western democracies, "to provide a clear and comprehensive definition of the concept of 'terrorism', which would distinguish between freedom-fighters, based on the right to self-determination, and blind terrorist acts of fanaticism." He drew attention to the fact that the Tigers had embarked on the peace initiative even before September 11 and, what is more, they even issued an official statement "condemning the September 11 attack."

Of equal significance was the growing convergence of views between the LTTE and the UNP Government. The two sides, as stated earlier, had their own compulsions to seek a negotiated settlement. They wanted to follow a step-by-step approach. Each step would be an end by itself and would pave the way for the next step. Why should ordinary Tamils be subjected to severe hardships? Lift the embargo, remove the irksome security restrictions and let normalcy return. People, irrespective of ethnic affiliations, would develop a stake in peace. When normalcy is restored, negotiations could commence for the formation of an 'interim administration' in the North-East.

Once an interim administration is in place, the Tigers would get 'domesticated' and negotiations for a final settlement could follow. Prime Minister Ranil Wickremesinghe and his close advisers believe that the interim period would lead to the formation of a constituency among the Tamils committed to a peaceful solution. They would, if the need arose, act as a pressure group. This interregnum would also enable the UNP leaders to prepare the ground in Sri Lanka's South for meaningful negotiations with the Tigers. What is more, Colombo believes that it could win international support for a peaceful solution, and also mobilise resources from abroad for "regaining Sri Lanka".

Prabhakaran won the early rounds. The ban on the LTTE was removed, in Sri Lanka the Tigers were recognised as the sole representative of the Sri Lankan Tamils and the provisions of the ceasefire agreement as analysed by the author elsewhere were weighted in favour of the Tigers. These provisions converted the LTTE - controlled areas into a 'State within a State'. From Colombo's point of view, despite occasional hiccups, the ceasefire has held the ground. The current 'no-war situation' has given the citizens some breathing space, and the country is experiencing a "degree of normalcy" never experienced during the 'Third Eelam War'. What is more, in Oslo the LTTE committed itself to negotiating a federal solution within a united Sri Lanka.

Self-Determination in a Multi-Ethnic State

The 'Thimpu Principles', especially the concept of self-determination, are likely to dominate the constitutional talks, as and when they take place. In this context, Balasingham's elaboration of the concept of 'self-determination' requires close scrutiny. At the April 2002 news conference in Kilinochchi, Balasingham pointed out that self-determination has two dimensions – internal and external. Balsingham added: "By self-determination, we mean the right of the people to decide their own political destiny – it can also apply to autonomy and self-government. If autonomy and self-government are given to our people, we can say, to some extent, it is matched. But if the Sri Lankan Government rejects our demand for autonomy and self-government, then, as a last resort, we opt for secession."

Rohan Edrisinha, Director, Centre for Policy Alternatives, Colombo, in a discussion paper, has rightly pointed out that "recognising a 'Tamil nation', a traditional 'Tamil homeland', and its right to 'self-determination' could certainly imply the recognition of an independent Tamil sovereign State." Edrisinha has cogently argued that Tamil legal experts like Rudrakumaran and Sornarajah — both participated in the recent Paris conclave to finalise the LTTE's response to the Government's proposals on interim administration — have argued that devolution and autonomy are stages *en route* to the final destination of an 'independent sovereign Tamil Eelam'. Rohan Edrisinha quotes Sornarajah as arguing for "the acceptance of a confederal political arrangement as a strategic ploy to further the goal of an independent Tamil nation-State."

To quote Sornarajah: "The making of a confederacy recognises the distinctness of the Tamil people and their homeland. It will also lead to the demarcation of the boundaries of the homelands in a constitutive document. These are gains to be had. It will bring the war to an end, and ensure that the confederate arrangements works, as there is the threat of resumption of war. ... Strategically, a confederation may be considered for the reason that it gives the Tamil homeland clearly defined borders, and creates a breathing space for some time. Generally, confederation as a solution has not worked. It was suggested in the Vance-Quen Pact in Yugoslavia, but never got off the ground. Confederations have generally not worked as a solution to ethnic crises."

As Edrisinha pointed out, scholars like Sornarajah advocate confederacy because they believe that it is doomed to fail. Balasingham's statement that while Ranil Wickremesinghe is the Prime Minister of Sri Lanka, Prabhakaran is the "Prime Minister and President of Tamil Eelam" assumes significance in the backdrop of this analysis. If the concept of self-determination is to be rationalised and accommodated in any constitutional settlement, there must be iron-clad guarantees that self-determination does not imply secession. In this context, the example of South Africa may perhaps be of some relevance to Sri Lanka.

Interim Administration, or *de facto* 'Tamil Eelam'

It must be pointed out that in the earlier round of talks, the two parties refrained from discussing the core political issues of the ethnic conflict. However, they have agreed to seek a political solution within a federal framework. Given the constitutional limitations under which the present Government works, its proposals for an interim administration are framed within the 1978 Constitution. Thus, on volatile issues like land and police, control would still remain with the Central Government. Obviously, these proposals fall short of the LTTE's aspirations. The only silver-lining is that the Tigers have not rejected these proposals outright.

The ideologues of the LTTE assembled in Paris in early September to finalise their response to the Government's proposals. Very likely, these will be submitted to Colombo through the Norwegian mediators in mid-October. If the

LTTE's response goes beyond the confines of the present Constitution, which is very possible, a political deadlock will ensue. The fact of the matter is that there is a big hiatus between what any Sri Lankan Government can offer and what the LTTE will be prepared to settle for. The essential fragility of the peace process flows from this dilemma.

The stark reality must be underlined. Colombo is negotiating with an organisation that is administering a 'de facto State'. The LTTE has a well-organised 'army' and 'navy'. They administer their territory with their own civil service, law and order machinery, taxation system and judicial apparatus. When the peace process started, the LTTE believed that they could extend their administration to the whole of the North and the East, which they consider as the 'traditional Tamil homeland'. However, unforeseen developments — the Sri Lankan Supreme Court decision on the respective powers of the President and Parliament, the simmering discontent among the Muslims and the ongoing Muslim-LTTE clashes, and also the determination of the armed forces not to allow the High Security Zones to be dismantled — have acted as stumbling blocks to Prabhakaran's quest for unbridled supremacy.

One thing is certain. The LTTE will not, in the near future, agree to any arrangement that would involve the laying down of arms and demobilisation of its armed forces. Prabhakaran, like Mao, believes that power flows from the barrel of the gun. From the point of view of the peace process, with its objective of working out a federal model, the irony is that there is no federal State in the world where the federating units are permitted to have their own armed forces. Nor has the LTTE so far spelt out the constitutional framework that would fulfil its political aspirations. However, a few years ago, Prof. A.J. Wilson referred to the constitutional proposal drawn by a firm of London solicitors – Bates, Wells and Braithwaite – at the request of a 'group of concerned citizens of Sri Lanka' in

England. Entitled, "A Proposal for Peace with a Framework for the Constitution of Ceylon", it had the tacit approval of the LTTE and was presented to President Chandrika Kumaratunga. The proposal did not even refer to the country as Sri Lanka, but by its old name, as Ceylon.

According to Prof. Wilson, the gist of the proposal is the creation of a confederal structure comprising "two States, each being internally autonomous and each having its own internal Constitution". A central council, consisting of equal number of representatives of each State, would act as the channel of communication and coordination between the two States. The Council will deal with foreign affairs, external defence and security of the Union, monetary policies, including the maintenance of a common currency and a central bank. It can be emphatically stated that such a constitutional arrangement will not receive any favourable response from even the moderates in the Sinhalese political spectrum.

The other part of it is that even the Indian writing on Sri Lanka and most of the Sri Lankan writing on Sri Lanka, refer to the conflict as being between the Sinhalas and the Sri Lankan Tamils. Not much attention is paid to the smaller minorities — namely the Muslims, and the People of Indian Origin (PIOs) in Sri Lanka. Devenesan Nesiah has pointed out that the Muslims form a Tamil-speaking community that seeks its identity not in terms of language, but in terms of religion, a community which is spread throughout the island but is concentrated in the Eastern Province, in Amparai and so forth. They used to support the UNP and are now being used to extract concessions. With the escalation of the ethnic conflict, they have felt the need to form a political party of their own, namely the SLMC. The SLMC (Sri Lanka Muslim Congress) has had a crucial balancing role in the earlier Government as well as in the present one. Rauf Hakim, who now leads the

Muslim community, does not belong to the East, and is a Kandyan.

Ambassador Rasgotra has rightly pointed out (in his inaugural address here) that the Muslims in the East are in a state of ferment. The Sri Lankan Tamils and the LTTE allege that they are discriminated against by Colombo, but the fact of the matter is that the LTTE has discriminated against the Muslims. We all know how the 'ethnic-cleansing' took place in the Jaffna peninsula. The tragedy is that all parts of Sri Lanka are, in varying degrees, multi-ethnic, but the only part of Sri Lanka which is nearly mono-ethnic is the Jaffna peninsula. How many Muslims have gone back to Jaffna after the cessation of hostilities? Have any of them gone back? Very few have. I think the wounds are deep. What is even more significant from the Indian point of view is that international forces would exploit the 'Muslim factor'. For a long time, their ideological inspirations and contacts have been with Keezhakarai in Tamil Nadu, and powerful forces who are likely to fish in troubled waters. So, when it comes to the question of a constitutional settlement, there have to be safeguards for the Muslims as well as the Sinhalas in the East.

The other community about which also there is no mention made, are the People of Indian Origin (PIO). This was a matter of great concern for New Delhi in the early years of Independence, but now both New Delhi and Tamil Nadu seem to have forgotten that community. Even the question of citizenship to the residue of the Sirimavo-Shastri Pact, which was agreed to and incorporated in the draft Sri Lankan Constitution of 2000, and to which the JVP, PA and UNP are committed, has not been passed into law. I do not know why is the delay about the whole thing.

Devanesan Nesiah points out in his interesting paper that in times of crisis, the 'Malaiyaha Tamils', as many of them would like to call themselves, can go to the North-East and live safely, and can retain their identity there. The experience of the 'plantation Tamils' who have gone to the North-East has not been very benign. There was movement of the people from the plantation areas in the mid-Sixties, and they have been cannon-fodder in the struggle between the Sinhala lions and the 'Tamil Tigers'. I have visited the relief centres in Vauvuniya, and more than 60 per cent of the people there are PIOs. Neither New Delhi cares for them, nor does Tamil Nadu. If you look at their concentration, they were 42 per cent in Nuwara Eliya, and used to be smaller minorities elsewhere. Now in Nuwara Eliya perhaps, if there is further devolution from the provincial council to the pradeshiya sabhas, their rights could be taken care of. But what about the other constituencies where they are in miniscule minority? There should be constitutional proposals where they get their representation in employment, and wherein their linguistic rights are also enshrined.

Need of the Hour : Bi-Partisan Consensus

Any settlement to be successful or effective has to go beyond the 1978 Constitution. If the interim administration has to be acceptable to the LTTE, it has to go beyond the proposals under the 1978 Constitution. No Tamil party will agree that the control of land and police should be with the Centre. This necessitates a constitutional amendment, and this could take place only when the President and the Prime Minister work together. However, both have been playing partisan politics. You know the fate of the 2000 draft Constitution, which was a consensus document. Choksi had played a big role in its preparation, and TULF leaders like Neelan Thiruchelvan and Sampanthan had also played big roles. When it was brought to Parliament, it was torn up.

Attempts have been made to impeach the President. The President occasionally says that the Prime Minister or the UNP wants to kill her. It is in the area of bringing about a bipartisan consensus that India, the US and various other countries can work together. They could perhaps drive home the point to the two great leaders of the Sinhalese people, Ranil Wickramesinghe and Chandrika Kumaratunga — both of whom are not chauvinistic and have not inherited the legacies of the past — that they should come together to talk to the LTTE, if the LTTE is willing to talk. But if the LTTE is not willing to talk, they should tackle it together.

Indian observers of the Sri Lankan scene are convinced that the need of the hour is a bi-partisan Sinhala consensus. The issues of war and peace should not be subjected to the vagaries of competitive Sinhala politics. The LTTE is interested in widening the divide between the UNP and the PA so that they could tell their followers that the Sinhalese would never give a fair deal to the Tamils. Whatever may be the criticism against President Chandrika Kumaratunga, she is not a chauvinist. Throughout her political career, she has shown empathy and sensitivity towards the minorities. Sri Lanka can ill-afford the present confrontational politics between the President and the Prime Minister. Let not posterity judge that both sides missed another chance for enduring peace. As Maya Angelou, the Black American poet, wrote a few years ago: "History, despite its wrenching pain, cannot be unlived. But, if faced with courage, need not be lived again".

Discussion

On the issue of why the Muslims have not contributed to the Tamil movement, it was pointed out that there is a controversy regarding the High-Security Zones. The Tamils, the LTTE, demand that the HSZs should be dismantled so that the Tamils can go back. Most of the Muslims in Jaffna do not live in the High-Security Zones. They live in Big Street and all, outside the High-Security areas. But it is not clear why Muslims are not going back to Jaffna, though fear of the LTTE may be one reason.

Others said that the Muslims need assurances regarding security. A few hundred families have come, but not even those families have come fully. Some of them have restarted their trade, but many are waiting and watching. Although the LTTE has given some kind of qualified expressions of regret for having chased them out, the welcome has not been very warm and they are still not sure whether there will be more trouble later.

Moreover, for some of them their houses are no longer there. So, it means a big investment. You don't invest in a large house – most of them had very good houses – unless you are sure it won't be broken again. Also, the Tamils, displaced from the High-Security Zones, have occupied the Muslim houses. The Muslims had been displaced to Puttalam. The whole thing has to be settled at one shot, and it has to be a comprehensive solution, in which the LTTE will also have to come up and say that they would guarantee the security of the Muslims.

Intentions, Capabilities Of The Sri Lankan Govt. and The LTTE

Security Implications for Sri Lanka, India and the South Asian Region

Iqbal Athas

Sri Lanka: One Year After The Peace Accord is indeed a significant topic to focus on from Chennai. In the past several days, this historic milestone has been drawing a great deal of attention in Colombo and several world capitals. Since the truce, to the not-so-discerning, the gruesome memories of a bloody separatist war have almost faded. The absence of bomb explosions, assassinations and curfews has not only brought calm but also an aura of newfound freedom. Many seem to be captivated by the belief, though not truly realistic, that peace has already arrived.

There were the sceptics who claimed that the ceasefire would not last beyond a few months, but it has held for 19 months. This in itself is the qualitative difference between the earlier attempts at cease-fire and the current one. If it has come about with foreign facilitators, it has served well to raise the limits of tolerance towards the settlement of the long-drawn ethnic conflict. This also underscores the threshold of tolerance, predicated on Sri Lanka remaining united and sovereign. The firm belief is clearly that no settlement should result in the vivisection of the country, neither de facto nor de jure. To the discerning, the ceasefire and the year-long peace talks have also posed many questions with more being added to the list as the days pass by.

After five rounds of peace talks with the Government of Sri Lanka (GOSL), the LTTE has suspended them since April 2003. In between, the LTTE had rejected the first two of the three Government proposals on an 'interim administration' in the Tamil areas, but agreed to consider the third – the offer of a provisional interim administration sans power over the police, security, land and revenue.

Although the proposals do not meet what the LTTE called the "Tamil aspirations", and contained very little powers, they did not reject it outright. This has led to the LTTE busying itself with the formulation of a comprehensive set of proposals – for the first time since the ethnic conflict commenced – for the Government's consideration. The LTTE has made it unequivocally clear that the future of the Ceasefire Agreement and its survival will depend on the Government's response. Its proposals, when made, would see the emergence, for the first time, of 'core issues' – matters that would have to be resolved if permanent peace is to dawn in Sri Lanka.

Two weeks ago, in Oslo, members of the Norwegian Government facilitation team told me, "The upcoming talks would be the most difficult phase of the negotiating process. We will have to face very tough challenges." During their visit to Colombo last week, one of the tasks that reportedly engaged their attention was on how to "re-design" their facilitator role, and thus the negotiating process. In talks with the main Opposition People's Alliance, as well as moderate Tamil political parties, they raised this issue, and invited their proposals for this purpose.

It is clear from their assertions and action that the Norwegians are gearing themselves for tough times ahead. It would be logical to expect a plethora of new, knotty issues. New controversies between the Tamil-dominated North and the Sinhala-dominated South will follow.

The 19-month-long ceasefire, and a year of peace talks, has yielded very little results. Yet, it has helped prevent violence, spurred economic activity, given rise to increased tourist arrivals – in short, created a climate of normalcy. The Ceasefire Agreement, and the resultant period of truce, has also led to changing scenarios. Nowhere is its importance felt more than in the sphere of security and defence-related issues. These are of particular concern not only to Sri Lanka, but also to India and even the South Asian region in a broader sense.

The two hallmarks of the near 20-year-long ethnic war are that it has been conducted almost entirely under a state of emergency. That meant the normal laws of the land did not apply in most circumstances. The other is the heavy restriction imposed on the media. The result – both Sri Lankans and the outside world were told of developments concerning the war only through sketchy news releases put out by the Ministry of Defence. The casualty figures of the rebels were heavily exaggerated. Hence dissemination of information about the war, leave alone creating a crisis of credibility for successive governments locally, failed to tell the world what was going on.

As personal experience would show, the complexities of the protracted war reporting on this conflict have had its dangers in my 38-year-long career. In 1993, after I criticised a major military offensive in the North where the Army suffered heavy losses, both of men and material, armed men raided my house and there were threats to kidnap my only daughter, four years old then. A funeral wreath was delivered to my home. It came purportedly from the unit that had suffered the reversals.

Pressure was brought to bear on the publisher and the Editor of my newspaper to force me out of my job, but they did not yield.

After the People's Alliance of President Chandrika Bandaranaike-Kumaratunga was voted to power in 1994, I wrote extensively on large-scale corruption in military procurements contributing to mortar-locating devices purchased for millions of dollars that did not function, helicopter gunships that were non-airworthy, and vintage naval craft that were non-operational. One night in February 1998, a group of well-built men, all armed with automatic pistols, broke into our home and threatened us. Later, under mounting pressure, the Government ordered an investigation and two persons were arrested. They turned out to be the chief bodyguard of the then Air Force Commander and the head of the Special Airborne unit, respectively. They were indicted in a High Court in Colombo. After a trial that lasted over four years, they were sentenced to nine years of hard labour. The case is now in appeal.

The media still remains accused, this time as the main stumbling block to peace. Either due to a total reliance on the faith, or due to naïve unfamiliarity with the negotiating tactics of other rebel groups, the Government now accused us of trying to sabotage the peace talks. This was when reports reflecting the changing ground realities came to be highlighted periodically.

The 19-month-long ceasefire is governed by a set of modalities which both the security forces and the rebels are required to adhere to. Needless to say, the primary purpose is to ensure that there are no hostilities. An equally important aspect is that the "balance of power", of both the security forces and the rebels, should remain at the level that existed on 22 February 2002, when the Ceasefire Agreement was signed. In other words, the agreement seeks to freeze the military-balance.

While there have been no large-scale hostilities, has the balance of power remained static since the ceasefire and the resultant truce? Let us examine some of the salient features of the Ceasefire Agreement, and how the ground realities have changed:

CEASEFIRE AGREEMENT: MILITARY OPERATIONS

1.2. Neither Party shall engage in any offensive military operations. This requires the total cessation of all military action and includes, but is not limited to, such acts as:

a) The firing of direct and indirect weapons, armed raids, ambushes, assassinations, abductions, destruction of civilian or military property, sabotage, suicide missions and activities by deep penetration units;

b) Aerial bombardment;

c) Offensive naval operations.

1.3. The Sri Lankan armed forces shall continue to perform their legitimate task of safeguarding the sovereignty and territorial integrity of Sri Lanka without engaging in offensive operations against the LTTE.

Ground Reality: Assassinations and abductions have become a major irritant in the enforcement of the Ceasefire Agreement. The Sri Lanka Monitoring Mission (SLMM), a body of Scandinavians, and the Norwegian facilitators both raised the issue with the LTTE over the increasing number of killings.

A misguided police raid into an intelligence cell located in a Colombo suburb led to the discovery of weapons and explosives in January 2002. The Government was made to believe that this was a secret hideout, from which ruling UNF leaders were to be assassinated by a military group. In an unprecedented move, the Army Commander, the Director of Military Intelligence and his senior officers were indicted in courts for storing dangerous weapons and explosives. My newspaper revealed that the hideout was in fact a Military Intelligence Forward Cell from which assassination of rebel leaders in the East was carried out before the ceasefire. We named some of the victims, key rebel leaders in the East. The case was withdrawn but the revelations outraged the public. An angry President Kumaratunga appointed a Commission of Inquiry to probe the matter. It is now in the process of concluding its findings.

In retaliatory attacks that have been going on in the 19-month-long ceasefire, the rebels killed 44, and attempted to murder 31 and abducted 17. This included five military intelligence operatives, nine other service personnel and 13 civilian informants. Three soldiers and a civilian escaped death, but a soldier, a civilian and three other servicemen were abducted. The LTTE was also accused of killing 17 persons from rival Tamil political parties and abducting nine. At least 26 attacks on them failed or only caused minor injuries.

The task of "safeguarding the sovereignty and territorial integrity of Sri Lanka" has become a contentious issue for the Navy. The Navy is prohibited by the Ceasefire Agreement from engaging in "offensive military operations against the LTTE". However, in March and June 2003, the Navy sank two LTTE vessels in the deep seas off north-east Sri Lanka. It is no secret that the help of the Indian Navy was sought and obtained in tracking down these vessels. The Sri Lanka Navy said the LTTE was bringing in military hardware, and their gunboats opened fire after being attacked. Admitting for the first time that they were cargo vessels of the LTTE heading for an Indian port, the rebels denied the charge.

A bizarre twist to the incident came when Government and the LTTE leaders were talking peace in the Japanese capital of Tokyo. They asked the Scandinavian peace monitors to work out modalities to prevent future clashes at sea. After consultations with the two sides, the SLMM came out with a set of proposals. My newspaper revealed how the monitors asked the Navy to confine their exercises, particularly live-firing, to specified areas at sea. The SLMM wanted to carve out separate areas for 'Sea Tigers', the sea-going arm of the LTTE, for training and live firing – and repeated the call to recognise them as a "*de facto* naval unit". No detection or inspection of 'Sea Tigers' vessels were to be permitted for the Navy in these 'carved-out areas' without SLMM monitors. In effect, for the Navy, these areas were to be "no-go" zones unless the monitors were with them.

The call to restrict exercises by a sovereign nation's Navy, tasked to protect the country's territorial integrity, raised serious questions on whether the SLMM had the mandate to make such a recommendation. Such a call, in accordance with the Sri Lankan Constitution and other laws of the land, could be made legally only by the President, who is the Commander-in-Chief, the Minister of Defence, the Commander of the Navy, or those in the subordinate command authorised by them. These proposals, shocking enough on their own, were accompanied by a map clearly marking out areas in the western and eastern territorial waters, where the 'Sea Tigers' should be allowed to conduct exercises and live-firing. These proposals generated a controversy in the security establishment and among the opposition political parties. There were concerns in New Delhi too, for India was seeing signs of the emergence of a third navy in the Palk Strait. The proposals have not been pursued since then. The LTTE is, however, determined to seek formal recognition for its sea-going arm, which has expanded both in terms of men and material.

Now to another provision in the Ceasefire Agreement : Separation of Forces

1.4 Where forward defence localities have been established, the GOSL's armed forces and the LTTE's fighting formations shall hold their ground positions, maintaining a zone of separation of a minimum of 600 metres. However, each party reserves the right of movement within 100 metres of its own defence localities, keeping an absolute minimum distance of 400 metres, no such right of movement applies and the parties agree to ensure the maximum possible distance between the personnel.

1.5 In areas where localities have not been clearly established, the status quo as regards the areas controlled by the GOSL and the LTTE, respectively, on 24 December 2001 shall continue to apply pending such demarcation as it is provided in article 1.6.

Ground Reality : In the North, security forces positions are clearly defined by a bunker-line and an obstacle-belt with a fence. Accordingly, demarcation of "cleared" (security forces - held) and "uncleared" areas have been established, keeping the forward defence lines (FDLs) as the guideline.

The areas held by the security forces were defined as High Security Zones (HSZ). During the peace talks, the LTTE has repeatedly demanded the security forces withdraw from the HSZ to enable refugees to resettle, and for the rehabilitation programme to recommence. When the security force commanders in the North steadfastly refused to pull out, expressing fears that they would become vulnerable to attack, the help of a distinguished retired Indian Army officer was sought with the concurrence of the Government and the LTTE. Lt-Gen Satish Nambiar, with experience in battles and peace-keeping operations, declared that if these zones are dismantled without securing "reasonably foolproof assurances", the shortcomings of deployment and equipment (of the security forces) would be evident to the LTTE. He cautioned that re-capture of areas lost to LTTE "would entail much loss of life", and the Army "is desperately short of state-of-the-art equipment".

In the East, the security forces maintained independent military bases in tactically-important localities. They conducted operations in the jungles to flush out the LTTE. There were no FDLs in areas defined on the ground. Since the ceasefire, all this has changed in the East, which includes the port city of Trincomalee, which the LTTE has declared is the capital of their so-called separate State of 'Tamil Eelam'. Recruitment of fresh cadres, training camps, new rebel bases, police stations, court houses, administrative systems, tax collection mechanisms have all fallen in place.

When the ruling UNF signed a Ceasefire Agreement with the LTTE, which officially marked the end of Phase III of hostilities in 'Eelam War III', that fierce phase had accounted for the largest losses in human and material terms. The Government was keen to undo what their own political predecessors had done. They leased out the sprawling World War II oil tank farm to State-owned Indian Oil Corporation (IOC), a move that ensured not only an Indian presence in the area but also cleared their apprehensions. It is relevant to mention that in the Indo-Sri Lanka Peace Accord of 1987, which saw the arrival of Indian Peace Keeping Force, the Sri Lankan Government was prohibited from leasing these storage tanks sans India's imprimatur.

The importance of Trincomalee continues even after the ceasefire, as a naval, political and economic centre. It remains the lifeline for some 40,000 troops and policemen deployed in the Jaffna peninsula. It is only a few hundreds who travel in and out of the peninsula by the daily flights. The bulk moves about by ships from Trincomalee after traversing along the main A-8 highway. Military supplies and provisions for their sustenance take the same route. Hence, crippling Trincomalee or choking Alpha Eight highway can be fatal to the troops holding the peninsula.

My newspaper revealed how the rebels have opened up new military camps, re-occupied ones they had abandoned earlier, and set up a string of satellite camps around the bases that existed. The accompanying map gave graphic details of the changing environment. Newly-recruited cadres have been trained and moved in, we said. New weaponry and communication equipment have been widely distributed. The report noted: "This rapidly developing scenario in and around Trincomalee is signalling a marked shift to the military balance. The Tiger guerrillas are continuing to become stronger militarily, whilst the ground they dominate is expanding. This is in the backdrop of the security forces being plagued with desertions, hit by lack of resources and forced to maintain an inactive profile lest they should be accused of sabotaging the peace process." The report added: "They are yet to receive even the three months' requirements to replenish their dwindling stocks of ammunition and other items. The long-term impact of this change may lead to a virtual siege of Trincomalee – a move that will threaten not only Sri Lanka's but now India's own interests."

The main opposition People's Alliance of President Kumaratunga raised the issue. Her former Foreign Minister and now Senior Advisor on international affairs, Lakshman Kadirgamar, was in New Delhi two weeks ago and apprised the Government and Opposition leaders in India of this fact. In Colombo, the Government's chief peace negotiator and spokesman, Cabinet Minister G.L. Peiris, denied new camps had come up, surrounding Trincomalee. The only exception, he said, was one at Manirasakulam (or, Kuranku Paanchan Kulam) where the LTTE had constructed a camp in a Government-controlled area after the ceasefire. The SLMM had ruled that this violated the ceasefire. Even as the shadow-boxing between the Government and the Opposition over this contentious issue continued, Prime Minister Ranil Wickremesinghe conferred last week with security chiefs over threats to Trincomalee. Contingency measures to meet the threats have been discussed, and the need to further strengthen the Navy decided upon.

Force Strength

Besides the changing ground realities, there are several other important aspects from matters arising out of the Ceasefire Agreement. The total strength of armed LTTE cadres that stood at 9,390 before the ceasefire, according to Sri Lankan intelligence, has increased to 19,750. This is both in respect of the North and the East, and includes members of the so-called 'Eela-Padai', a civilian militia.

Intelligence officials say that at least 30 per cent of the strength are child soldiers. Japan's Special Envoy to the Sri Lankan Peace Process, Yasushi Akashi, raised the issue last week with LTTE Political Wing leader S.P. Tamilselvan at the rebel-held northern town of Kilinochchi. Tamilselvan's reply was that children were joining the rebel ranks out of great enthusiasm, and were not being forcibly conscripted. He said that even UNICEF had been told of this position. In response to a query over political killings, Tamilselvan replied that such incidents were taking place in Government-held areas. Hence it was a matter for the State agencies.

According to Sri Lankan intelligence, more than 19 new camps have been set up in the Eastern districts of Trincomalee and Batticaloa since the ceasefire. The strengthening of the LTTE is in marked contrast to the Sri Lankan security forces, which are hamstrung by the provisions of the Ceasefire Agreement, which aims at retaining the status *quo*. It is manifestly clear that only one side is observing the rules. There is also provision in the Ceasefire Agreement requiring that the Sri Lankan military pull out from the several installations that were located in schools, places of worship and so on. This compelled them to pull out of several places in the North, thus diminishing their presence. Those conversant with security will appreciate that it also diminishes their role in some sense.

Procurement of military hardware for the security forces remained frozen until the recent months. Ammunition stocks dwindled because they were expended for training purposes. President Kumaratunga went public at her party's annual sessions, to declare that the Army was left with only nine days of ammunition. However, when she made the declaration, stocks had been adequately replenished with emergency assistance from India.

Desertions from the Army have been higher during the ceasefire than during times of war. In the year 2000, the number was 4,972. The number increased in the succeeding years: 2001 : 6,018, 2002 : 7,326 and 2003 : 4337 (for the first five months). Recruitment drives after the ceasefire have also fallen far short of targets. In 2002, the Army launched a drive to recruit 10,000 soldiers but ended up listing only 2,503. In August 2003, a drive to recruit 5,000 yielded only 2,300, with the drive still under way. The top brass has asked the Government to raise salaries and also find placements for troops in UN Peace-Keeping Forces, to make the career attractive.

What do these changing realities mean? Has not the LTTE become militarily stronger than the security forces in the 19 months of ceasefire? Have they not become stronger politically too? That is even before the core issues are discussed. How much more will these ground realities change if there is a delay in discussing the core issues? Would such delays, which will make the LTTE much stronger, downgrade the 'core issues' to a matter of low priority? Cannot a much stronger LTTE ask a government, which has neglected its security forces and its security preparedness, to take it or leave it?

The Indian Angle

Amidst these and many other questions, one other important aspect should not be left unsaid. That is the repercussions on India, Sri Lanka's closest neighbour, and the South Asian region.

Very soon the first set of comprehensive proposals of the rebels will be known. At that stage, discussion would cease to be academic, and would involve *real politik* considerations. In this context, there are two important factors to be considered:

i. The impact of a weakened Government security situation in Sri Lanka on India's vital interests – especially control of the Trincomalee harbour, international shipping lanes, and the presence of a third navy in the Palk Straits.

ii. Possible constitutional configuration in Sri Lanka. When the LTTE's counter-proposals are made public, India will have to naturally take a public stand.

The legality, political wisdom and feasibility of having an interim administration dominated by the LTTE, without any assurances that they would be party to a satisfactory final solution, is also a matter of concern. More so, without any hint even of the decommissioning of arms. Will such an interim administration become a permanent feature of the political architecture of Sri Lanka? India has repeatedly stated that it will never countenance a separate State in Sri Lanka.

There would appear to be three options available to the rebels, all of which will have an effect on India.

An indefinite stand-off between the LTTE and southern Sri Lankan polity. This is on the basis that the South is both unwilling and unable to grant them all that they want, leaving them with the alternative of continuing the status quo. This would continue to be to their advantage.

Demanding that the Sri Lankan Government agree to a near sovereign-autonomy that the LTTE may demand. If the Sri Lankan Government of the day and, indeed the other parties, make it clear that the price demanded by the LTTE for permanent peace is too high and cannot be paid, the LTTE will have to fall back either on the stand-off option or, the war option. This means breaking the ceasefire and being the first to start the fighting again.

The final agreement may have to take existing ground realities into account, which suggest that the LTTE may already control a greater part of the North-East and has the necessary political infrastructure to support it.

Even if the Tamil issues are settled, the failure either of the Government or the LTTE, or both, to accommodate the Muslim aspirations may sow the seed for a religious war in the East of the island, where a sizeable number of Muslims live. Signs of seething Muslim discontent are surfacing. The police who investigated recent killings of Muslims in the East found that all the victims had used third parties to make contacts with the LTTE to procure weapons. The killings were reportedly by the LTTE. As a police official involved in the investigations said, "Unlike the LTTE, they (the Muslim youth) need not wait long to raise funds to buy weapons. They already have the currency. All they have to say is '*Allahu Akbar*', and there are groups ready and waiting to help them".

It needs to dawn on all sections, both in Sri Lanka and abroad, that no durable solution to the problem is possible without the involvement of India. The 'South India factor' has a special place in these equations. The question is whether a Tamil Nadu Government will idly watch these ominous developments, in the light of the visceral hatred of the LTTE. Any discussion of the peace process must take all these into account.

Discussion

Some participants suggested that the hardliners within the LTTE are taking control and Balasingham found it embarrassing to go to peace talks and defend the LTTE's position, particularly on issues such as tax on ships, weapons being brought in and the assassinations. It is also known that he has complained about his faxes to the leadership not reaching the destination. Sometime back, the belief in Colombo was that the role he played as translator during the first visit of Akashi was very different from the role that he played at Prabhakaran's news conference on the 10 April 2002. This time, he distinctly cut himself off from the Paris discussions.

Other participants wondered whether India was not losing the strategic autonomy because of the presence of the foreign powers in the region, given the greater involvement of the US, Japan, Norway and the European Union, and not just in Sri Lanka. Others said that that was the reason why any settlement without India's concurrence will not be possible at all. Based on the Sri Lankan Prime Minister's assertions over an 'international safety-net', there is a popular belief in some sections of the Sri Lankan Government that should something go wrong, you would probably be seeing the American GIs parachuting into the Vanni and shoot every member of the LTTE.

Others wondered about the condition of the Sri Lankan Army. The Army is not only demoralised but also fatigued. In such a situation, it was not clear if the Army was capable of fighting if the LTTE decides to go back to war. One of the main causes for the UNF Government to enter into negotiations with the LTTE was the Sri Lankan security forces. In 1995, when they launched a series of military operations, they were able to secure Jaffna and push the LTTE into the Vanni. Had that not happened, the military equations would have changed and, perhaps, the need for negotiations as we see them today would not have arisen. The Army has not been able to ready itself to the levels of preparedness that it had on 22 February 2002, replenishing what it required. As against this, the LTTE has been allowed to acquire state-of-the-art equipment.

It is very well known that when the defences of the Vanni fell in 1999, the LTTE did not need to re-equip itself by procuring weapons. They had artillery shells, they had a very large stock of assault rifles and ammunition and so on. So, what they are procuring is state-of-the-art material. For example, in April 1995, they were known to use surface-to-air missiles only in the Jaffna peninsula, because of restricted quantities. We now know that they have been spread out to the East. The LTTE is also known to have used certain types of equipment in this war which the security forces did not posses. The equation is worrying. There is another aspect that has been going on in the past 19 months. That is the building up of the cells in the cities, the suburbs and also in certain strategic areas like the Hill Country. We are talking of the suicide cadres coming in. We are talking of the smuggling of explosives and weapons. Ahead of the attack on the Colombo airbase, a cell had been in operation there for one year, and it was responsible for that attack. That was under restricted conditions. Now they have a free run because there are no check-points.

Regarding the relationship of Muslims with Tamils and the Sinhalese, it was pointed out that Muslims are not inimical to either of them. In the East, unlike in the North, where there is preponderance of LTTE following, the picture has changed considerably. There is no political leadership in the East. If you hear the Friday *jumma* prayers now, mullahs are talking of measures to protect their own areas. There is a feeling that the Muslims have been let down by the Government on the one hand, and their own leadership on the other.

Intentions and Capabilities of Reluctant Partners

Col. R. Hariharan, VSM (retd)

An infallible method of conciliating a tiger is to allow oneself to be devoured," said Konrad Adenauer, the first-Chancellor of post-War Germany, while speaking on the response to the Soviet designs in Europe. Prophetically, these words appear to be so relevant in the Sri Lankan political context.

The word "negotiate" has three meanings – to try to reach an agreement by discussion, to get or give money value for an instrument, or to get over an obstacle or difficulty. In the Sri Lankan peace process, the negotiations appear to be relating to all the three meanings of the word. Going by the international record of peace negotiations between democratic governments and insurgent organisations, the Sri Lanka peace process has not gone off badly. If Latin American experience is the yardstick, it has gone off well. If our own Indian record with the Naga insurgents is the benchmark, the Sri Lankans have done better. But to thousands of Tamil refugees the world over, now forming part of the 'Eelam Tamil Diaspora', these statements are odious. To thousands of Tamils and Muslims living as refugees in their own country, what has been achieved is too little.

This is not the first time that the Sri Lankan Government and LTTE have spoken of peace at the same time. In the past, such experiences built up high expectations only to deceive in the end. Among the pundits on terrorism and insurgency, and international think-tanks that analyse the global dimensions of irregular warfare, the expectations are not very high. Thus, there is a lot of cynicism in any analysis of the Sri Lankan peace moves. One cannot help but draw a parallel between the failed peace initiatives of the past between the Palestine people and Israel on the one hand, and the 'Tamil Tigers' and the Sri Lankan Government on the other. Both are human tragedies of gross dimensions, with hardened attitudes and intransigent minds, where egotism and politics have over-ridden compassion for the common man. In comparison, durable peace appears to have a better chance of sustaining in Sri Lanka than in Palestine.

One fortunate fall out of 9/11 tragedy is that globally people and nations are coming to understand the true dimensions of terrorism. The rules of the game of people's movements and liberation struggles have changed forever. We need to explore new ways of tackling terrorism, whatever be its cause. In the words of Prof Valentin Daniel, "We have heard it told, and told ourselves of acts of terror in ways that incite rage and revenge, hate and pride, pity and compassion, action and stunned repose. But we need to find new ways of speaking of terror so as to hold terror itself at bay, to check its advance into the general and the commonplace, to restrict it to the particular." We can only hope that both the antagonists, the LTTE in particular, come to terms with this changed global reality and avoid recourse to yet another round of warfare.

As one whose family has had first-hand experience of the catastrophe of 1983 and the war in Sri Lanka, and as one who had actively participated in the Indian Peace-Keeping Force (IPKF), it is not a pleasant feeling to visualise renewed operations by the LTTE and the Sri Lankan Government. While discussing the military scenarios in this paper, I do not consider a military solution by itself bringing an end to the problem. No soldier wants a war. Like all mankind, he would rather live in peace than die in war. As an old soldier, this is also my firm belief.

The peace process has two reluctant participants, and a third unseen presence. The two main participants do not appear to be there at the table as a result of the fine art of diplomacy of the Norwegian interlocutor. They are there, pushed by the urgency of two "watershed events", one local and the other global. The first "watershed" was the 24 July 2001 LTTE attacks on the Katunayake air base. Undoubtedly, it was a resounding success for the LTTE in military terms – and disaster for the Sri Lankan war-machine in terms of counter-LTTE operations. To the Sri Lankan establishment, it brought home the grim reality that the LTTE was capable of causing colossal damage in the heart of the national capital of Colombo, well outside the killing fields of peninsular Jaffna or the coastal areas of Trincomalee-Batticaloa. As Dr V. Suryanarayan has mentioned in his writings, the 'Katunayake' attack was a significant turning-point in the Sri Lankan attitude to finding a military solution against LTTE. It would appear to have been the last straw on the Government's back – already over burdened with a crippled economy, a demoralised armed force and a disenchanted population.

In democratic societies, terrorism and insurgency give politicians wonderful opportunities for scoring brownie points when the country goes to the polls. Sri Lanka is no exception. The Tamil insurgency issue has been the staple fare for Sri

Lankan politicians. President Chandrika Kumaratunga made her political debut on this issue. However, after her disastrous efforts both at pursuing peace and making war, the UNP Opposition cashed on the promise of brokering a lasting peace.

The UNP's record in this aspect had been dismal, two party Presidents having tried their hands at peace and war rather ineffectually. Having won a parliamentary mandate on the issue of peace, the UNP coalition has now been called upon to show results. Luckily for Sri Lanka, in Ranil Wickremesinghe, it appears to have a political personality who genuinely believes that the negotiating table is the only way to tackle the LTTE. He has shown an uncanny understanding of the need of the people when he said in a recent interview, "People want a peace dividend now". [2]

Sri Lanka could ill-afford to prolong the agony of fighting a well-seasoned outfit that has the dubious distinction of being billed as the No 1 terrorist force in the world.[3] Every President, including incumbent President Chandrika Kumaratunga, has gambled his or her political fortune on brokering peace and waging war to "usher in peace". So, when Wickremesinghe chose to opt for the peace process, was he merely repeating the set piece? No. I think, he represents the ever-growing, enlightened thinking of the people of Sri Lanka who would go through an agonising (and at times painful) peace process rather than take up arms once again. The Norwegians had been brokering peace for quite sometime in Sri Lanka with no great success. This time around, with Ranil Wickremesinghe leading the peace moves, they can hope for better results to show.

Fortunately for Sri Lanka, its well-wishers like Japan are also keen to see the fruition of the peace process. On many occasions in the past the LTTE had talked of peace and ceasefire, only to use the interregnum to carry out its four R's (rest, recoup, recruit and re-train). So, its profession of desire to talk "peace" had always been looked upon with suspicion.

But this time around, the LTTE's environment of global operation has changed. So now, when it talks of peace, Sri Lanka can afford to take it seriously.

Why is the LTTE at the peace table when there is no definite possibility of a free and independent, 'Tamil Eelam' emerging at the end of it all? Having laid waste thousands of lives in its two-decade-long struggle, is the Tiger changing its stripes? Has LTTE given up its 'Eelam quest', probably to gain a little more than what was offered on a platter by Rajiv Gandhi 15 years earlier? These are some of the questions that come to the mind when we look at the LTTE's history. I think it is the second 'watershed' event that brought about this seemingly difficult change in LTTE's mindset. I am not sure if it is a change of mind as regards the concept of an 'independent Eelam'.

The second 'watershed' event – 9/11 attack on the Twin Towers and the Pentagon in the U.S., had a global ripple-effect. Till 9/11, for the western world terrorism and insurgency were happenings 'elsewhere', reserved for parlour discussions at coffee breaks when the intelligence fraternity met. Their recent encounters with terrorism were limited to tackling the Real IRA planting a bomb and warning the police when it was about to explode. But 9/11 was a traumatic experience for the world's richest nation, which has assumed the role of universal policeman in a unipolar world. It brought home the fact that terrorists can strike the world's mightiest power at the time and place of their choosing.

Unfortunately for the LTTE, 9/11 happened too soon after the 'Katunayake attack'. Since then a few key U.S. decisions, taken in close collaboration with its allies in the West, have made the prosecution and direction of terrorism from distant lands more difficult than ever before. In fact, the U.S. has worked out an integrated, and at times even draconian system to combat terrorism both at home and abroad. In the words of US Secretary of State Colin L. Powell, "Nations everywhere now recognise that we are all in this together. None of us can combat terrorism alone. This global threat demands a global response. Concerted action is essential, and together we are taking that concerted action."

The inclusion of LTTE in the US list of global terrorist organisations alongside Al-Qaeda called for an end to its 'legitimate' operations in the West. The UK in particular is at the very heart of the LTTE's overseas activities. The nearly half a million strong 'Eelam Tamil diaspora' scattered across 50 countries is the backbone of LTTE's vast resources. It funds the LTTE's vast global network, and provides the resources to carry on its war. Mulling over the hard options, the LTTE appears to have come to the conclusion that it has to revamp its approach to the 'Eelam struggle' in view of the changed global realities. Entering the peace process was handy for the LTTE to internationally 'legitimize' its existence to a certain extent. It has also provided the strategic breather that the LTTE needed to come to terms with the hard realities of changed global perceptions of insurgencies and terrorism and work out a new equation for its survival and sustenance.

The climate was right, and the two parties to an adverse situation became reluctant partners in a peace process. India, as the major power of the region, with a huge Tamil population having links with the Sri Lankan Tamils, always looms large in any political equation in Sri Lanka. It had been reluctant to take any active part in the peace moves after its bitter experience in 1987, muddled further by the LTTE's assassination of Rajiv Gandhi. Despite Prabhakaran terming the killing of Rajiv Gandhi as "a tragic incident", it has been difficult for India to grant legitimacy to the LTTE by actively participating in the current peace process.

This has not diminished the important role India can play in ensuring peace in the island. Thus, in spite of its seeming reluctance, India's could be called the third unseen presence at the talks, as the other two partners want and need its blessings to underwrite lasting peace in Sri Lanka.

Intentions and Capabilities

Intentions are generated out of visions and goals. Capabilities decide whether the intents go beyond the realms of visions and dreams. Strengths and weaknesses embedded in the characteristics of both the Sri Lankan Government and the LTTE will determine whether the capabilities are rooted in reality. In the light of my own background as a military intelligence analyst, I have examined the characteristics of both the parties to evolve possible intentions and capabilities. Of course, my focus is by no means limited to the military aspects, because military options are exercised not in isolation but only as a part of overall power projection. However, my purpose is to outline issues that would affect the military option, leaving out the issues on the political thought process to the other scholars on the subject.

In the case of the LTTE, which is essentially an autocratic armed movement, the armed wing holding positions of primacy has been dictating the political process. I do not visualise any change in this scheme of things. Thus its political and military processes are closely intertwined and indistinguishable. Unlike this, in the Sri Lankan State, the military is only a creature of a democratic and representative Government accountable to its people and parliament.

Political

With a democratic Government operating within the realms of international law, the Sri Lankan Government enjoys global legitimacy. This gives it access to the global forums, the UN and other nations. Sri Lanka's international image, which was tarnished in the Nineties due to gross human rights violations, has become better now. Over the years, it has been able to pro-actively network with its neighbours, particularly India, to evolve a pragmatic foreign policy. It has progressively built strong links with India commercially, economically and politically. In recent times, Sri Lanka has emerged as India's strongest ally in South Asia next only to Bhutan. Therefore, the potential source of succour to LTTE from India stands curbed.

As democracies go, Sri Lanka has a fairly good record of elections and parliamentary practices, barring insurgency-swept areas. It has a hybrid Constitution that attempts at having a presidential form of government in the setting of a parliamentary system. This dual system is at best a compromise and, like all compromises, does stifle the functioning of both the President and the Prime Minister. So, vital national decisions tend to be delayed, negotiated between parties. This has been compounded by the two major political coalitions led by the UNP and the SLFP not seeing eye-to-eye even on issues affecting the vitals of the nation. The LTTE and minority political groups have time and again exploited this inherent weakness of Sri Lankan polity.

Despite this weakness, both the major political parties appear to have successfully put other internal issues, rooted in inter-party frictions and constitutional contradictions of President-Prime Minister confrontation, on the back-burner for the time being in order to take up the peace process. However, this potential flash-point to burn up the peace process is very much there. With the pragmatic leadership of Ranil Wickremesinghe as the Prime Minister, the peace process has solid political backing in the Government. It is to President Chandrika Kumaratunga's credit that she has given a fairly free run for the Prime Minister to have his way in the peace talks, at least for now.

The JVP is against any liberal provision of autonomy to the Tamils, lest it should affect the unitary structure of Sri Lanka. Its growing strength could adversely reflect on the political fortunes of both the UNP and the SLFP in the elections, whether the peace process succeeds or not.

There is a lack of credibility in the minds of the Tamil population about the sincerity of Sinhala politicians due to failure of past 'peace exercises' by successive Presidents from the late J.R. Jayewardane to Chandrika Kumaratunga, belonging respectively to the UNP and the SLFP. The 'surrender' of their identity to the LTTE by the Tamil political parties, barring a few, reflects the political despondency among them.

Social Characteristics

The Sri Lankan population is officially divided into ethnic groups of Tamils, Sinhala, Moors (Muslims), and Burghers, etc. To an outsider, it is difficult to understand the rival claims of Aryan, Dravidian or Arabic lineage of these groups. The fostering of Sinhala chauvinism from early Sixties, and its culmination in the anti-Tamil conflagration of 1983, were the result of majoritarian politics practised for nearly three decades of independence. However, having suffered the LTTE insurgency for nearly two decades since, the majority Sinhala population appears now to have a better understanding of the Tamil grievances. Though this has come at an enormous human and economic cost, a majority of Sri Lankans appears to have veered round to the belief that a peaceful solution was the only answer to the Tamil insurgency.

Optimistically, this should see the emergence of a broad, majority consensus within the country that the peace process should take precedence over an armed conflict to resolve the 'Eelam issue'. So, peace rather than war with the Tamil insurgents has become a political issue, and not by a mere social paradigm. Sri Lanka has had a poor human rights record as the use of brute force against the Opposition and civil population was common. However, there appears to be a conscious effort to improve this, and by South Asian standards it has made definite progress in this respect.

There is a widespread war-weariness among the population. The prolonged blood-letting has cost the nation dearly, both in terms of national morale and developmental effort. The weakened economy makes fresh prosecution of war a very unviable national proposition.

Military Terrain

Being an island-nation, Sri Lanka's terrain lends itself only to limited strategic military manoeuvrability. The Jaffna peninsula falls within the dry belt, unlike the rest of Sri Lanka, which has heavy rainfall. Thus, it is comparatively barren. In military terms, this calls for highly mobile operations due to lack of cover. The insurgent hideouts in the peninsular part have to be urban, imposing limitations on the size of their operations. In this setting, selective assassination and effective use of land-mines and non-conventional explosive devices can pay better dividends than classical guerilla operations. Being totally dominated by the Tamils, the North had been out of the main stream of the nation's life except for military operations. Thus, it would perhaps cause greater impact if the LTTE carried out terrorist operations in areas in the island other than the peninsula.

Inevitably, insurgent bases for training and recuperation have to be well protected. The Vanni area, up to the Mullaitivu coast with its lush jungle offers ideal hideouts for large guerilla forces. Elephant Pass, the narrow causeway linking Vanni to peninsular Jaffna, therefore becomes vital for any force operating in the region. This also provides easy accessibility from the Alampil Sea on the Mullaitivu coast on the East to the western coast of Jaffna. In military terms, the deep waters of Alampil Sea facilitate free movement of ships to unload supplies and take them to Jaffna proper, which has shallow waters on the west. This was perhaps the reason why the LTTE prioritised capturing this area, instead of Jaffna town itself.

The northern coast of Jaffna peninsula (Madagal-Point Pedro) has deeper waters and provides the easiest access to the 'Tamil areas' of South India on the eastern seaboard – the Indian coast is just an hour away by speed boat. Kankesanturai provides good draft for bringing in ships. The Palali airfield has facilities to launch limited air operations, though it is within artillery range from the South and the East. Most of Jaffna peninsula also has built-up areas, which canalise military operations along major road axes. A smaller force occupying the built-up areas can inflict higher damage and casualty on any assaulting force. This would call for the effective use of armour, to be deployed imaginatively to support typical infantry operations in built up areas.

The axis, Jaffna-Chavakacheri-Elephant Pass-Kilinochchi-Omanthai-Vavuniya, is vital for the sustenance of Jaffna peninsula and its domination. Anyone who controls this axis has better sustainability of military operations. This axis can come under effective insurgent operations between Vavuniya and Kilinochchi, due to the dense forest-cover on the eastern side. Elephant Pass is a bottleneck, which can be interfered with by effective covert operations. Jaffna is the second biggest town in Sri Lanka, and the cultural capital of the Tamils in the country. It has been the strong focal-point of Tamil ethos and sentiments. It has well-built infrastructure, though mostly not in operation due to sustained military operations. As the capital of 'Tamil Eelam', its possession is directly linked to assertion of Tamil supremacy.

In the Sri Lankan mainland, the Eastern Province, including Trincomalee and Batticaloa, are considered traditional Tamil areas. This coast has good beachheads for troops. Trincomalee is an excellent natural port with good berthing facilities. It provides an eastern gateway to the ASEAN countries and India's east coast. This province has a strong presence of Sinhala and Muslim minorities. It has good links with the rest of Sri Lanka, which makes movement of reinforcements easy. Trincomalee has a modern airport. Both the towns have good infrastructure and thriving commerce. Though the Muslims are Tamil-speaking, the LTTE's 'ethnic-cleansing' operations of the past have antagonised them. In fact, the Muslims have been alienated from the Tamils over the years, due to social and political compulsions.

The Sri Lankan Armed Forces

The three-division strong Sri Lankan Army (SLA) has been fighting the Tamil insurgents for the last two and a half decades, with varying degrees of success. Except for a three-year respite during the IPKF operations against the LTTE, it had enjoyed only brief periods of calm during the intermittent peace processes. Considering its moderate size, it has limited options to rotating troops in counter-insurgency operations. This is considered vital, lest the troops, hunting the insurgents intermingled with civilian populations continuously, should become brutalised. Considering this inherent limitation, the SLA has improved its human rights record over the years. Its rank and file is perhaps now more aware that the civilian population needs to be kept neutral if they are to succeed against the insurgents.

After the IPKF left Sri Lanka in 1990, the SLA has had two major spells of operations against the LTTE. It managed to capture Jaffna, and open up the axis Jaffna-Kilinochchi-Vavuniya for most parts in 1995. This proved that the SLA is capable of launching successful operations against the LTTE. While it could hold on to Jaffna, lack of strategic manoeuvrability against the LTTE in the Vanni region cost it dearly. After initial successes, SLA suffered heavy casualties during 1997, progressively losing Omanthai and Kilinochchi in a series of LTTE counter-attacks, culminating in the loss of Elephant Pass in early 2000. The loss of this Pass, which had been under the SLA control for over a decade, resulted in the LTTE taking a large number of prisoners, and capturing artillery guns and ammunition. These operations proved profitable for the LTTE as it added conventional artillery to its arsenal. These massive casualties have undoubtedly affected the Army's capability. High rate of desertion further demoralised the armed forces, but military setbacks alone are not the reason. The political ambivalence in finding a solution to the LTTE insurgency for over two decades is clearly a cause for the lack of strategic direction to the SLA, resulting in its demoralisation. Moreover, the loss of experienced senior officers has denuded of its seasoned leadership.

On the positive side, the SLA has been making deliberate efforts to train its troops specifically for counter-insurgency with the help of India, the UK and other friendly countries. While its officer cadre is as good as any in South Asia, the troops have the limitations of inadequate training and motivation. It is a land-bound Army as against the LTTE, which is equally capable of using the sea to its advantage. Added to this, it has limited tactical mobility in the absence of adequate airlift capability and heliborne firepower. The Navy and Air Force in particular need more infusion of money, equipment, aircraft and ships for launching effective operations afresh. The Sri Lankan armed forces are also war-weary, reflecting the mood of the people. They will need tremendous motivation to relaunch operations against the LTTE. To achieve this, a resurgent national leadership needs to rebuild the armed forces with special attention to motivation, strategic decision-making and tactical operational mobility so essential in counter-insurgency warfare as well as conventional warfare. Of course, they have to be provided with modern weapons and sophisticated equipment needed in modern counter-insurgency operations.

The SLA has limited transport capability so essential to move troops from one sector to another. It has depleted fighter squadrons to support ground operations. Unless it is modernised, it will not be able to make a mark in any future conflict. Its vulnerability to LTTE missile attack is well known. Likewise, the Sri Lankan Navy has been able to operate in the east coast with some success. However, it has not been able to counter the high-speed 'Sea Tigers' operations in shallow waters, or effectively prevent the LTTE's cargo ships from bringing in supplies. The Navy needs strong political support and freedom to operate to bring out its best.

LTTE's Characteristics

The LTTE has a proven military capability as an effective guerilla force, with a unified command capable of launching successful operations. Its colossal success in the Elephant Pass operations against the conventional defences of a large Sri Lankan force has shown its newly-acquired ability to conduct large-scale conventional operations also. It is now capable of conducting guerilla operations along with conventional warfare.

The LTTE's forces have generally been estimated at 8,000-10,000 with about 6,000-armed fighters. It has women's battalions and a naval wing, the 'Sea Tigers', which has progressively been built up in strength (estimated at 2,000) and capability. Highly-motivated elite troops, known as 'Black Tigers', form the core of the 300-500 strong suicide-squad. The LTTE figures among the world's top 12 insurgent groups that have specialised in suicide attacks. It had accounted for two-thirds of all suicide-bombings across the world up to 2002, according to one estimate. Child-soldiers taken in at a tender age and indoctrinated to the LTTE's cause form the source of 'Black Tigers'. With the result, the LTTE had been ruthless against its foes, whether political or military. Its assassination victims include a whole galaxy of intellectuals, bureaucrats, politicians, military leaders, leaders of other Tamil militant groups, prime ministers and ministers, apart from common criminals, wayward women and ordinary mortals who fell out with the organisation.

The LTTE has excellent radio communications and an organised system of intelligence-gathering. It controls most of the Northern Province, barring some important towns, including Jaffna. Its bases in Mullaitivu area are yet to be penetrated by the Army. It has been running areas under its control with an administrative machinery, including police and courts, cobbled together mostly from its cadres. As the LTTE exercises physical control of vast areas of North and East, free exercise of governance by any legitimate Government is not possible unless it regains control of these areas. Militarily, the LTTE is now placed in an advantageous position as it has the freedom to switch forces from the eastern seaboard to western seaboard through control of the crucial Elephant Pass-Vettilakeni area.

The LTTE has no democratic pretensions. Decision-making rests with a single person – Prabhakaran. Thus, the built-in delays of democratic decision-making that an elected Government faces are absent. Prabhakaran has repeatedly demonstrated the LTTE's strong commitment to the ideology of creating an independent 'Tamil Eelam', even though in the past he had a number of opportunities to accept legitimate compromise solutions (e.g. Indo-Sri Lanka Accord, 1987). This has created a strong impression among the Tamils all over the world on his sincerity to the cause of 'Eelam'. On the other hand, non-LTTE Tamil leaders in Sri Lanka have lost their credibility through compromises of their stand on various occasions. This has built up Prabhakaran's image as the only leader who can deliver Tamil Eelam.

The LTTE has been able to achieve a few remarkable firsts in the current peace process:

- For the first time, the LTTE has gained recognition from the Sri Lankan Government itself as the sole arbiter of the fate of 'Eelam Tamils'.
- The LTTE has managed to cow down all major Tamil political parties into towing its line. For the first time, the Tamil political opinion is orchestrated to play the LTTE tune, with dissent muted to a few organisations. This has strengthened the LTTE's position in the dialogue process.
- The 'Sea Tigers' has proved its superior capability with some notable successes against the Sri Lankan Navy. Even the Norwegian mediators have informally recognised the 'Sea Tigers' as a naval entity.
- For the first time, the LTTE has put forward a plan on its own initiative, unlike its negative response in earlier peace efforts. Though it has spelt out its commitment to three of the four points in the 'Thimpu Principles', it has indicated the feasibility of fitting its 'Eelam demand' within the ambit of a federal Sri Lanka.

Despite all this, there are inherent flaws in the LTTE. These are:

- The LTTE enjoys low credibility, both internally and internationally. Past experiences of dealings with the LTTE has not enhanced its reputation as an organisation that one can confidently deal with. This affects its dealings not only with Sri Lankan political parties and leaders of Sinhala, Tamil and Muslim polity, but also with the policy-makers in India and in countries like Norway, who have an interest in the success of the peace process.
- The LTTE has always pronounced its strong commitment to the cause of creating an independent 'Tamil Eelam'. Thousands of lives of Tamils have been sacrificed in its struggle. To compromise on that in the peace process would be considered a betrayal by the rank and file. Thus, if the 'Eelam cause' is diluted in the current negotiations, it can rebound on the organisation and Prabhakaran, though the rank and file may not vocalise it immediately – for fear of brutal repression of dissent.
- With the assassination of Rajiv Gandhi, the LTTE has totally antagonised India, losing its strong support base in Tamil Nadu. So, in any resumption of LTTE operations, India may figure as a strong factor in support of Sri Lanka, to the tremendous disadvantage of the LTTE.
- The LTTE is more feared than endeared by the Tamil population. With no democratic practices or processes to his credit, "Prabhakaran commands a *Führer*'s awe rather than the mere respect accorded to ordinary leaders", as the *Economist* says. It has no transparent mechanism for consulting different shades of public and political opinion. It has continued to exhibit its

intolerance of dissent. Therefore, it will find it difficult to fit in as a political force in a federal democracy.

- The LTTE's strong anti-Muslim posture over a long period of time has alienated large sections of Tamil-speaking Muslims, who see their future only in the Sri Lankan mainstream. Prabhakaran's recent averment that "the Tamil homeland belongs to the Muslim people" as well, does not carry much conviction among the Muslims as they have been attacked and killed by the LTTE even after the peace talks commenced.
- The LTTE has no clear-cut political or economic ideology. Its record of administration of the areas under its control has not made life comfortable for the people. It has a strong image as an anti-intellectual organisation with fascist convictions – totally unsuited to participate as a political segment in a federal democracy.
- The LTTE's systematic elimination of Tamil intellectuals and moderate leaders has placed it at a disadvantage in evolving negotiating strategies. By eliminating them, it has also closed all avenues of communication with foreign governments to put across its case effectively to muster their support.
- It lacks good political leadership. Its military leadership had always taken precedence over political elements. Unlike in many other insurgent movements, the political cadres do not command respect in the LTTE. Invariably, they are identified as part of the propaganda and administrative machinery rather than as decision-makers.
- While the LTTE has a strong and self-activating second-line military leadership to execute military operations, there is a void in the leadership required to

meet the political and administrative needs of peacetime.

- The LTTE has a whole generation of youth that have no avocation other than that of militancy. The burden of retraining and rehabilitating them in socially useful non-military occupations will be a heavy one for the LTTE and its 'government', when peace is ushered in.
- The LTTE has been included in the US list of global terrorist organisations. It has a poor human rights record with its child-soldiers, summary killings, 'kangaroo courts' and public executions even for comparatively trivial crimes. This has not endeared it internationally, and it will be a long time before the LTTE is taken out of the list of terrorist outfits. This will be a major handicap for obtaining supplies and support from overseas, in case the LTTE wants to restart hostilities.
- War-weariness of the Tamil people. By and large, there is a great expectation among the Tamils that this time the LTTE would usher in peace, rather than restart military operations. The Tamils would like to normalise their fractured lives after two decades of struggle.
- In spite of holding large areas of 'Eelam' under its control, key components like Jaffna town, Palali airfield, and Kankesanthurai are not under the LTTE control. Launching military operations to capture these would require huge resources.
- Though the LTTE has exhibited its success in conventional operations in Elephant Pass, it has to make serious efforts to convert its guerilla force into a conventional force. In the present context, it may not be possible to capture a sprawling area like Jaffna by guerilla operations against a conventional army – because it would be a time-consuming process. The lack of conventional capability for such an operation

is a weakness of the LTTE. Limited artillery capability is yet another weakness.

Government's Intentions and Capabilities

Obviously, the Sri Lankan Government's intention would be to work out an acceptable formula for power-sharing with the LTTE. Even if it does not succeed, the aim would be to prolong the peace, and avoid yet another round of military operations against the LTTE. But the democratic polity imposes certain limitations on how far the 'no-war-no-peace' interregnum could be prolonged, and how much concession could be extended to the LTTE. Three critical issues would need an internal consensus among the non-Tamil polity of Sri Lanka if another round of military confrontation were to be avoided. These are:

(1) level of autonomy for an 'LTTE government' in the federal format,

(2) delineation of the areas that would constitute the Tamil province, or provinces, and

(3) the future of LTTE's armed cadres and their rehabilitation.

However, even if there is no consensus on their side, the Sinhala polity may be driven to the military option by the LTTE. Past negotiating techniques of the LTTE indicate that impossible demands on intransigent issues normally precede resuming the military option. The LTTE, having had more than a year to recuperate its resources, should be ready to exercise its military option any time. Without sounding pessimistic, any stalling of negotiations by the LTTE at this juncture, on comparatively trivial issues thrown to the fore, would indicate that it is approaching the point of no return.

Militarily, the Sri Lankan Government should be able to hold on to defensive positions in Jaffna, contiguous areas of

Valikamam and the line Kankesanthurai-Point Pedro, with its existing forces. However, it will have to estimate required force-levels based on the discerned LTTE target areas. If the armed forces were to defend its areas in Jaffna peninsula with the required force levels, its ability to respond to the defence needs to counter the LTTE threat to the mainland would be seriously affected. If there is a long invest by the LTTE in Jaffna peninsula, the SLA would require air and naval support in much greater terms than its current capabilities. Thus, it might not be within Sri Lanka's capabilities to sustain such operations with its existing force levels. But, given the post-9/11 anti-terrorism scenario, the Government would perhaps bid for and succeed in getting some external support to compensate this.

LTTE's Intentions and Capabilities

Despite Prabhakaran's April 2002 statement, it is difficult to believe that LTTE is giving up its vision of lording over an 'independent Tamil Eelam'. If it does so, it would be considered a betrayal of the tremendous sacrifices made by thousands of Tamils at the altar of 'independence'. So it cannot prolong the current impasse of no-freedom-no-war. It has to come out with a tangible package to show its achievement at the current peace negotiations. In the areas administered by it, the LTTE has a flag, a national anthem and a police force. It also dispenses summary justice. The LTTE collects taxes in these areas, which Colombo terms as extortion.

These are not mere trappings, but an exercise of LTTE power in 'Tamil Eelam' that is already there on the ground. The LTTE has to gain legitimacy not only for this exhibition of visual symbols, but also its exercise of power. Otherwise, it would lose its reputation as the vanguard organisation fighting for Tamil independence. How can it do this without loss of face? The LTTE has three courses:

1) Avoid war, by opting for a confederation rather than a federal format (somewhat like Montenegro) by leveraging its willingness to give up insurgency.
2) Maximise its demands and thus play to the gallery, and scale it down at the negotiations. This logical methodology goes against the grain of LTTE.
3) Maximise the demand to such an extent that no self-respecting government would be able to concede it – and let the peace talks flounder. This would enable the LTTE to blame the other parties and resume operations at a time of its choosing.

Conventional wisdom would dictate that the LTTE adopt the first or second course. However, to induce the LTTE to do this, probably the West will have to make it unequivocally clear that the safe havens of the LTTE in Europe and the U.S. would be no more tenable. As a face-saving device, this can perhaps be linked up with an economic package for rehabilitation of the cadres and people in the affected areas. Can this kind of solution be evolved?

In normal circumstances, resuming military operations would not be a logical option for the LTTE. However, insurgent forces, which put faith in acts of terrorism, do not follow normal paths of logic and reasoning. They have their own convoluted logic outside normal reasoning. The LTTE in the past has exhibited this aberration repeatedly, in its pattern of behaviour with India. To quote one instance, it antagonised a whole nation by assassinating Rajiv Gandhi for reasons best known probably to none other than Prabhakaran. Thus, the LTTE exercising the military option is a real possibility. How will this military option be exercised? It could be a cocktail of actions:

- Terrorist operations outside 'Eelam areas', which could be disclaimed by the LTTE
- More incidents in the territorial waters of Sri Lanka

- Selective assassinations of key personalities

The targets in mainland Sri Lanka would be economic ones like Colombo Port and the oil terminal being revived at Trincomalee, now leased out to IOC, tying down a large segment of Sri Lankan forces. This could be followed by the LTTE building military pressure on Palali and Valikamam, cutting off the Vettilakeni-Elephant Pass line, thus culminating in seizing control of Jaffna, Palali and Kankesanthurai – in that order of priority. The LTTE has the capability to sustain such an operation for a short duration against each of these target areas. So it could take them on piecemeal, one after the other.

But with the present global line-up of nations willing to combat terrorism, it will not be easy for the LTTE to resume operations in Sri Lanka, and pass it off as 'freedom struggle'. The LTTE's hard options are unlikely to succeed as easily as it might expect or hope. As the U.S. Deputy Secretary of State, Richard Armitage said the LTTE has to "unequivocally renounce terrorism in word and deed". While the US could see a future for the LTTE, it has been left to the Tigers to show they were worthy of 'legitimacy'. Otherwise, it may end up as an international untouchable. It is evident from the change of guard in the LTTE at the negotiating table that the military option could be under serious consideration. To ward off this suspicion, the LTTE will have to device ways by which the onus or responsibility for breaking the peace process will fall on the other party. Will it do so? As I said earlier, terrorist movements have their own logic. So, we have to wait and see what the LTTE has in mind, just as millions of Tamils all over the world do.

What are the chances of peace negotiations continuing for a long time, to evolve a viable solution? With no political group having an outright strength to move a constitutional amendment bill in Parliament, nobody appears to be in any hurry. Will the negotiations drag on till December 2005, when the incumbent President retires, leaving the field open for Wickremesinghe? Is it in the realm of probability? Well, I quote an AFP report datelined Colombo, 13 July 2003, and you be the judge: "During the early days of the process, Norway's Deputy Foreign Minister Vidar Helgesen warned that a final settlement could take up to 10 years, and that Oslo as the facilitator was ready for the long haul". Democratic regimes could be as fickle as insurgent groups. So we are in for a period of wait and watch.

REFERENCES

1. Prof E Valentin Daniel at Neelan 'Thiruchelvan Memorial Lecture' June 28 2003
2. Ranil Wickremesinghe in an interview, *Time Asia*, September 2003
3. In fact, Prof Rohan Gunaratne rates LTTE as far superior to both Hamas and Al-Qaeda in terms of capability, organisation and resources. "International regional implications of the Sri Lankan Tamil insurgency", 2 December 1998.
4. Colin L. Powell while releasing the report "Patterns of Global Terrorism 2002", US Dept. of State, 30 April 2003.
5. *'The Tiger Comes out of its Lair", Economist Global Agenda,* 12 April 2002.
6. *Economist Global Agenda* ibid
7. *The Hindu*, 12 April 2002.
8. "LTTE must denounce terrorism in words and deeds: US", *The Hindu*, 14 April 2003.
9. "*Sri Lanka Talks set for a long haul*" by Amal Jayasinghe, Colombo, Agence France Presse,12 July 2003.

Discussion

A participant pointed out that of all the suicide-bombing incidents in the last 20 years, the LTTE's contribution has been more than 40 per cent. This is despite the increase in suicide-bombings by various Islamic militant groups.

The discussion also focussed on the tendency to overrate the so-called international opinion. The international opinion is rather late in forming, and even later in acting. It takes two to three weeks before international opinion starts to have any bearing on the internal situation, or what happens in any region. Because of 9/11, international opinion may dry up a little bit of the funding, and a little bit of the arms procurement. It may make it a little more difficult.

The discussion also touched upon the LTTE's intentions. A participant pointed out that even now it is very clear that the LTTE's aim is to have an 'independent Tamil Eelam'. Things like the interim administration are part of a tactical stop, a halt to replenish, to carry on talks, and to regroup. They never ever stated that they had any long-term intention other than a 'Tamil Eelam'. Everything else, be it a strategic or a tactical manoeuvre, as may be distinguished by some experts, would merely be stops en-route, to change the engine, to take on additional fuel or whatever.

The LTTE has already refined its old terrorist tactics to get close to a *de facto* 'liberation war'. First, by equipping itself with modern arms. Secondly, by a confrontational approach, directly confronting the Army, and not merely indulging in hit-and-run tactics. They will be able to justify their campaign as coming under the definition of a 'liberation movement', rather than a terrorist movement. Also, the LTTE has nearly wiped out the rest of the Tamil movement and has, in fact, become the de facto sole representative of the Tamils - whether we recognise it or not. Militarily, they are definitely the sole representatives of the Tamil movement. However, the LTTE does not have the capability, as of now, to enforce its will to achieve its objective of an 'independent Tamil Eelam'. What are the intentions of the Government of Sri Lanka? Given the best of circumstances, "stop all secessionist movements and have an integrated and secure unitary government in Sri Lanka". The Government of Sri Lanka does not have the capability to wipe out the entire militant capabilities of the LTTE, either.

So, what is the present peace process? It is nothing but the recognition, by the LTTE and the Government of Sri Lanka, of the limits of their present capabilities. They cannot achieve their objectives, so they have got to compromise. Either reach a workable and long-standing compromise, or reach a patchy and temporary compromise, to gain time to re-equip and regroup and fight again.

The Role Of External Powers

Of Phases and Paces

Dr Gamini Samaranayake

The role of 'External Powers' is a vital factor in the on-going peace process in Sri Lanka. The actors and roles have changed over time in all peace attempts, but the parameters of basic expectations and interests are common. So much so, the involvement of 'external powers' in the form of third parties to the Sri Lankan peace process can be divided into two periods. The first period was India's involvement from the mid-Eighties to the early Nineties. The second period of involvement began from year 2000 with interfaces by Norway. The role of external powers led by Norway became pronounced after the signing of the Ceasefire Agreement between the United National Front Government and the LTTE in February 2002. Although there has been a plethora of literature on the ethnic conflict, research on the international involvement in conflict-resolution is minimal.

To understand the role of external powers in the peace process of Sri Lanka, it is necessary to study 'third parties' that intervene as mediators to resolve conflicts of the kind. According to Chris Mitchell, 'third parties' can be defined as parties "who help adversaries open negotiations and (perhaps) end a dispute in a mutually satisfactory agreement".[1] Third parties can be a State or groups of States, international organisations such as governmental agencies/organisations, UN bodies, non-governmental organisations, or individuals. The roles of third parties tend to change from conflict to conflict. In a real conflict–resolving situation, third parties are expected to offer the following services:

a. Good offices, to act as a mailman or a medium to communicate in initiating the peace process. In other words, to contact those in dispute in order to find out whether it is worth making an effort to bring them into a dialogue.

b. Mediation, to reopen quiet communication between the adversaries, and take part in discussions focussed on the resolution of the related conflict.

c. Conciliation, to come forward with practicable settlement proposals acceptable to the adversaries involved.

d. Adjudication to make other parties agree in handing over their conflict to the third-party for a solution. It can be done either by law and/ or by force.[2]

This analytical framework will be utilised to examine the role of the international actors in the conflict in Sri Lanka. However, it is the premise of the study that the roles of the international actors are conditional upon the nature of the conflict in the country. Therefore, it is necessary to examine the background of the conflict in Sri Lanka.

---

1. See, Chris Mitchell, *Mediation*, in Paul Smoker et el. (eds) Reader in Peace Studies, Oxford, Pergamon Press, 1990, pp.26-32.

2. *M.L. De La Roca, et el.* " Comparing Third Parties in Peace Processes: Afghanistan, Guatemala and Sri Lanka", in Experiences from Conflict Resolution in the Third World, Goran Lindgren, Kjell-Ake Nordquist and Peter Wallensteen, (eds.) Dept, of Peace and Conflict Research, Upsala University, Uppsala, 1993, p.4.

BACKGROUND OF THE CONFLICT

The Sri Lankan conflict is unique since it is confined to a dual armed conflict beginning from the early Seventies. The first facet of conflict was a Left Wing insurrection waged by the Janatha Vimkuthi Peramuna (JVP) to establish an 'egalitarian socialist society' in the country. It was responsible for waging war in 1971, and later in 1987-1989. At present, the JVP is a significant radical force, having 16 members of Parliament in mainstream politics. However, its continuation in parliamentary politics and rejection of violence depends on the nature of the polity in the country.

The second aspect of the conflict is the ethnic insurrection waged by the LTTE. It is based on Tamil ethnic grievances, resulting from socio-economic and political changes during the post-independence period. The popular term is "discrimination". It is not always confined to ethnic discrimination. It is ethnic and political discrimination with various other forms, which have contributed to the conflict between the Sinhalese majority and the Tamil minority. But unfortunately the most popular aspect is the ethnic. In a way, 'ethnic discrimination' has contributed to the conflict in the North and the East, and the 'political discrimination' has contributed to the origin and the development of the conflict in the South. Many have – and much has been – written about the causes of ethnic conflict. Very few have written on what has contributed to transform the ethnic conflict into an armed conflict, using a strategy of rural guerrilla warfare-cum-terrorism. The Tamil youth unrest due to unemployment and university admission policies based on a district-wise quota system were key factors, which transformed the ethnic conflict into a protracted armed conflict since the mid-seventies.

However, the following two factors are precipitators of the origin and development of Tamil youth insurgency. The first was the April 1971 JVP insurrection. The insurrection displayed the weaknesses of the security forces of the State and stressed the importance of violence to achieve political objectives. When the insurrection occurred in 1971, the North and the East were peaceful areas. The Government captured all JVP leaders, including their chief, Rohan Wijeweera, and kept them in a northern Jaffna prison. Though the JVP had not originally planned to attack police stations at Jaffna and other places in the North and in the East, it had to revise its plans in order to rescue Wijeweera.

The second was the creation of Bangladesh as an independent State. The separation from Pakistan, with military assistance from the Government of India, was an example for the Tamil secessionist groups. The latter indicated the significance of Indian intervention in creating a separate State in South Asia.[3] The LTTE has been waging war since the mid-Seventies to establish a separate State encompassing the North and the East of the country. This protracted struggle continued until the signing of the Ceasefire Agreement between the Government headed by United National Party and the LTTE in February 2002. Unlike the Left Wing insurgency in the South, the ethnic conflict was a forum for international mediation – first by India, and later by Norway. It is obvious that when a State loses its ability to regulate an ethnic conflict, the problem can become a regional dilemma because it creates an opportunity for external intervention.

The Role of India

In analysing the role of external powers in the peace process of Sri Lanka, it is necessary to examine the role of India in

3 See, Urmila Phadnis, "Tamil Bangla in Ceylon", *Hindustan Times,* March 6th 1972.

conflict-resolution in Sri Lanka. Due to the geo-political reality, the most important external actor in the peace process of Sri Lanka is undoubtedly India. India is the only country in the region that is affected by the ethnic conflict in Sri Lanka. After the ethnic riots of July 1983, until the withdrawal of the Indian Peace-Keeping Force (IPKF) in March 1990, India played a significant and active role in the peace process of Sri Lanka. However, it is evident that India did not have a cohesive role in the ethnic conflict, and this has changed from Government-to-Government, and from Prime Minister-to-Prime Minister.

The period from 1977 to 1983 can be cited as the first period of India's mediation in the conflict of Sri Lanka. This period covers the Janata Party Government of 1977 and the Congress Government under Indira Gandhi, until the ethnic riots of July 1983. In the initial stages of ethnic insurrection, the Janata Party Government abstained from any form of involvement in the conflict. India treated the conflict as part of Sri Lanka's domestic politics, rather than an issue for diplomatic or political intervention. Furthermore, India strongly believed that the solution to the ethnic conflict in Sri Lanka had to be found within the framework of the sovereignty and integrity of Sri Lanka. India did not support the Tamil demand for a separate State also because it was not a favourable example for her own experiences of conflict in Punjab, and Jammu and Kashmir. However, this policy of non-participation changed into indirect participation with the change of Government at the Centre, from the Janata Party to the Congress in 1980. The following two factors contributed to the change of India's role as an indirect participant in the conflict in Sri Lanka.

The first factor could be attributed to India's regional interest in South Asia. India's perception of South Asia as a security zone – which New Delhi alone was entitled to dominate and manipulate – did not in the opinion of the Government of India permit the involvement of other external forces within the region. The following statement by the then Prime Minister Indira Gandhi vividly articulates India's regional policy for South Asia:

> "India will neither intervene in the domestic affairs of any State in the region unless requested to do so, nor tolerate such intervention by an outside power. If external assistance is needed to meet an inter-crisis, States should first look within the region for help".[4]

Secondly, the overspill of Sri Lanka's ethnic conflict to the South Indian State of Tamil Nadu compelled India to take a strategic interest in the Sri Lankan conflict. It was during this period that the Tamil guerrilla groups set up bases in southern India following the imposition of emergency in the Northern Province of Sri Lanka in August 1979.

Thirdly, the ethnic strife of July 1983 caused the direct intervention of India as a mediator in the conflict. The ethnic riots of 1983 were a reaction of the South of the country, where the Sinhala majority predominantly resides, towards the on-going guerrilla war in the North. Because of the riots, more than 15,000 Sri Lankan Tamils took refuge in Tamil Nadu. Therefore, the State of Tamil Nadu pressured the Central Government in India to mediate with the Government of Sri Lanka.[5]

Since 1984, the Government of Sri Lanka, with India as a third party, has made several approaches and attempts – such as the All-Party Conference in 1984, the Thimpu Talks in 1985, the Political Party Conference in 1986, and the Indo-Sri Lanka Accord of 1987 – to seek a peaceful resolution to the ethnic conflict. What was expected by the LTTE from India was armed intervention similar to that in East Pakistan, which resulted in

4. P. Venkateshwar Rao, "Ethnic Conflict in Sri Lanka: India's Role and Perceptions", *Asian Survey*, Vol. 28, 1988, p. 422.

5. See" Internationalisation of Sri Lanka's Ethnic Conflict: The Tamil Nadu Factor", K.M. De Silva and R.J. May, (eds) Internationalisation of Ethnic Conflict, London, Pinter Publishers, 1991.

the creation of Bangladesh as a separate independent State in 1971. The 1987 Accord proved India's rejection of a separate Tamil 'Eelam State' in Sri Lanka. India's third-party mediation was successful only in terms of being able to initiate a process of devolution of power as a result of the Indo-Sri Lanka Agreement. However, the attempt was futile, mainly due to the intransigence of the LTTE, the second insurrection of the JVP from 1987-89, and the opportunistic politics within and outside the UNP Government.

Initially, the LTTE accepted the Accord along with other Tamil militant groups like the EPRLF, PLOTE, TELO and EROS. However, within one week of the signing of the Accord, the LTTE refused to disarm. It revived its armed struggle with the IPKF, who were stationed in Northern and Eastern Provinces to supervise the implementation of the Agreement. The LTTE waged war against the IPKF until the latter's withdrawal at the end of March 1990. Furthermore, Rajiv Gandhi, the former Prime Minister of India, was assassinated by the LTTE, in a suicide-bombing at an election rally near Chennai in May 1991. It was this incident that forced India to play a neutral role as a third-party in the conflict of Sri Lanka.

The presence of the IPKF in the country was a blessing in disguise for the JVP to stage its second insurgency from 1987-89. The JVP resented the Government, believing that the Government had betrayed the sovereignty, independence and territorial integrity of Sri Lanka. It was an open secret that under the UNP Government in 1987, Prime Minister Ranasinghe Premadasa and Defence Minister Lalith Athulathmudali opposed the Indo-Sri Lanka Agreement. Later, President Premadasa tried to undermine India and the Agreement through negotiations with the LTTE. The outcome was the withdrawal of the IPKF and the reduction of the Indo-Sri Lanka Accord of 1987 to a dysfunctional document. The assassination of President Premadasa on 1 May 1993, by a suicide-bomber of the LTTE, compelled the Government to revise the view that the conflict is not ethnic, but terrorist – and could be solved only by a military strategy.

Background to the Role of Norway

The favourable background to the second involvement of international mediation was created with a change of power from the United National Party (UNP) to the People's Alliance (PA), at the general and presidential elections in 1994. The PA Government was of the view that the conflict was primarily political in nature with an ethnic character, and therefore, a negotiated political settlement was necessary to resolve the problem. The Government and the LTTE were able to agree upon a ceasefire on 8 January 1995, and three rounds of talks were held. All talks were supplemented and effectively driven by an exchange of over 40 letters between the President and the LTTE.

When the Government was preparing for the fourth round of talks, the LTTE demanded lifting of the embargo, allow all fishermen to fish in the northern coastal waters, remove military camps located in a strategic position in the North, and permit the LTTE cadres to carry guns for their own protection when in Government-controlled territory in the East.[6] Although the Government agreed to the first two demands, it did not accede to the others. As a result, the LTTE withdrew from negotiations, and began 'Eelam War III'. Thereafter, the PA Government's objective was to defeat the LTTE militarily, even while offering political concessions and socio-economic rehabilitation to the Tamil community. The PA Government's

6 Marshall R. Singer, " Sri Lanka's Ethnic Conflict: Have Bombs Shattered Hopes For Peace?" *Asian Survey*, Vol. Xxxvi, No. 11, !996, p. 1150.

strategy for solving the conflict was based on the following three elements:

(a) To isolate the LTTE from the Tamil population, and use the military to reduce the fighting capability of the LTTE sufficiently to bring them to the negotiating table for a peace settlement

(b) To design and negotiate a political solution based on greater devolution of power to the regions and

(c) To provide for economic rehabilitation and reconstruction in conflict-affected areas after peace has been restored.[7]

In December 1995, the Government forces re-captured Jaffna city, the capital of the so-called 'Eelam State'. In 'Eelam War III', the Government forces launched various operations: 'Operation Riviresa', (Sunshine), 'Operation Sath Jaya' (True Victory), 'Operation Edibala', (Gallant Force), 'Operation Jayasikuri' (Sure Victory), 'Operation Revibala' (Sun Power), 'Operation Ranagosa' (Battle Cry), 'Operation Revikirana', (Sun Ray), and 'Operation Kinihara' (Anvil).[8] While being engaged in war with the LTTE thus, the Government concentrated on rebuilding the civil administration in the North. Given the two-track policy, the PA Government did not welcome outside mediation in the conflict in Sri Lanka. However, the LTTE was willing to accommodate international intervention in the form of a third-party mediator.

While the war continued, the Government of Sri Lanka requested aid agencies and donors to support its "Triple-R" approach of rehabilitation, reconstruction and reconciliation in the war-ravaged areas of the North-East. It is a debatable issue as to whether the donor community used aid to influence

---

7. Arve Ofstad, " Countries in Violence Conflict and Aid Strategies: The Case of Sri Lanka" *World Development*, Vol 30, No. 2, 2002, p. 166.

8. See Appendix 1 for the Table with summary of above-mentioned military operations.

the approach and policies of the Government in the peace process in Sri Lanka. It is evident that all donor countries hoped to see a peaceful settlement of the conflict rather than a continuation of the civil war. They argued that the civil war had hampered developmental activities, and the escalating defence budget was not acceptable. Consequently, emphasis was laid on the fact that efforts must be made to accelerate a political solution to the ethnic conflict.

Initially, the Government of Sri Lanka strongly opposed any political conditionality in the aid debate. However, the PA Government toed the line, with the aid agencies adopting the policy of "war for peace". The PA Government was pushed to a position where it blamed the LTTE for forcing them to continue the war while the Opposition led by the UNP, continued to destabilise the political proposals to bring about a solution to the conflict.

It is evident that pressure from the donor-countries was exerted through a dialogue between the Government and aid-donors at the Consultative Group (CG) meeting organised by the World Bank in Paris in 1995. From May 1998, this forum came to be known as the 'Sri Lanka Development Forum'. The major donor-countries adjusted the overall aid package to exert pressure and influence on the Government to move forward with its peace process. The donor-countries claimed to promote a peaceful solution to the war. Of these countries, Sweden and Norway took the lead in reorienting their aid package to support a movement towards peace.[9]

This approach provided active support to the Government's effort to create a national consensus for its political proposals. Peace initiatives were included in their poverty-reduction and employment-generation programmes. Support for many peace-promotion programmes such as

9. See, Arve Ofstad, Countries in Violent Conflict and Aid strategies, *World Development*, Vol. 30, No. 2, pp. 165-180.

2.1 The Parties shall in accordance with international law abstain from hostile acts against the civilian population, including such acts as torture, intimidation, abduction, extortion and harassment.

2.2 The Parties shall refrain from engaging in activities or propagating ideas that could offend cultural or religious sensitivities. Places of worship (temples, churches, mosques & other holy sites etc) currently held by the forces of either of the Parties shall be vacated by D-day + 30 days and made accessible to the public. Places of worship which are situated in their respective "high security zones" shall be vacated by all armed personnel and maintained in good order by civilian workers, even when they are not made accessible to the public.

2.3 Beginning on the date on which this Agreement enters into force, school buildings occupied by either party shall be vacated and returned to their intended use. This activity shall be completed by D-day + 160 at the latest.

2.4 A schedule indicating the return of all other public buildings to their intended use shall be drawn up by the Parties and published at the latest by D-day + 30.

2.5 The Parties shall review the security measures and the set-up of checkpoints, particularly in densely populated cities and towns, in order to introduce systems that will prevent harassment of the civilian population. Such systems shall be in place from D-day + 60.

2.6 The Parties agree to ensure the unimpeded flow of non-military goods to and from the LTTE-controlled areas in accordance with Annex A. Quantities shall be determined by market demand. The GOSL shall regularly review the matter with the aim of gradually removing any remaining restrictions on non-military goods.

2.7 In order to facilitate the flow of goods and the movement of civilians, the Parties agree to establish checkpoints on their line of control at such locations as are specified in Annex B.

2.8 The Parties shall take steps to ensure that the Trincomalee - Habarana road remains open on a 24-hour basis for passenger traffic with effect from D-day + 10.

2.9 The Parties shall facilitate the extension of the rail service on the Batticaloa-line to Welikanda. Repairs and maintenance shall be carried out by the GOSL in order to extend the service up to Batticaloa.

2.10 The Parties shall open the Kandy - Jaffna road (A9) to non-military traffic of goods and passengers. Specific modalities shall be worked out by the Parties with the assistance of the Royal Norwegian Government by D-day + 30 at the latest.

2.11 A gradual easing of the fishing restrictions shall take place starting from D-day. As of D-day + 90, all restrictions on day and night fishing shall be removed, subject to the following exceptions : I) fishing will not be permitted within an area of 1 nautical mile on either side along the coast and 2 nautical miles seawards from all security forces camps on the coast; ii) fishing will not be permitted in harbours or approaches to harbours bays and estuaries along with coast.

2.12 The Parties agree that search operations and arrests under the Prevention of Terrorism Act shall not take place. Arrests shall be conducted under due process of law in accordance with the Criminal Procedure Code.

2.13 The Parties agree to provide family members of detainees access to the detainees within D-day + 30.

Article 3: The Monitoring Mission

The Parties have agreed to set up an international monitoring mission to enquire into any instance of violation of the terms and conditions of this agreement. Both Parties shall fully cooperate to rectify any matter of conflict caused by their respective sides. The mission shall conduct international verification through on-site monitoring of the fulfilment of the commitments entered into in this Agreement as follows

3.1 The name of the monitoring mission shall be the Sri Lankan Monitoring Mission, hereinafter referred to as the SLMM.

3.2 Subject to acceptance by the Parties, the Royal Norwegian Government (hereinafter referred to as the RNG) shall appoint the Head of the SLMM (hereinafter referred to as the HOM), who shall be the final authority regarding interpretation of this Agreement.

3.3 The SLMM shall liaise with the Parties and report to the R N G.

3.4 The HoM shall decide the date for the commencement of the SLMM's operations

3.5 The SLMM shall be composed of representatives from the Nordic countries

3.6. The SLMM shall establish a headquarters in such places as the HoM finds appropriate. An office shall be established in Colombo and in Wanni in order to liaise with the GOSL and the LTTE, respectively. The SLMM will maintain a presence in the distrcts of Jaffna, Mannar, Vavuniyua, Trincomalee, Batticaloa and Amparai.

3.7 A local monitoring committee shall be established in Jaffna, Mannar, Vavuniya, Trincomalee, Batticaloa and Amparai. Each committee shall consist of 5 members, two appointed by the GOSL, two by the LTTE and one international monitor appointed by the HoM. The international monitor shall chair the committee. The GOSL and the LTTE appointees may be selected from among retired judges, public servants, religious leaders or similar leading citizens.

3.8 The committees shall serve the SLMM in an advisory capacity and discuss issues relating to the implementation of this Agreement in their respective districts, with a view to establishing a common understanding of such issues. In particular, they will seek to resolve any dispute concerning the implementation of this Agreement at the lowest possible level.

3.9 The parties shall be responsible for the appropriate protection of and security arrangements for all SLMM members.

3.10 The Parties agree to ensure the freedom of movement of the SLMM members in performing their task. The members of the SLMM shall be given immediate access to areas where violations of the Agreement are alleged to have taken place. The Parties also agree to facilitate the widest possible access to such areas for the local members of the six above-mentioned committees, cf Article 3.7.

3.11 It shall be the responsibility of the SLMM to take immediate action on any complaints made by either Party to the Agreement, and to enquire into and assist the Parties in the settlement of any dispute that might arise in connection with such complaints.

3.12 With the aim of resolving disputes at the lowest possible level, communication shall be established between Commanders of the GOSL armed forces and the LTTE area leaders to enable them to resolve problems in the conflict zones.

3.13 Guidelines for the operations of the SLMM shall be established in a separate document.

Article 4: Entry into force, amendments and termination of the Agreement

4.1 Each Parties shall notify their consent to be bound by this Agreement through a letter to the Norwegian Minister of Foreign Affairs signed by Prime Minister Ranil Wickremasinghe on behalf of the GOSL and by leader Velupillai Pirabaharan

Annexure 1

Agreement on a Ceasefire Between The Government Of the Democratic Socialist Republic Of Sri Lanka And The Liberation Tigers of Tamil Ellam

Preamble :

The overall objective of the Government of the Democratic Socialist Republic of Sri Lanka (hereinafter referred to as the GOSL) and the Liberation Tigers of Tamil Eelam (hereinafter referred to as the LTTE) is to find a negotiated solution to the ongoing ethnic conflict in Sri Lanka.

The GOSL and the LTTE (hereinafter referred to as the Parties) recognize the importance of bringing an end to the hostilities and improving the living conditions for all inhabitants affected by the conflict. Bringing an end to the hostilities is also seen by the Parties as a means of establishing a positive atmosphere in which further steps towards a lasting solution can be taken.

The Parties further recognize that groups that are not

directly party to the conflict are also suffering the consequences of it. This is particularly the case as regards the Muslim population. Therefore, the provisions of this Agreement regarding the security of civilians and their property apply to all inhabitants.

With reference to the above, the Parties have agreed to enter into a ceasefire, refrain from conduct that could undermine the good intentions or violate the spirit of this Agreement and implement confidence-building measures as indicated in the articles below.

ARTICLE 1 : MODALITIES OF A CEASEFIRE

The Parties have agreed to implement a ceasefire between their armed forces as follows :

1.1 A jointly agreed ceasefire between the GOSL and the LTTE shall enter into force on such date as is notified by the Norwegian Minister of Foreign Affairs in accordance with Article 4.2, hereinafter referred to as D-day.

MILITARY OPERATIONS

1.2 Neither Party shall engage in any offensive military operation. This requires the total cessation of all military action and includes, but is not limited to, such acts as :

a) The firing of direct and indirect weapons, armed raids, ambushes, assassinations, abductions, destruction of civilian or military property, sabotage, suicide missions and activities by deep penetration units;

b) Aerial bombardment:

c) Offensive naval operations.

1.3 The Sri Lankan armed forces shall continue to perform their legitimate task of safeguarding the sovereignty and territorial integrity of Sri Lanka without engaging in offensive operations against the LTTE.

Separation of forces

1.4 Where forward defence localities have been established, the GOSL's armed forces and the LTTE's fighting formations shall hold their ground positions, maintaining a zone of separation of a minimum of six hundred (600) metres. However, each Party reserves the right of movement within one hundred (100) metres of its own defence localities, keeping an absolute minimum distance of four hundred (400) metres between them.

Where existing positions are closer than four hundred (400) metres, no such right of movement applies and the Parties agree to ensure the maximum possible distance between their personnel.

1.5 In areas where localities have not been clearly established, the status quo as regards the areas controlled by the GOSL and the LTTE, respectively, on 24 December 2001 shall continue to apply pending such demarcation as is provided in Article 1.6.

1.6 The Parties shall provide information to the Sri Lanka Monitoring Mission (SLMM) regarding defence localities in all areas of contention, cf. Article 3. The monitoring mission shall assist the Parties in drawing up demarcation lines at the latest by D-day + 30.

1.7 The Parties shall not move munitions, explosives or military equipment into the area controlled by the other Party.

1.8 Tamil paramilitary groups shall be disarmed by the GOSL by D-day + 30 days at the latest. The GOSL shall offer to integrate individuals in these units under the command and disciplinary structure of the GOSL armed forces for service away from the Northern and Eastern Province.

Freedom of movement

1.9 The Parties' forces shall initially stay in the areas under their respective control, as provided in Article 1.4 and Article 1.5

1.10 Unarmed GOSL troops shall, as of D-day +60 days, be permitted unlimited passage between Jaffna and Vavuniya using the Jaffna - Kandy road (A9). The modalities are to be worked out by the Parties with the assistance of the SLMM.

1.11 The Parties agree that individual combatants shall, on the recommendation of their area commander, be permitted, unarmed and in plain clothes, to visit family and friends residing in areas under the control of the other Party. Such visits shall be limited to six days every second month, not including the time of travel by the shortest applicable route. The LTTE shall facilitate the use of the Jaffna - Kandy road for this purpose. The Parties reserve the right to deny entry to specified military areas.

1.12 The Parties agree that as of D-day individual combatants shall, notwithstanding the two-month restriction, be permitted, unarmed and in plain clothes, to visit immediate family (i.e. spouses, children, grandparents, parents and siblings) in connection with weddings or funerals. The right to deny entry to specified military areas applies.

1.13 Fifty (50) unarmed LTTE members shall, as of D-day + 30, for the purpose of political work, be permitted freedom of movement in the areas of the North and the East dominated by the GOSL. Additional 100 unarmed LTTE members shall be permitted freedom of movement as of D-day + 6-. As of D-day + 90, all unarmed LTTE members shall be permitted freedom of movement in the North and East. The LTTE members shall carry identity papers. The right of the GOSL to deny entry to specified military areas applies.

Article 2 : Measures to restore normalcy

The Parties shall undertake the following confidence-building measures with the aim of restoring normalcy for the all inhabitants of Sri Lanka :

- The parties will facilitate restoration and rehabilitation of places of worship in the north and the east belonging to all religious communities.

On the basis of their firm conviction that the maintenance of law and order in the north and east is of paramount importance, the parties agreed to request the Sub-Committee on De-escalation and Normalization to propose a common approach to settling cases involving the disputed use of private property, where such use has been impeded by the conflict. Furthermore, the LTTE will ensure that the activities of their law and order mechanisms will not be extended beyond the areas dominated by the LTTE.

The parties strongly underlined the need to move rapidly on humanitarian and rehabilitation efforts in the north and east. For this purpose, the early establishment of the North-East Reconstruction Fund will be critical. The parties agreed that the custodian of the fund should be selected and modalities for its operation agreed at the next meeting of the Sub-Committee on Immediate Humanitarian and Rehabilitation Needs. The parties expressed their appreciation of the strong support extended by several governments to the peace process at the Sri Lanka Support Meeting held in Oslo on 25 November, and urged these governments to rapidly release funds needed for humanitarian and rehabilitation efforts.

The parties acknowledged the need to ensure that the priorities and needs of women are taken into account in all aspects of the peace process. To this effect, they agreed to establish a permanent advisory committee which will, on a regular basis, submit proposals relating to women's interests to the sessions of negotiations and to the sub-committees of the peace process. The committee will consist of four representatives of each party.

As a priority area identified by the parties for humanitarian action, the parties stressed the need to improve the situation for children affected by armed conflict. Inspired by the international norms protecting the rights of the child, the parties underlined that children belong with their families or other custodians and not in the workplace, whether civilian or military. The LTTE will engage in a partnership with the United Nations Children's Fund (UNICEF) to draw up an action plan for restoring normalcy to the lives of children, and the parties called on the international community to provide financial support for such an action plan.

The GOSL will, in order to arrive at the broadest possible consensus, establish an appropriate mechanism for consultation with all segments of opinion as part of the ongoing peace process.

http://www.peaceinsrilanka.org/insidepages/Pressrelease/RNG/RNG5thDec.asp

Annexure 2

Parties have decided to explore a political solution founded on internal self-determination based on a federal structure within a United Sri Lanka

Oslo, 5 December 2002

Statement of the Royal Norwegian Government

The third session of peace talks between the Government of Sri Lanka (GOSL) and the Liberation Tigers of Tamil Eclam (LTTE) was held in Oslo, Norway on 2 to 5 December 2002. In a frank, open and constructive manner, the parties focused on three major areas :

– Consolidation of the ceasefire

– Humanitarian and rehabilitation action

– Policical matters

The Parties agreed on a working outline defining the objective as well as a number of substantive political issues for negotiation.

Responding to a proposal by the leadership of the LTTE, the parties agreed to explore a solution founded on the principle of internal self-determination in areas of historical habitation of the Tamil-speaking peoples, based on a federal structure within a United Sri Lanka. The parties acknowledged that the solution has to be acceptable to all communities.

Guided by this objective, the parties agreed to initiate discussion on substantive political issues such as, but not limited to :

– Power-sharing between the centre and the region, as well as within the centre

– Geographical region

– Human Rights protection

– Political and administrative mechanism

– Public finance

– Law and order

The parties recognised that progress on political issues must be supported by the continued consolidation of the Ceasefire Agreement. Now concrete measures will be taken to facilitate further de-escalation and to improve normalcy :

The GOSL will shortly return one of the hotels in Jaffna to its original use.

The LTTE will ensure that all future transportation of area commanders will take place under the supervision of the Sri Lanka Monitoring Mission (SLMM).

The LTTE will accept the right of political groups to carry out political work, including in the Jaffna peninsula and the islands, provided that they are unarmed, as stipulated by the Ceasefire Agreement.

The GOSL will, in consultation with all relevant parties and groups, evolve a solution to the problems arising from recent developments in the Delft Island.

The parties will facilitate restoration and rehabilitation of places of worship in the north and the east belonging to all religious communities.

on behalf of the LTTE, respectively. The agreement shall be initialed by each Party and enclosed in the above mentioned letter.

4.2 The Agreement shall enter into force on such date as is notified by the Norwegian Minister of Foreign Affairs.

4.3 This Agreement may be amended and modified by mutual agreement of both Parties. Such amendments shall be notified in writing to the RNG.

4.4 This Agreement shall remain in force until notice of termination is given by either Party to the RNG. Such notice shall be given fourteern (14) days in advance of the effective date of termination.

Annexes :
Annex A: List of goods Annex B: Checkpoints.

Annex - A.

The Parties agree to ensure the flow of non-military goods to and from LTTE dominated areas of the Northern and Eastern Province, as well as unimpeded flow of such goods to the civilian population in these areas. Non military goods not covered by article 2.6 in the Agreement are listed below :

Non military arms/ammunition
Explosives
Remote control devices
Barbed wire
Binoculars/Telescopes
Compasses
Penlight batteries

Diesel, petrol, cement and iron rods will be restricted in accordance with the following procedures and quantities :

Diesel and Petrol

The Government Agents (GA) will register available vehicles; tractors and motorcycles in the LTTE controlled areas. The GA will calculate the required weekly amount of diesel and petrol based on the following estimate :

Trucks/Buses - 250 litre/week
4 wheels tractor - 310 litre/week
2 wheel tractor - 40 litre/week
Petrol vehicle - 30 litre/week
Motorcycles - 7 litre/week
Fishing vessel - 400 litre/week

Cement

Cement required for rehabilitation and reconstruction of Government property; registered co-operatives; or approved housing projects implemented by the GOSL and international NGOs and more affluent members of the society; will be brought in directly by relevant institutions under licenses issued by Government Agents. The GA shall stipulate the monthly quantities permitted for such project based upon planned and reported progress.

Cement required for individual shops/construction/house owners/rehabilitation- initiatives will be made available through the co-operations on a commercial basis. The monthly import for this purpose will be limited to 5,000 bags during the first month and thereafter 10,000 bags/month. Individual sales by the co-operatives will be registered and limited to 25 bags per household.

Iron rods

Iron rods for building constructions will be brought in to the LTTE controlled areas under licenses issued by the GA.

A monthly re-assessment will be made to assess the possibilities of removal of the above restrictions.

Annex - B.

Checkpoints agreed in Ch.2.7 are as follows :
- Mandur
- Paddirupur
- Kaludaveli Ferry Point
- Anbalantivu Ferry Point
- Mamunai Ferry Point
- Vanvunateevu
- Santhiveli Boat Point
- Black Bridge
- Sitandy Boat Point
- Kiran bridge
- Kinniyadi Boat Point
- Valachenai
- Makerni
- Mahindapura
- Muttur
- Ugilankulam
- Omanthai.

http://www.peaceinsrilanka.org/insidepages/Agreement/agceasefire.asp#A2

The third session of peace talks between the Government of Sri Lanka (GOSL) and the Liberation Tigers of Tamil Eelam (LTTE) was held in Oslo, Norway on 2 to 5 December 2002. In a frank, open and constructive manner, the parties focused on three major areas:

- Consolidation of the ceasefire
- Humanitarian and rehabilitation action
- Political matters

The parties agreed on a working outline defining the objective as well as a number of substantive political issues for negotiation.

Responding to a proposal by the leadership of the LTTE, the parties agreed to explore a solution founded on the principle of internal self-determination in areas of historical habitation of the Tamil-speaking peoples, based on a federal structure within a united Sri Lanka. The parties acknowledged that the solution has to be acceptable to all communities.

Guided by this objective, the parties agreed to initiate discussions on substantive political issues such as, but not limited to:

- Power-sharing between the centre and the region, as well as within the centre
- Geographical region
- Human Rights protection
- Political and administrative mechanism
- Public finance
- Law and order

The parties recognised that progress on political issues must be supported by the continued consolidation of the Ceasefire Agreement. New concrete measures will be taken to facilitate further de-escalation and to improve normalcy:

- The GOSL will shortly return one of the hotels in Jaffna to its original use;

- The LTTE will ensure that all future transportation of area commanders will take place under the supervision of the Sri Lanka Monitoring Mission (SLMM);

- The LTTE will accept the right of political groups to carry out political work, including in the Jaffna peninsula and the islands, provided that they are unarmed, as stipulated by the Ceasefire Agreement;

- The GOSL will, in consultation with all relevant parties and groups, evolve a solution to the problems arising from recent developments in the Delft island;

region of South Asia. It is referred to as a 'traditional third-party approach'. The second is the on-going, multi-third party involvement of Norway, the US, Japan, the EU and the other donor-countries based on aid and loans. It is referred to as a problem-solving approach.

Although the first was criticised as difficult, expensive and dangerous, it proved to be productive, laid the foundation for the devolution of power and for defining a solution to the ethnic conflict in Sri Lanka. Obviously, it did not succeed because of the inability to understand the overall conflict in the country. It is premature to analyse the third-party role of the Government of Norway and other allied countries. It is true that Norwegian mediation has brought the conflicting parties to a Ceasefire Agreement, or Memorandum of Understanding (MoU), and an end to the civil war, partially or temporarily. Though it has mustered international cooperation in assisting the peace process in Sri Lanka, it has excluded the major stakeholders in the conflict of Sri Lanka. What is lacking in conflict-resolution in Sri Lanka is national and regional consensus and cooperation of the nature and dynamics of conflict in the country.

Discussion

A participant pointed out that the July 1983 incidents were not a reaction of the South to the ongoing guerrilla war. There is ample evidence to show that it was a carefully-planned pogrom, by a section in the Government. There is evidence, some of which is reported in the Presidential Truth Commission, that has recently been released. It is unfair to blame the people for it.

Others agreed that it was organised, deliberately organised. Also, there were only incidents not war. But it is also true that the insurrections started in the mid-Seventies, with the assassination of Alfred Doraiappah. At that time there was no organisation called the Liberation Tigers of Tamil Eelam. They appeared in public after the killing of Bastion Pillai, and policemen in 1978. The year 1983 was a turning-point, but it is a myth that the problem started after 1983. It was partly caused by the Government and partly by the LTTE. The *Sama Peramuna*, the Peace Front, put up posters, asking political parties to apologise. Only the LTTE and the United National Party Government had to apologise, and nobody else did so. That was the difference between the 1958 and the 1983 riots. That is part and parcel of the ethnic insurrection in the North.

Some participants argued that Sri Lanka's problem is not confined to the northern situation. Unfortunately, both outsiders and insiders alike read the situation thus. For example, in the seventies, before the 1971 rebellion the JVP mobilised its cadre and sympathisers to achieve socialism using various Marxist jargons. Now they are not using any Marxist jargon. They are now more 'nationalistic' than 'socialistic'. Different actors are reacting differently. There are many sides to the conflict in Sri Lanka. That is true of any conflict, but Sri Lanka is different. There are more sides than usual, and each reacts the way it reads the situation.

APPENDIX - I

Peace Activities

International organisations, national organisations & local organisations

Organisations	Academic venues	Conflict resolution and / or training	Govt advocacy	Human rights	Inter-Ethnic Inter-religious education gatherings	Peace efforts	Rehabilitation
Academy for Educational Development (AED)	—	x	x	—	—	—	—
Asia Foundation Commission	—	—	—	x	—	—	—
Asian Human Rights Commission	—	x	—	x	—	—	—
Berghof Foundation for Conflict Studies	x	x	x	—	—	—	—
CARE	—	—	—	—	—	—	x
Caritas Sri Lanka	—	x	—	x	x	x	x
Centre for Policy Alternatives	x	x	x	x	—	—	—
Canadian International Development Agency CIDA	—	—	—	—	—	—	x

Organisations	Academic venues	Conflict resolution and / or Training	Govt advocacy	Human rights	Inter-ethnic inter-religious education gatherings	Peace efforts	Rehabilitation
Constrtium of Humanitarian Agencies	x	x	x	x	x	x	x
Dept. for International Development (DFID)	—	—	x	—	—	—	x
Diakonia	—	—	—	—	x	—	x
European Union	—	—	x	—	—	—	x
Family Rehabilitation Centre	—	—	x	—	—	—	x
Friends for Peace in Sri Lanka	x	—	—	x	—	—	—
Gesellschaft Fur Technische Zasammenarbeit	—	—	—	—	—	—	x
Human Rights Watch	—	x	—	x	x	x	x
INPACT	x	x	x	x	—	—	—
Institute of Human Rights	—	—	—	x	—	—	—
International Alert	—	—	x	—	—	—	—

Organisations	Academic venues	Conflict resolution and / or Training	Govt advocacy	Human rights	Inter-ethnic inter-religious education gatherings	Peace efforts	Rehabilitation
International Centre for Ethnic Studies, Colombo	x	—	x	—	—	—	—
International Centre for Ethnic Studies, Kandy	x	—	x	—	—	—	—
International Committee of The Red Cross	—	—	—	—	—	—	x
Janodaya Kendraya Uswetakeiyaw	—	—	—	x	—	—	x
Japanese Embassy	—	—	—	x	—	—	x
King's College (International Policy Institute)	x	—	—	—	—	—	—
Marga Institute	x	—	—	—	—	—	—
National Peace Council of Sri Lanka	x	x	x	x	x	x	x
Nowegian Embassy	—	—	x	x	—	—	x
Oxfam International	—	—	—	—	—	—	x
Peace & Community Action	—	—	—	x	—	—	—

Organisations	Academic venues	Conflict resolution and / or training	Govt advocacy	Human rights	Inter-ethnic inter-religious education gatherings	Peace efforts	Rehabilitation
People's Peace Front	x	x	x	x	x	x	x
Regional Centre For Strategic Studies	x	x	—	—	—	—	x
Resettlement and Rehabilitation Authy. of the North (RRAN)	—	—	—	—	—	—	x
Rural Development Foundation	—	—	—	—	x	—	x
Samasebaya, Anuradhapura	—	—	—	—	—	x	—
Sarvodaya Shramadana Movement	x	x	—	x	x	x	x
Save the Children	—	—	x	—	—	—	x
SewaLanka	—	x	x	—	x	—	x
Sri Lanka First	—	—	x	—	—	—	—
Sri Lanka Foundation	x	x	x	x	x	x	x
Sri Lanka Monitoring Mission (SLMM)	—	—	x	x	—	—	—

Organisations	Academic venues	Conflict resolution and / or training	Govt advocacy	Human rights	Inter-Ethnic inter-religious education gatherings	Peace efforts	Rehabilitation
Survivors Assn	—	—	—	—	x	—	x
Swedish Embasy	x	—	x	x	—	—	x
Thirumarai Kalani Mandrum	—	—	—	—	x	x	—
UNICEF	x	x	x	x	x	x	x
UNHCR	—	—	—	—	—	—	x
US AID	x	—	x	x	—	x	x
University Teachers for Human Rights (Jaffna)	x	—	x	x	—	—	—
Uva Wellassa Govi Kantha Sansadaya Buttala	—	—	—	—	—	—	x
YATV	—	—	—	—	—	x	x

Dilemmas of External Actors

K. Venkataramanan

That prolonged domestic conflicts, especially of an ethnic or sectarian nature, invite external intervention is an everyday experience for many affected nations in today's world. Foreign ingress in a nation's affairs can be due to opportunistic intervention by powerful nations, or a matter of choice exercised by its rulers, or even a matter of compulsion involving trade, development and security interests. In the case of Sri Lanka, all three are involved. Reeling under the throes of an ethnic conflict that seemingly defies solution, the tiny island-nation in the Indian Ocean has been forced by historical circumstances and military realities to court foreign help in various manners since 1983. There is probably something in the political system of Sri Lanka that makes it more amenable than most countries in the region to the opinion of the international community and foreign intervention.

While discussing the role of external powers, one should be conscious of the limitations of their usefulness and influence. Most sovereign nations and even sub-national parties that contribute to conflicts, and are an inevitable part of the process of resolving them, naturally seek to safeguard the autonomy of their respective political and policy-space, even while seeking outside support. When any extraordinary extent of space or scope is given to external players in a domestic conflict, one may assume that the nature of the conflict has reached such a critical stage that only international support and scrutiny can resolve it. Observers of the situation in Sri Lanka will not dispute that the prolonged ethnic conflict has reached such a hopeless stage that international opinion is often called upon for a regular audit of its peace process and adjudication of incidental issues that arise from time to time.

One hardly needs to be surprised that the current peace initiative in Sri Lanka has rendered the role of external forces all-pervasive. This has increased Sri Lanka's dependence on the international community, manifold. Its future and even its survival as a nation, is now firmly in the hands of the rest of the world. Unless the current ethnic conflict is resolved early without damage to its integrity, and its political and constitutional system is rebuilt on federal lines, Sri Lanka is in danger of being reduced to a state of permanent political pliancy. Such is the influence of external factors in the country that some even fear that it may be run one day by a consortium of nations. This is a situation that a sub-national or separatist movement would love. For, what would be more welcome than unlimited international exposure, proximate opportunities for presenting problematic aspects underlying the conflict on the world stage, and for seeking approbation for the cause and the tactics used in pursuing the cause?

The role of external forces, however, does not always conform to a settled notion of invited attendance, consensual ministration, or, to use an expression currently much in vogue, to act as a 'safety-net' for domestic interests. Foreign involvement not merely gives rise to domestic political resentment or resistance, but to multiple dilemmas for both the external actor and the national leadership. These dilemmas, essentially political and strategic, have created a set of bipolarities in the Sri Lankan context. There is also the larger political question involving the obvious contrariety between sovereignty and internationalisation. A large portion of the country is under a non-elected armed group that has tried to set up its own institutions of governance, administration and judicial administration. The domestic leadership and the political parties will have to make a conscious effort to retain the national sovereignty in the face of the necessity to internationalise the resolution of this issue. The current peace process is remarkable for the battering that the nation's sovereignty has taken in the course of its acceptance of world support for its peace efforts.

There is a second bipolarity in the 'cohabitation' conflict between the executive President and the Prime Minister that is manifest as a conflict between domestic politics and world opinion. The power-crisis is not so much due to Sri Lanka's unique Constitution as it is due to the respective personalities. If at all this cohabitation is working today, is functional today, and has not reached its logical conclusion, either in the impeachment of the President or the sacking of the Prime Minister, it is largely due to the international community. The pressure of world opinion is on the two leaders, and they have apparently let their respect for it overrule their political instincts.

The external factor has perhaps helped keep the 'cohabitation' afloat, even though the President enjoys vast powers to sack the Prime Minister or the legislature itself, and has often expressed an inclination to exercise such powers. This possible inhibitory role of external forces can also be extended to the matter of political alliances such as the one that failed to materialise between the Sri Lanka Freedom Party

(SLFP) and the JVP. Though the President says it is because of differences over portfolios, the JVP says it is because of the President's refusal to give up her position on the 'devolution of power' as a solution to the ethnic conflict. Surely, President Chandrika Kumaratunga would have caused dismay even among friendly nations, if she had rescinded her party's support for 'devolution of powers' to Tamil-speaking people in pursuit of an electoral alliance.

A third issue that arises from the need or request for external intervention is a dilemma faced by the foreign actors – whether their role should be marked by reticence or activism. In this, the external forces face different expectations from different domestic parties, and have to strike a balance between showing their concern or support and avoiding assumption of intrusive roles. One example of this dilemma is discernible in the attitude of the 'international community' towards the LTTE, a necessary party to the peace talks that has now withdrawn from the negotiating table. There are many who believe that the 'international community' has been much too soft on the LTTE, confining its occasional critical observations to generalities. Both individual diplomats and consular missions often voice their opinions on the status of the peace negotiations and even comment on occasional truce violations, but they are careful, according to these critics, not to offend the United National Front Government and its negotiating-partner, the LTTE. The simple truth may be that they do not want to derail the peace process.

While examining this aspect of external participation in Sri Lanka's peace process, viz., the dilemma of foreign entities called upon to play a central or supportive role in ushering in peace to the island, these entities are often clubbed together under various terms like the ubiquitous 'international community', often a one-phrase substitute for the US, European Union, Norway, India and Japan in the Sri Lankan context, or more generally, as 'world opinion'. Prof. Jayadeva Uyangoda has recently added to this discourse the term 'global State'. The term 'international community' may be required to refer to the body of world opinion that seems to influence developments within the peace process, though it is safer to use the names of individual nations, agencies and institutions.

India's Dilemma

India was the earliest and most significant external player in the Sri Lankan arena. Despite this, or (more accurately) because of this, India now displays the maximum reticence in the current peace process. Its approach towards the peace initiative has been marked mostly by silence, but it has given enough indication that it remains concerned about developments within the negotiation process as well as the ground realities under the prevailing truce. Not even the entry of big powers like the US and Japan into the political and economic aspects of peace-making has changed India's perception that non-interference is its best policy in the prevailing circumstances. There was a moment in the process when India appeared seriously concerned, after Japan announced a hands-on, activist approach to peace in Sri Lanka, but the Japanese have convinced the Indian establishment that they do not intend to make any inroads into areas of India's concern.

India figures in the Sri Lankan scene as a player with a huge baggage from the past. During 1983-90, it tried out all possibilities in external role-playing endeavour: supporting the Tamil cause, supporting militancy, supporting the Sri Lankan State by taking up the role of disarming the LTTE, besides signing a short-lived peace agreement with Colombo. In the process, it had on different occasions antagonised different segments in Sri Lanka, like the Government, the LTTE, the Sinhala nationalist Opposition, and the Tamils. Thus, the

Indian pendulum has swung both ways, pausing to seek a negotiated settlement midway. It has now settled down to a simple functional mode in support of the ongoing peace initiative. India stands by a few core principles that have the approval of the international community, and which are not inconsistent with the agreed principles on which the LTTE and the Sri Lankan Government have committed themselves to a peaceful settlement in future.

These principles – a commitment to the territorial integrity of Sri Lanka, a negotiated settlement meeting the aspirations of all sections of its society, the adoption of political pluralism, and respect for human rights and democracy – have found great resonance among other countries and institutions backing Sri Lanka's efforts to return to peace. These norms have now evolved into a one-sentence global policy on Sri Lanka. India's non-participation in the peace process, its maintenance of a ban on the LTTE and refusal to give up its demand for extradition of LTTE leader Prabhakaran are all considered necessary not only by policy-makers in India but also by many supporters of the process in Sri Lanka. This is because India's position is deemed helpful in maintaining international pressure on the ruthless rebel group that has the reputation for walking out of talks and reneging on its commitments.

The Government-LTTE agreement in Oslo in December 2002 also reflected these norms, when the parties decided that they would together explore the possibility of a federal solution based on the principle of 'internal self-determination' within a unified Sri Lanka. The Oslo session also adopted a key phrase from the 1987 Indo-Sri Lanka Accord when it referred to Sri Lanka's North-East as 'areas of traditional habitation of Tamil-speaking peoples'. India possibly had some reason to be satisfied that two key principles it had advocated – preservation of the island-nation's unity on the one hand, and assuring the Tamils of an administrative unit in a merged North-East on the other – continued to form the basis for a negotiated settlement. In the normal course of events, India, or indeed any other country, would not have had any reason to be excessively anxious and concerned about the direction of the peace process, given the overall framework within which it is taking place, under world media glare and maximum international scrutiny. However, the past and the present have a way of coming together to conspire against any vision of a tranquil future. Together they mandate that the world be justly concerned over what is happening in Sri Lanka today.

India faces quite a few predicaments and dilemmas as part of this process. It faces a general predicament in the form of an eternal suspicion about its motives among both the Tamils and Sinhalese in Sri Lanka. One has heard allegations in Colombo that India would always want war in Sri Lanka because the advent of peace would mean that it might have to give up its demand for the extradition of the LTTE leader Velupillai Prabhakaran and reconcile itself to the prospect or reality of an LTTE-run administration. If the difficulty in deciding what to do or say in the event of peace was the war-time dilemma, the present 'neither-war-nor-peace' situation may well create its own conundrum. Given the fact that confidence in the peace process is at its lowest ebb today, the question as to what India would do if there is a return to war will keep speculation going as long as the present truce lasts.

India has frequently said that it has certain constraints in playing an active role in any peace talks involving the LTTE, in a reference to the legal problem of Prabhakaran's extradition and the proscription of the LTTE in India. The problem of dealing with an outlawed group, that too one with a proven tendency towards fascism and a hideous record of terrorism, and led by someone wanted for assassinating a national leader, is no doubt a difficult proposition.

Yet, there is some merit in the argument that a country confident of its position and stature in the world ought not to let its regional policy be held hostage to just one issue. One is tempted to ask if it is not possible for India to engage itself in a constructive way in the current peace process, putting aside bitter memories of the past, given the fact that more than a decade has elapsed since the assassination. I think that this was the point that Velupillai Prabhakaran was trying to make at the Kilinochchi news conference, when he said that the assassination of Rajiv Gandhi was an "old incident that took place more than a decade ago", and a "tragic incident" at that.

However, any merit in these contentions is defeated, not by any external argument, but by the inherent nature of the LTTE and its conduct during the present ceasefire. Despite observing a formal truce for 18 months, the LTTE has shown no signs of cleaning its blood-soaked record, or changing its policy of eliminating Tamil political rivals. Besides the visible violations of the truce, like rampant child-conscription, abduction and murder of disarmed former militants and Tamils working for the Army or the military intelligence, they have robbed the Tamil masses of any sense of peaceful existence with their frequent dire warnings of a return to war. Their obvious politico-military consolidation, the expansion of their parallel institutions like police force, judiciary, banking and revenue systems, and their refusal to disband their feared suicide squads collectively mean that the LTTE is practising a policy of deliberately causing an erosion for the southern support for peace. This has not been adequately considered. Why is it that all this is taking place under a rubric of a peace process for 19 months? It is because the LTTE does not want the constituency for peace in the South to extend beyond a particular level because, ultimately, it needs the plausible excuse that the peace process collapsed because of political bickering in the South.

Of particular concern to India has been the group's attempt to drive non-LTTE Tamil parties like the Eelam People's Democratic Party (EPDP) and Eelam People's Revolutionary Liberation Front (Varadaraja Perumal faction) out of the North-East. These parties had backed the Indo-Sri Lanka Accord, given up militancy and joined the political mainstream. By these actions, the LTTE has made it easy for India to stay away from the peace initiative, and remain sceptical about its outcome. It has also given India a chance to articulate its concerns, and highlight political pluralism and democracy. It was after a visit by Foreign Secretary Kanwal Sibal to Sri Lanka in 2002 that India added the words 'political pluralism, human rights and democracy' to its routine statements on the ethnic conflict.

This situation naturally leads to the question concerning what India would do in the event of an outbreak of hostilities again. This has to be answered in conjunction with the question what the world will do in such an eventuality. The idea of an 'international safety-net', first introduced as a crucial pillar supporting the current peace process by Prime Minister Ranil Wickremesinghe in a speech in Sri Lanka's Parliament in January 2002, becomes relevant in such a context. As an individual nation, India is unlikely to change its policy of aloofness, and may restrict itself to a statement of regret. The strengthening of Indo-American relations in recent times has given rise to an expectation, not always explicitly stated, that the 'global super-power' and 'regional super-power' will come together to intervene militarily against the LTTE. Contrary to this expectation, as well as the widely-held belief that the international community will at last have its say in such a situation, nothing of that sort is likely to happen.

India and the US have stepped up military cooperation with Sri Lanka. According to Wickremesinghe, measures have been worked out for strengthening the country's armed forces with help from these two countries. In such circumstances, it is unlikely that Sri Lanka itself will ask for overseas military presence. However, in the event of such a request, any realistic assessment of what India will do must take into account a set of dilemmas that India will have to resolve before it can send forces into the island-nation again. The foremost of these inhibiting factors is its past, some of it very dubious. Its experience of sending peace-keepers and the resultant pain and humiliation it suffered will preclude any possibility of a second intervention, even if invited again by the Sri Lankan Government.

Writing in *The Island* recently, former Sri Lankan diplomat Bernard Tillakaratne disclosed that in a one-on-one discussion he had arranged between the late Sri Lankan President Ranasinghe Premadasa and then Indian Prime Minister P.V. Narasimha Rao, the latter had categorically said that India would never intervene in Sri Lanka again, 'even if invited'. While this is no declaration of policy of permanent import, it certainly shows the extent to which the Indian State and polity are weighed down by their bitter experience in Sri Lanka. After all, the events of 1983-90 are not easily lived down. India's covert support for Tamil militancy, which extended to military training and providing arms and finance, had been exposed. India had been trapped into fighting a directionless war against the LTTE, and humiliated by a political and military alliance between the Premadasa regime and the Tigers. Ultimately, the IPKF, which lost nearly 1200 men, was summarily asked to leave. This is the first inhibiting factor.

The second inhibiting factor that militates against the idea of a second intervention by India is the recent debate on sending troops to Iraq to assist the US. This becomes relevant because it reveals a clear opposition within the country, both in the establishment and among the public, to any ill-advised deployment of Indian soldiers on foreign soil. Parliament has passed a unanimous resolution opposing the US-led invasion of Iraq. There may, as many will immediately point out, be nothing in common between the situation in Sri Lanka and Iraq. But what ought to be emphasised is the general aversion in the country to military missions without sufficient cause.

The war in Sri Lanka has been going on for too many years for another breakdown of peace to matter greatly to the Indian people. Yet, it should be noted that the current peace initiative does mark such a decisive phase in the neighbouring nation's history that if the truce is ended by the LTTE arbitrarily, there may be a global clamour for decisive and punitive action against the LTTE. India may then add its voice to world opinion. None knows this better than Prabhakaran, and one can·reasonably expect that he will not call off the ceasefire except under conditions in which a neutral observer will find it difficult to blame the Tigers alone.

In sum, India's choices are severely limited by its multiple dilemmas, and the country is effectively precluded from either joining the current peace negotiations in a meaningful manner or embarking on any future initiative in the event of the collapse of the talks.

The American Voice

The hands-on approach of the US towards the Sri Lankan peace process, marked by regular statements on important events relating to the ceasefire or negotiations, is seen by the United National Front Government as its surest guarantee for success in its peace efforts. The US presence is seen to impart stability to the global support enjoyed by the initiative, as well as keep the process honest by acting as a deterrent against the LTTE abandoning the negotiating table. In contrast to the opprobrium and charges of partisan behaviour that the US attracts elsewhere in the world, the American role in the island enjoys goodwill and support. However, the Tamils have deep suspicions about the US approach, given the fact that most of the statements relating to the peace process since early 2002 have not been confined to expressions of support, but have extended to trenchant criticism of the Tiger rebels. The latest was issued on 17 September 2003 asking the LTTE to renounce 'terrorism' and make 'realistic' demands. Earlier statements include a remark by Deputy Secretary of State Richard Armitage that the US might 'hunt down' the LTTE if it failed to renounce violence and terrorism.

E. Ashley Wills, former US Ambassador in Colombo, spelt out the American position on Sri Lanka in a speech at Jaffna in 2001. The US, he said, rejected the idea of a separate State, opposed a military solution, supported the Norwegian facilitation, and deemed the LTTE a 'terrorist organisation' which was not the sole representative of the Tamil people. He refrained from advocating a solution, saying the parties themselves at negotiations must work out the exact political form by which 'Tamil rights', equality and dignity should be protected.

The speech evoked condemnation from the Tamils, mainly for the American characterisation of the LTTE as a 'terrorist group' that does not solely represent them. There is an undercurrent of hostility in Colombo's Tamil media against what they perceive is an Indo-US design against the Tigers. The Americans have openly attacked the LTTE for continuing with child-conscription, political assassinations and refusing to go by the rulings of Nordic monitors. State Department spokesman Philip T. Reeker accused the LTTE in August 2003 of 'undermining the confidence' in the peace process. He went on to refer to a controversial Vennirasakulam military camp that the LTTE is refusing to vacate even after being told by the SLMM monitors that its existence is in violation of the ceasefire accord.

The current impasse over the nature of the proposed interim administration for the North-East has overshadowed the fact that the Tigers pulled out of the peace negotiations on 21 April this year mainly because they were kept out by the U.S. from a seminar on the peace process in Washington. The United States put the LTTE on its terrorism list in 1997, while Britain did so in early 2001. The LTTE statement of April 21 did not blame the United States, but rather assailed the Colombo Government and Norway for letting the seminar – which was a preparatory meeting ahead of an important peace-aid conference in Tokyo in June – be hosted by the US. However, the U.S. was not averse to sending Armitage to both the peace support conference held on 25 November 2002 in Oslo and the Tokyo Aid Conference on 9-10 June 2003.

After the Tokyo meet announced a huge aid of $ 4.5 billion over four years to rebuild Sri Lanka, especially the war-ravaged North-East, and linked such aid to clear progress in peace talks, the LTTE showed growing disenchantment with the international profile of the peace initiative. They accused the Wickremesinghe Government of welcoming 'undue and unwarranted interference by extra-territorial forces' in the conflict, and thereby complicating what was essentially an 'internal affair'. There is bound to be endless speculation on whether all this means there is a possibility of an American military intervention in the event of a return to war. It will be futile to debate the question whether Sri Lanka is of 'sufficient strategic interest' to the US to warrant such an intervention, given the apparent convergence of interests between the US and India in the region. It will be safer to conclude that the Americans, like the Indians, will let the currents of world opinion decide their course of action.

Facilitators and Monitors

President Kumaratunga inducted Norway into the peace efforts in Sri Lanka as a third-party facilitator in 1999. The Norwegians were credited with great finesse and capability in peace-making and mediation, primarily based on their experience in the signing of the Oslo Peace Accord between Israel and Palestine in 1993. Norway's role has attracted commendation from the international community for its skillful handling of a sensitive assignment. Much of the credit for the survival of the Sri Lankan peace process should go to the Norwegians. However, sections of the Buddhist clergy, the President and her party, the JVP and some Colombo-based newspapers are highly critical of the Norwegian involvement.

Norway faces frequent street-protests, angry denunciation, and calls for ending role its as a facilitator. The primary charge against Norway is that it is acting in a blatantly partisan manner in the LTTE's favour, and turns a blind eye to its multiple ceasefire violations. Prime Minister Wickremesinghe likened the campaign to the opposition faced by India in 1987 when it sought to mediate between the Government and the LTTE. "What was said of India then is now being said of Norway by the same detractors", I tell them, "Do not make the same mistake again", he said in an address to Parliament on 4 March 2002.

The dilemma faced by Norway is specific to all intervening third-parties in conflict situations, however well-meaning they may be in playing their role. It is not as though exacting standards of impartiality is what their detractors want. Rather, what they desire is that in moments of crisis within the negotiation process, the mediators should tilt to their own side. Given such a situation, the Norwegians have borne up well to all kinds of provocation and insults, without being forced into walking out of the peace efforts. However, there may have been one or two instances when their actions gave the impression of proving their detractors right. These may not have been intentionally partisan acts but *bona fide* mistakes that they could have avoided with better judgement and anticipation.

A major error committed by Norway in the course of the peace process was the assumption of the role of monitoring the ceasefire, through the Sri Lanka Monitoring Mission (SLMM), a team of observers drawn from Nordic countries, but answerable to the Norwegian Embassy in Colombo. There was an obvious conflict of interest between their role as facilitators of the peace talks and as the adjudicator of ceasefire violations. As moderators in the peace process, the Norwegians cannot be expected to be critical of either party, especially in sensitive matters like truce-violations. Yet, they chose to bring the Monitoring Mission under their own purview. The University Teachers for Human Rights (Jaffna) pointed to this conflict of interest in the early days of the ceasefire, especially in the context of the widespread instances of 'child conscription' and abduction of young adults by the LTTE. In recent weeks, Amnesty International has expressed doubts whether Norway's role as peace-facilitator was affecting the performance of the Monitoring Mission headed by it.

Norway clearly feels the effects of glaring contradictions between the high-profile, internationally visible, plenum of negotiations, and the less-acknowledged ground realities that constitute a parallel dimension neutralising the gains at the negotiating table. As months pass without the resumption of direct talks, it is becoming increasingly obvious that there has always been these two mutually-contradictory dimensions within the current peace process. Perhaps, the current stalemate in the talks is an honest phase, as there is greater acknowledgement today of the gulf that separates the euphoria of truce and the disillusionment over the ways in which it is floundering.

An episode that showed the Norwegians in poor light was their disingenuous act of providing diplomatic cover to the import of a radio transmitter brought into the country by the LTTE for its 'Voice of Tigers' radio. The ostensible reason was that the Government, unable to waive the customs duty on the equipment, wanted the Norwegian Embassy to clear the consignment in the interest of promoting the peace process. It passes understanding how the Government could be so inflexible that it did not want to waive a levy for the sake of peace, and yet expect the Norwegians to abuse their diplomatic privilege of duty-free import. It was subsequently announced that Norway would pay the relevant duty, but that only begged the question why the LTTE, which could afford to import the equipment, could not pay it on its own. Norway's Ambassador in Colombo, Jon Westborg, who was closely associated with the peace moves for over two years, earned a public rebuke from President Chandrika Kumaratunga for his role in clearing the LTTE's equipment. Norway was perhaps being over-zealous in protecting the peace process rather than consciously white-washing the LTTE. This highlights the need for understanding on the part of external actors towards the sensitivities of a sovereign nation.

In contrast, the truce-monitoring group has tried to play an even-handed role between the parties. The SLMM, comprising truce observers from Norway, Sweden, Denmark, Finland and Iceland, has been wildly accused of being pro-LTTE, and turning a blind eye to depredations by the Tigers, especially their frequent ceasefire violations. However, neutral observers will not agree with such a characterisation. The SLMM has serious limitations in terms of its mandate and manpower. Moreover, being part of the Norwegian project is a further handicap. A relevant factor is that the ceasefire monitors appear to be conscious that they are part of a sensitive peace process and that their work cannot be pursued with judicial zeal to the detriment of relations between the negotiating parties. The SLMM's presence remains a great source of strength to the Tamils of the North and East, going by the thousands of complaints with which people have approached the monitors after over-coming their initial fears. That most of these were against the LTTE speaks both of the people's courage and the confidence that the SLMM has inspired amongst the people there. In terms of numbers, the SLMM rulings were only a small percentage of the complaints that flowed, but the fact that they found the LTTE guilty in nearly 90 per cent of the investigated ceasefire violations shows that much of the criticism that it is pro-LTTE is misplaced.

The Monitoring Mission attracted a lot of flak for suggesting demarcation of separate areas in the sea for the 'Sea Tigers' to conduct naval exercises, and for blaming a mysterious 'third force' in the north-eastern seas for the slaying of 13 Chinese fishermen in March. These were baffling decisions, indeed. However, few commended the SLMM for holding that the Sri Lankan Navy was well within its rights as per the global Law of the Seas when it sank LTTE vessels in international waters. Nor were the truce monitors thanked for a detailed expose of the rebels' attempt to smuggle in an anti-aircraft gun in a 'fishing vessel'. The details given in the SLMM's final report on the 7 February 2003 incident were such as to nail every lie in the LTTE's version. In fact, the SLMM indirectly exposed as untrue a Norwegian statement from Berlin, where talks were taking place then, that the suicides of three militants in the incident was due to a 'communication failure'.

It was a case in which the LTTE leadership over-ruled decisions agreed on in Berlin to resolve the 'Delft stand-off', and directed the cadres to blow themselves up. More recently, the SLMM asked the LTTE to remove a controversial camp at

Kurankupanchankulam in Trincomalee district, holding that even the rebel maps showed that the territory fell within the Government-controlled area, but the Tigers have flatly refused to accept the ruling.

A significant criticism of the SLMM's functioning pertains to political killings by the LTTE in the last few months. The monitors were even castigated by global human rights groups like Amnesty International and Human Rights Watch for not doing enough to investigate these targeted killings. The SLMM pleaded that these crimes ought to be investigated by the police as they took place mostly in Government-controlled areas. The role of the SLMM is thus indisputably one of reining in the parties during the ceasefire, and the trend so far has been that the LTTE finds itself seriously discomfited in the process. The SLMM released a few statistical summaries of pending complaints and those disposed of until the end of last year, but appears to have given up the practice in the last few months. It is a poor commentary on the international community that the SLMM rulings are not backed up by diplomatic measures to enforce them. The findings do not seem to have any consequence on the negotiating process. Why cannot Norway and Japan take a firm view and refuse to interact with the Tigers unless they complied with the rulings?

There seems to be no explanation why the SLMM, a crucial component of the peace process, should find itself ignored and humiliated, and its findings not being factored into the progress of talks. After all, it is only the Sri Lankan Government that cannot afford to antagonise the LTTE for fear of the latter walking out of talks and calling off the ceasefire. The rest of the world is in a better position to ensure compliance with the truce with more coercive diplomacy. The monitors can also consider a more activist role such as breaking through LTTE barriers to reach camps to which they have been denied access, while Norway and Japan can refuse to meet LTTE representatives. This is not too much to expect from external actors after 19 months of committed pursuit of peace negotiations.

International Opinion

"A solution to the North-East problem will be through international opinion. We must focus our attention accordingly... If international opinion, is with us, we could protect the territorial integrity and unity of our nation", Prime Minister Wickremesinghe said in an address to Sri Lanka's Parliament in January 2002, prior to the signing of a formal ceasefire agreement. True to his words, he has been assiduously cultivating world-opinion in favour of his peace efforts, and has ensured that this is also the best opportunity for finding a peaceful solution. The present truce is the longest ever in the history of this conflict. His strategy has largely paid off, but it remains to be seen if the ultimate denouement is in his favour. The merit of this approach will depend on the extent to which the LTTE will respect and fear world opinion. There are signs that the guerrilla outfit remains impervious to such opinion until now and may not be averse to defying it, when the need arose.

Wickremesinghe's detractors, headed by President Chandrika Kumaratunga, are convinced that his gambit has failed, and that the LTTE has strengthened itself enormously under the peace process, besides ingratiating itself to large sections of the international community. An important feature of the peace effort has been the progressive legitimisation of the LTTE, something that the Government seems to have consciously worked towards in the last one year. It is well known in the Peace Secretariat circles in Colombo that, far from keeping the LTTE's relative lack of legitimacy alive, the Government's intention is to usher the rebels into the global community as part of 'mainstreaming' them.

The Opposition in Colombo, the nationalist media and LTTE detractors caught on to this strategy early on, when it was announced that the Government and the LTTE would make a joint appeal for funds from the world in a 'Peace Support Conference' organised by Norway in Oslo in November 2002. The Government stuck to its guns, arguing that the LTTE would have to commit itself to globally acceptable principles while on the international stage. The unspoken defence for the Government acting as an escort to the rebels was that they would find it impossible to return to terrorism after making their debut in a multilateral stage involving powerful nations of the world. Long-time LTTE-watchers, however, are aware that the group not only knows how to exploit such a forum but also how to wriggle out of any implied multilateral commitment that its participation may entail. This was amply demonstrated when the LTTE boycotted the Tokyo conference of 9-10 June 2002.

In the run-up to the Tokyo meet, there was tremendous pressure on the LTTE leadership to attend the conclave and revive direct peace talks. Those who were pushing included Norway, the main aid-giver and host Japan, the United States, and countries from the European Union. They were dangling the carrot of large-scale infusion of foreign funds, and the prospect of the LTTE being allowed the final say in its disbursement and in other development-related work in the North-East. The LTTE was not impressed. It bunched together all its grievances into a single demand: an interim politico-administrative structure for the North-East, in which the LTTE would have full control and which will apparently be outside the purview of Sri Lanka's constitutional and parliamentary systems.

The world thought that the LTTE was playing its familiar game of brinkmanship so that they could extract the maximum out of the compelling need of the Government to make a success of the Tokyo conference. With the country yet to get out of its economic crisis, and having no public funds to revive its economy, leave alone prepare for another war, the Government had no choice except to plead with the LTTE to come to Tokyo and participate in the joint appeal for aid. The conference ended with a peace bonanza for the reconstruction of the country, quantified at over $ 4.5 billion. The donors, expectedly, linked the actual delivery of aid to a number of conditions, including a steadfast commitment to peace, a settlement that will ensure human rights, democracy and the rule of law. The final statement also spoke of full compliance with the ceasefire by both parties, and continuous monitoring by the donor-community. In another aspect that would certainly have upset the LTTE, it said a separate Muslim delegation should be allowed to participate at the negotiating table.

By now it was clear that the initial assessment of the LTTE's refusal to come to Tokyo was wrong. The rebels, far from using their attendance as an instrument to extract concessions, were actually placing demands that could not be met, in order to avoid going to Tokyo. The LTTE saw the Tokyo meet as a plot to thrust a solution on it, along with a monitored regime of human rights, political pluralism and democracy, principles alien to its philosophy and practice. The LTTE's reaction confirmed this. "The Colombo Government, with the active assistance of the facilitator and its international 'tactical allies', has formulated this strategic paper to super-impose its own agenda on the LTTE. This is unacceptable to us," said a statement from the LTTE headquarters. It also hit out at the 'Colombo Government' for allowing unwarranted interference by its international allies. It explicitly objected to the global 'safety net' devised by Wickremesinghe to bolster his efforts.

It is now amply clear that the LTTE is uncomfortable under the glare of the 'international community'. It would rather deal with Colombo on its own terms without external forces breathing down its neck. Its immediate agenda is to get the external element ousted, but given the global scale on which the peace initiative has been undertaken, it's not easy to come by.

Safety-Net for Whom?

What is commonly referred to as an 'international safety-net' was originally spoken of by Prime Minister Wickremesinghe in an address to the Sri Lankan Parliament in January 2002, when he used the phrase 'security-net' in the context of 'two factors' concerning the LTTE. He explained these two factors as first, a guarantee for the LTTE's honesty towards the peace talks, and second, the prevention of any adverse effects on the outfit's 'international ban' if there were any change in its domestic proscription. It was clear from his formulation that he wanted the ban on the LTTE elsewhere in the world to stay, while his own country would lift it. The United States, the United Kingdom, Australia and, of course, India, have so far retained their respective legal measures against the LTTE, but it is difficult to speculate whether there is any guarantee for the LTTE's 'honesty' as regards the peace talks.

The foremost question that has arisen after a quantum leap in the peace process last year and a prolonged stalemate this year, is whether the LTTE has given up its demand for a 'separate State' and is willing to settle for regional autonomy in its 'homeland'. Detractors of the peace process, ranging from well-meaning sceptics to chauvinist forces, have begun to ask whether Sri Lanka will emerge undivided from the peace process, as it moves towards political and diplomatic empowerment of the LTTE who are unlikely to disarm. There are many in the island-nation today who believe that the world is watching, if not being a party to the process of 'creeping Eelamisation' of the country. Instead of acting as a restraining factor, the international community's presence is seen by these detractors as an endorsement of the politico-military consolidation of the LTTE. In this context, the question arises as for whom the 'safety-net' is intended. Is it for the peace process, the Government, or the LTTE? Is the world being influenced into formalising the territorial control already enjoyed by the LTTE? After all, Balasingham said at Sattahip in Thailand after the first round of peace talks that the LTTE already had an administration in place, and the aim was to gain international recognition for it.

That such a question should arise exposes the predicament faced by the international community. The world – or, at least the countries actively interested in Sri Lanka's fortunes today – have shown a collective resolve so far not to allow the country's dismemberment. Sceptics are not convinced that they are all equally committed to this objective. On the other hand, they remain convinced that in the event of a return to war, the diplomats now criss-crossing the world in the name of peace in Sri Lanka may not turn up to help the State, and may even quietly accord recognition to a putative 'Tamil Eelam'. There is obvious confusion among these external players who think they are being helpful when they see the LTTE's actions in a positive light. Be it the LTTE's keenness to import an FM transmitter, or its demand that international lending institutions come to the Vanni region to discuss direct funding for development and reconstruction projects there, the world has a tendency to feel encouraged by any steps by a former outlaw towards peace and eagerness to engage the international community.

Applying pressure through seemingly critical and harsh statements against the LTTE while, at the same time, deputing consular mission heads to the rebel political headquarters at Kilinochchi, important Governments are sending out ambivalent signals to both the Sinhalese and the Tamils. This is LTTE supremo Prabhakaran's biggest strength. Whatever the turn of events, whatever the nature of ceasefire violations, and howsoever strong the condemnation of his organisation's actions, it is unlikely that the world will gang up against him. He was once seen as a guerrilla leader caught in a bind, for neither could he continue with his war indefinitely, especially in the post-9/11 era, nor could he return to a peaceful civilian existence. However, he seems to have made full use of international opinion and a friendly Government's gestures to make his way towards personal emancipation. Whether the Tamils get a fair deal or not, it is clear that Prabhakaran will get a fairer deal from the world.

Japanese special envoy Yasushi Akashi recently described international attention as 'fickle', suggesting that if the peace talks do not resume soon, other conflict areas like Iraq could be the focus of donor-nations. One can only hope that the LTTE does not take a cue from this, and stall the talks for some more time in a bid to get itself out of world focus. The 'Tokyo Declaration' adopted by countries and institutions out to help Sri Lanka, linked the grant of aid with progress in peace talks, believing that this will be an incentive to the Tigers to resume negotiations. Have they, on the contrary, provided the LTTE leadership with a rare incentive for wreaking economic ruin in southern Sri Lanka? The benign international community has given the LTTE a choice. It can resume the talks and carry them towards fruition, while at the same time rebuilding the devastated north and east. Or, it can choose to deny much-needed aid to the Government under the belief that an economically weak South, headed by a politically weak regime, will be forced to concede the maximum. What will be the Tigers' policy for the immediate future: will it be 'Save the Talks and build the country', or 'Stall the talks and starve the State'? The world's preference is clear.

DISCUSSION

One participant suggested that the US has already learnt its lesson in Afghanistan and Iraq, and it may not want to burn its fingers in Sri Lanka. He also asked as to what would happen to the 'sovereignty' of Sri Lanka if everybody was expected to come to the rescue of Sri Lanka in case of a crisis.

Others argued that there can be no optimism about any military intervention, either by India or the US. It is exactly the opposite – that India is unlikely to intervene in case of a conflict, and it will be wishful thinking in Colombo if someone feels that way. About Sri Lanka's sovereignty, this is something that the Sri Lankan Government ought to be more concerned with, and they do not seem to be concerned at all. About two weeks back, the Government Agent for Vavuniya wanted to know from the Minister for Public Administration whether to allow Government servants to participate in the LTTE's *Pongu Tamil* festival. The reply came that he should consult the SLMM in its regard. This was a simple matter concerning the civil service rules of Sri Lanka. First he said that he will consult the SLMM and then he later said that it would not be a violation of the civil service rules if Government servants participated in an LTTE-backed event.

Another incident happened about three weeks ago in a meeting in 'Temple Trees', where Tamil and Muslim parliamentarians were present at the Prime Minister's residence. Mr. Hezbullah reportedly pointed out that the LTTE was levying taxes of Rs. 500 on Muslim traders in Batticaloa. The

US Ambassador was on a visit to Batticaloa at that moment and the Prime Minister contacted him on the phone, and asked if it was true.

Others pointed out that India cannot continue the policy of non-interference, or the *status quo* in Sri Lankan affairs. A former Prime Minister has been killed, and it has been proved beyond doubt that the LTTE leadership had a hand in it. Had it been the Americans, or for that matter, any other country, the situation would have been different, and the killer would have been probably hunted like Osama bin-Laden. Secondly, there is the proximity of the Sri Lankan territory to India. Third is the ethnic affinity of the Tamils in India to the Sri Lankan Tamils. Fourthly, foreign powers would play a predominant role, which in turn would affect the security of India. Taking all these into consideration, in the event of the peace accord failing, India should play a more vibrant role rather than keep mum as it is doing now.

Others suggested that though in general terms there are security concerns and there are developments across the Palk Straits that India has to legitimately be concerned with, it is not advisable to advocate a specific policy that India should either keep mum or play an active role in the event of what could happen in the foreseeable future. India is aware of what is happening and is closely monitoring the situation, and it may have its consequences. It all depends on the circumstances in which a possible collapse of the peace talks, would happen. This is the essence of what the Foreign Secretary of India said in a brief conversation, the last time he was in Colombo. Though India has not explicitly said anything, it is aware of these concerns.

Others argued that it is not so much the question of what India will do in the event of the peace talks failing, but as what India should do in the event of the peace talks succeeding. What sort of attitude will India adopt towards the LTTE? Will India press for the extradition of Prabhakaran?

But other participants disagreed on advocating a specific policy for India. In the event of the end of a peace process, India will naturally be expected to raise the following issues:

a) The issue of the extradition of Prabhakaran. India's position for the past 12 years has been that they would press for the extradition only if the circumstances are conducive - only when the Sri Lankan Government's jurisdiction extends to Prabhakaran's lair. That is the first constraint that Prabhakaran would face. Until that happens, India may not make a specific request and embarrass the Government of Sri Lanka.
b) India's attitude towards the LTTE is unlikely to change. If there is an interim solution, they will probably wait for the conduct of the LTTE to be revealed as the days go by. There is a big opportunity for the LTTE to legitimise itself in the eyes of the international community.
c) In the event such a solution is not available and there is a return to war, India can retain its present position of waiting for the war to subside, or waiting for a situation to emerge for playing a more effective role. There are doubts about the scope for another military intervention. India's policy will be reflected in actions, and it may or may not make a statement.

Another participant suggested that the entire Sri Lankan Tamil problem was totally caused by the Americans. Just for the record, a hundred years ago or so, the American missionaries came and contributed to what is now the Jaffna College, and a superb educational system in Jaffna which produced enough civil servants, bureaucrats and clerical staff to feed the

Government of Ceylon. Not very long after, another American, somebody we are a little more familiar with, a man called Col. Olcott, turned up in Colombo and was responsible for the revival of Buddhism and the 'Sinhala cause'. So with the American revival of Buddhism and the Sinhala cause at the one end, and the Jaffna-trained Government servants at another end, we had a problem starting a hundred years ago. It is as far back as that that external powers in this region have played a role.

On the "Role of External Powers", it was pointed out that there is this question of India's role and the matters within India which concern Tamil Nadu in particular. There are some other issues that need to be looked at, at some other point in time, namely, Kachachatheevu and the fishing rights. These are major issues at the moment. There is the "Sethusamudram scheme", which is another major issue. There is the Palk Straits bridge, against which Tamil Nadu Chief Minister Jayalalithaa has put her foot down. There is the traditional business route, for a thousand years now, between Velvettithurai and Kodiakarai. These are issues which have to be thought about, not merely in terms of Indian involvement, but also Tamil Nadu's involvement.

The diaspora issue also came up for discussion. The issue arises not just out of the 600,000 Sri Lankan Tamils in Norway. The issue of the diaspora stretches from New Zealand at the one end to Vancouver at the other. In Toronto, for instance, there are over 250,000 Tamils in a small area, where street after street has Tamil signs. They are making good money, and are in good businesses. There is certainly an international dimension to the flow of money into Sri Lanka's North and East. Whether that money is going into the pockets of the LTTE or going to the families is another question. It is good to remember that the largest number of deposits at the Bank of Ceylon, outside Colombo, is in the Jaffna branch.

A connected issue was of the money flowing in. Why, it was asked, is all this money flowing into Jaffna, only into 'the war effort', and why not into the peace effort and rebuilding industry? Why has not the money gone into the Kankesanthurai cement factory, or the Paranthan chemicals, or for new factories to resurrect the economy? In the past, when Ceylon was at its worst in terms of foodstuff, Jaffna was green. People from those parts will remember the growing of onion and all other things. Why are we not back at that again? It was suggested that if we looked at some of those issues rather than war all the time, maybe we will begin to forget war at some point in time. The diaspora needs to play a much greater role in this kind of thing.

Another issue raised was about the role of Japan and Norway. What are their special interests in this? Are Japan and Norway interested in the Indian Ocean fishing rights? Is this one of the issues involved? Norway is also an oil country. Is it looking for oil rights around Sri Lanka? What is its special interest other than these? 'Pure altruism' is something that is very hard to swallow. There are other interests there, where the Indian interests will impinge on.

Certainly after 9/11, the pressures on militant groups has been more than ever before. The pressure on the LTTE indirectly from several other countries around the world would tend to restrain the US. The LTTE could thumb its nose at whatever money that has been promised. At the end of the day, international pressures will be such that we will have a long road to peace, at least no war. The kind of low-level wars that we are talking about, the preludes to other things, will continue for some time more. However, a major outbreak of hostilities and 'surgical operations' is very unlikely for the next few years.

Where From Here?

Peace Dynamics

M. Rasgotra

The indulgence being shown by the Sri Lankan Monitoring Mission (SLMM) to the LTTE is an issue which needs mentioning. The navy of any country is an attribute of its external projection. What is involved there is not internal self-determination, but an aspect of external sovereignty. This monitoring mission has to its discredit a grave failure, even in suggesting that there should be an area of the sea around Sri Lanka earmarked for exercises by the 'Sea Tigers'. Who are they in any case to offer this kind of opportunity in a critical situation? This is highly objectionable. They have been negligent, they have been worse than that in actively promoting this kind of activity on the part of the LTTE.

As to whether India will intervene again or not, I am not a prophet. When this unfortunate trouble in Sri Lanka erupted, I was the Foreign Secretary in the Government of India. It caused us great unhappiness. It caused us great trouble also in due course. Our policy then was very clear. This was a domestic problem of Sri Lanka. India, as a friend keenly interested in the stability, integrity, peace and development of Sri Lanka, should exert its influence on both parties in friendly ways. The aim would be to bring both parties together, or at least bring them to the table for a cordial, peaceful, cooperative and creative discussion, which would bring out a solution to the problem. However, the most critical part of that policy was, no matter what happens, India will not physically intervene in Sri Lanka. This policy remained in operation until Rajiv Gandhi succumbed to an act of political seduction by President Jayewardane. He said that there was a terrible situation and that he had a discussion in his Cabinet, with then Prime Minister Premadasa present. The Cabinet, had decided that Sri Lanka on its own could not handle this problem and so India's support should be sought.

I think that if Indira Gandhi had been the Prime Minister at that time, she would have said, "No, thank you. Go ahead and try again, and we will help you. We will use our political persuasion or even pressure to bring the LTTE around to the view that this is a matter that is to be sorted out politically. After all Sri Lanka is a democracy, a humane democracy. Sri Lankans are a highly evolved political people and there is no earthly reason why this matter cannot be resolved through talks."

Rajiv Gandhi, being new to governance, had unfortunately discarded everyone who had been involved in the Sri Lankan situation during Indira Gandhi's time. There was P.V. Narasimha Rao, the Foreign Minister, G. Parthasarathy and myself. There were not many others. Indira Gandhi was personally and acutely interested in the day-to-day developments. Rajiv Gandhi shunted Narasimha Rao out to Human Resources Development, and discharged G. Parthasarathy for whatever reason, and I retired from service. He was surrounded by people who had no clue about what was going on in Sri Lanka. They had no direct experience about our neighbourhood. Such things happen in many countries. Rajiv Gandhi was dragged into the situation and jumped into it.

I know what profound regrets Rajiv Gandhi later had about the policy he had adopted at that particular time. One may call that intervention a mistake or a blunder, but I think the IPKF would have sorted matters out but for unfortunate things that developed on our side, in New Delhi, in internal politics. V.P. Singh, never a man of any great vision, carried on a personal vendetta against the Nehru-Gandhi family, and Rajiv Gandhi, personally. He defeated Rajiv Gandhi in an unfortunate election, only to be thrown out himself seven or eight months later. President Premadasa of Sri Lanka had a pathological fear or hatred of India. That is the story of the past.

What is likely, or not likely to happen in the future is dependent on the view that India takes of the Sri Lanka situation. What are India's interests? India is committed to the integrity and the unity of Sri Lanka, and I think if there is a grave threat to that position. India's options will be open. I do not want to spell this out any further. Secondly, India's security is very closely intertwined with Sri Lanka's security because of the proximity of the two countries, because of the traditional, cultural, political, economic and other linkages between them. If circumstances arise in which a security threat of one dimension or the other arises from this country to India's own security, then again India's options are open.

Now, you know metaphysics is a very vast area of intellectual gymnastics. What will the international community do? You see what is going on in Nepal. The Americans are as far away from Nepal as they are from Sri Lanka, but they have come in. The United States is a very exceptional country. It is one country in the world today whose interests span the globe. Wherever there is a terrorist threat in the making, potential or real, and the US feels that its interests or security is under some kind of a threat, it moves in different ways. Iraq is a different case. Nepal is the right kind of example to bear in mind. The LTTE is under a ban in the United States. It is described as a violent terrorist organisation. India takes the same view. Prabhakaran, in the eyes of Indian law, is personally a criminal, an assassin, responsible for Rajiv Gandhi's murder and a number of other murders. So, how circumstances turn and at what stage, I am not prepared to take a conclusive view one way or the other.

The situation in Sri Lanka has been described in various ways. There is comparative peace in the country. Because the people are enjoying this spell of peace, a peace-dynamic could develop. A democratic government in power there. It faces elections periodically. It cannot ignore the people's feelings, the people's desire for peace. That applies, to some extent at least, to LTTE supremo Prabhakaran's thinking, and his organisation's thinking. This peace-dynamic, at least in the hearts of the people, the ordinary people, the common people will influence thinking on both sides. We will move from non-peace to a small degree of peace, a small measure of peace to greater peace, and to permanent peace.

If that does not happen and this campaign of assassinations and violence continues, then I think we are heading for very dark times. How will the international community react? How will India react? These are all open questions. But this is a situation, because of Indian interests, Indian commitments in relation to Sri Lanka, which we have to keep constantly under watch, under monitoring, under study.

No Alternative, But...

B. Raman

One point that everybody seems to agree is that there was no alternative to the present peace process in Sri Lanka. At the same time, there are concerns whether the peace will endure. The answer to this will depend on what the LTTE's will be response to the 'interim administration' proposal. The LTTE has been very adamant in insisting that any interim administration should have responsibility not only for humanitarian relief and economic development, but also for the maintenance of peace and security. Having studied the statements coming from the LTTE over a period of time - and you read between the lines - it is very clear that the LTTE's particular objective is the formula of 'one-nation, two States, two armed forces, two administrations'. Whether any Government in Sri Lanka, whichever party is in power, will be able to accept this is the question.

So, if the LTTE again insists that security, and law and order should be its responsibility – in the interim administration, and it puts it as a take-it-or-leave it proposal and, not as a proposal that is negotiable, we are going to come to the end of the road in the peace process. On the other hand, if it says that it is prepared to negotiate, this is its position and it is prepared to negotiate with the government on that, then there is a possibility of further movement in the peace process.

Let us look at the experience of the Soviet Union in Afghanistan, the experience of India in Sri Lanka in the Eighties, the experience of the United States in Somalia, Afghanistan and Iraq, the experience of the US troops which went to the assistance of the Philippines, in the Mindanao Islands. They have shown that no external power can play an effective counter-insurgency role in another country, however powerful it may be, and whatever capability it may have. It has to be dealt with by that country. India for instance, supports the concept of unity and integrity of Sri Lanka. Whether the unity and integrity of Sri Lanka is maintained or not, it is not going to depend on what the external powers are prepared to do to support that, but only on the will, the motivation, the capability and the determination of the Government of Sri Lanka. If that determination is lacking, if the will is lacking, even if the entire international community supports Sri Lanka, it will not be able to maintain unity and territorial integrity.

One feels concerned about the way the present Government in Sri Lanka has been handling the peace process and the way it is reacting – it allowed, it conceded, the LTTE's demand for bringing in some broadcasting equipment into the country through the Norwegian Embassy.

We have this UN Resolution 1373, one of the important provisions of which is action against the flow of funds to terrorists. The Sri Lankan army does not have the capability to wrest control of the region which is at present controlled by the LTTE. But there are lots of other ways in which it can weaken its capability. One of the ways is preventing the flow of funds from abroad. There is a lot of funds pouring in from the diaspora. There is an opportunity for the Government of Sri Lanka to move for the seizure of the bank accounts. Every other country in the world, which is faced with the problem of terrorism, has made use of the provision to have the suspected funds of the terrorists frozen in different countries. Nearly $200 million have been frozen. One country that has not taken any advantage of this provision of 1373 is Sri Lanka. There is a fear that if they do anything like this, that may affect the peace process. If they take strong action against the LTTE, even if strong action is required, it may affect the peace process. This is something about which all of us have to be concerned.

The LTTE has not only the 'Sea Tigers' but also its own commercial fleet, which is run by the members of the Sri Lankan Tamil diaspora abroad. They have tremendous funds. The ships of this fleet are normally used for legitimate trade purposes. They take legitimate goods from one country to another. In between, they do a bit of gun-running.

There is no alternative to peace. One has to try for peace and, one has to keep the peace process going. However, the perception of an over-anxiety for peace, the perception that you are prepared to do anything, the perception that you are ready to concede the demands in the interest of keeping the peace process going, would ultimately damage the chances of peace, instead of bringing about peace. The Government of Sri Lanka should learn some of these lessons. Otherwise, they are going to face a difficult problem. Let us hope that ultimately the peace process comes through. It is in everybody's interest.

India is not disinterested, India may not be overtly active, but India is not disinterested. India has very legitimate, valid, security concerns. There are indications of the beginning of the radicalisation of the Muslim community in Sri Lanka. If this process of radicalisation continues, or is aggravated, it is ltimately going to have an effect – because we also have this roblem of radicalisation of sections of the Muslim youth in outh India, Tamil Nadu, Kerala, Andhra Pradesh, etc. If there s going to be a radicalisation of the Muslim youth in Sri Lanka, t is going have an aggravating effect on the similar process hat we are having in this country. So, from that point of view ılso, we have to closely monitor what is happening in Sri Lanka.

The Tsunami & The LTTE

B.Raman

Sri Lanka has suffered the most human fatalities (30,000 plus) and infrastructure and other property damage after Indonesia in the catastrophic tsunami disaster of 26 December 2004. According to reliable reports from independent sources, the Sri Lankan Tamil community in the Northern and Eastern Provinces has suffered the most in the tragedy, registering more than a half of the fatalities in the entire country. The roads and other infrastructure in the Tamil areas, which was already in an unsatisfactory state due to nearly 20 years of the Tamil insurgency for an independent Tamil State to be called 'Tamil Eelam' has suffered further damage, thereby hampering relief and rehabilitation efforts.

Since the tsunami has caused widespread damage or destruction of the fishing and other boats in the area and since the large number of mines planted by the security forces and the LTTE during the conflict have been loosened up by the water-surge, thereby causing serious danger to anyone moving on foot or by vehicle across agricultural and other fields, the only way of rushing humanitarian assistance to the Tamils is by road.

The repair of the roads and damaged culverts and bridges has, therefore, to be given priority. Unfortunately, the efforts of the Sri Lankan Government in this regard have been sluggish so far. It is alleged by the Tamils that the Government has been paying more attention to the repair and restoration of the damaged road and rail communications infrastructure in the Sinhalese-majority areas of the South.

The LTTE was the first on its feet after the disaster hit the area and lost no time in organising relief, in disposing of the dead bodies and initiating measures for the restoration of at least a semblance of normalcy in the areas under its control. The governmental agencies and the army were much slower to react in the Tamil areas, preoccupied as they were in the Sinhalese-majority areas. Pro-LTTE sources have alleged that President Chandrika Kumaratunga's Government, including the army, turned a deaf ear to the LTTE's request for urgently placing heavy earth-moving and other equipment at its disposal so that it could repair and restore road communications. The insensitivity of the Government to the tragedy suffered by the Tamils and its apparent attempts to draw political mileage out of it are also evident from the reported orders of Chandrika Kumaratunga to the army to take over the responsibility for running the relief and rehabilitation camps set up by pro-LTTE non-governmental organisations in the Tamil areas controlled by the Government.

When they found the governmental agencies slow to move into the affected Tamil areas under Government control, these non-governmental organisations took the initiative in setting up these camps. Instead of appreciating their efforts, and encouraging and helping them to continue their relief efforts, the Government has ordered them to hand these camps over to the army. This has been strongly resisted by the LTTE, which has threatened to continue to resist such moves at any price.

The Government has reportedly rebuked the Italian Embassy in Colombo for sending humanitarian relief directly to the affected Tamils, and has made it clear that all governmental assistance from other countries should be routed to the Tamils through it. It strongly opposed the wish of Kofi Annan, the UN Secretary-General, who was in Sri Lanka on 8 January 2005, to visit the affected Tamil areas in the Northern Province too and meet the Tamil leaders (meaning apparently the LTTE leaders) in order to express the solidarity of the international community with them, thereby forcing him to cancel his plans to go there. The Government reportedly took him only to the Tamil areas in the Eastern Province still under its control.

While repeatedly denying the LTTE's allegations of discrimination against the Tamils, President Kumaratunge has claimed that 80 per cent of all foreign medical assistance and humanitarian relief groups have been sent by the Government to the Tamil areas, but this is questioned by the Tamils. On the ground, the way the Government has been acting gives the impression that it is giving the first priority to the Sinhalese, majority areas, the second to the Tamil areas under its control and only the last to the areas under the control of the LTTE.

Independent reports from the Northern and Eastern Provinces indicate that the military infrastructure of the Government as well as of the LTTE has been seriously damaged by the tsunami, with the LTTE, which had a stronger and a wider presence than the Government, suffering a much greater damage. President Kumaratunga has been quoted in the media as saying that the possibility of the LTTE returning to insurgency due to its continuing differences with the Government was far more remote than it was before 26 December since, according to her, the LTTE had suffered heavy losses to its cadres and equipment. "Our camps have also lost a lot of equipment but physical damage to camp structures are less." she said.

It stands to reason that the LTTE's military infrastructure in the North as well as the East must have suffered considerably since the most devastating impact of the tsunami in Sri Lanka was reportedly in the Tamil areas. However, it has been difficult to quantify the losses suffered by the LTTE and to assess its impact on the LTTE's capability for resuming the insurgency and keeping it sustained. In the absence of reliable information, it is also difficult to estimate what effect the devastation has had on the LTTE's following amongst the people, particularly in the Eastern Province where its hold had been showing signs of weakening since March 2004.

While the LTTE has been more efficient than the Government in documenting the losses suffered by the Tamil civilians and in sharing the information with the international community, it has been playing down the losses suffered by its military infrastructure, and is giving figures that do not seem to be correct. On the other hand, the Sinhalese media, suspectedly fed disinformation by the military intelligence, has been reporting what appear to be highly exaggerated figures of the allegedly losses suffered by the LTTE.

The Reuters news agency, which one would presume to be independent, reported as follows in a dispatch from Mullaitivu on 29 December 2004: "The Tigers' main naval-base at Mullaitivu was devastated, as was part of its fleet. Bodies littered the ground like an upturned graveyard and the over-powering stench of death wafted over the area. Children accounted for the bulk of the victims in nearby fishing villages. All 135 children at an orphanage run by female Tigers were swept away to their deaths. 'We have only found bodies so far,' said Col. Soosai, head of the Tigers' naval arm, the 'Sea Tigers'. 'We have not received any aid from the Government yet. If the Government had warned us early when the quake struck, the devastation could have been partially avoided,' he said angrily. The rebels, whom the United States have placed on a list of banned terror groups alongside the likes of al Qaeda, said just 15 of their cadres were among the dead. A whole battalion of Sea Tiger cadres in fatigues collected bloated bodies and lined them at the roadside ready for mass burial. Some wearing white medical masks and gloves used leafy branches to swish away thousands of flies swarming over the dead. Few buildings on the coast were left standing. Mangled wreckage of trucks, mopeds and fishing boats lay twisted along the shore, and crumpled bodies were tangled in fishing nets. Telephone lines to the South were disrupted. Aid workers said that residents in the North-East now faced a new threat, from thousands of an estimated one million mostly plastic landmines sown across the region and now uprooted by floodwaters. Officials said just 12 of 1,500 local fishing boats were still seaworthy. More than 1,20,000 people in Tiger-held areas had been displaced from their homes, many now housed in makeshift refugee camps. Roofs sagged, walls crumbled and bricks littered the town. Many distraught survivors could only look on in desperation."

A website of the LTTE has quoted Soosai as follows on the losses suffered by the LTTE: "In Mullaitivu three of our fighters perished: Major Dharmendra, a fighter who was assigned to provide support to me and a civilian soldier we call 'Petrol Iyah' died in the calamity. In Vattuvagal and Chaalai, we didn't suffer any casualties. In Vadamaradchy East we lost three fighters manning the forward defence lines. An LTTE woman cadre who had come to Vadamaradchy East on leave died in the flooding. Loss of lives of our cadres was limited to those I have mentioned. We suffered some additional property damage. In Trincomalee and in Batticaloa two observation posts were washed away. The losses are not that significant."

However, non-Tamil and a number of non-LTTE sources have been giving differing estimates of the number of LTTE cadres killed, varying between 1,200 and 5,000. According to them, large quantities of arms, ammunition and explosives stockpiled by the Tigers have been destroyed. Tiger camps at Nagar Kovil in Jaffna, Mahalnadu, Velvetithurai, Thandamanarau, Malati, Mathagal, Mankarni, and 'Sea Tiger' camps at Mullaitivu, Nayaru, Chmmaale, Championpaththu and Chalai have been completely destroyed. Four Tiger radar centres positioned along the Mullaitivu coastal belt have been damaged beyond repair. About 200 boats belonging to the 'Sea Tigers' as well as 1,500 boats belonging to fishermen who are sympathetic to the LTTE, have also been badly damaged.

The tsunami has been a traumatic shock for the LTTE and its leadership, but there is no evidence to indicate demoralisation in the ranks of its survivors, or a weakening of their motivation. Unfortunately, only Ranil Wickremesinghe, the former Prime Minister, who initiated the peace process with the LTTE, has been conducting himself in a statesman-like manner in this hour of tragedy. He has been pointing out that despite the setback suffered by it, it was the LTTE which was the first to recover from the shock, and rush to the relief of the people. He has, therefore, been arguing in favour of routing all relief and rehabilitation through it and through organisations allied to it.

At this hour of national and regional tragedy, one could detect among sections of the Sinhalese signs of malign glee not only over the damage suffered by the LTTE, but also over the fatalities suffered by Tamil civilians. One only has to visit the internet chat rooms of many Sinhalese groups to have an idea of their mind-set. I am giving below random examples of the comments of the Sinhalese: "If we let them alone, disease will wipe them out. Sounds like the 'Seven Plagues' in Egypt to me. Let God do what man has been unwilling to do." "Nothing like a giant tsunami to ruin a good rebellion." "Those kids (children who were killed by the tsunami) would have ended up as child soldiers of the LTTE anyway." "Let them (the Tamils) rot. Perfect opportunity to go in and wipe out what's left of them." "Have their leaders strap on MEGA-bomb vests, then explode themselves. I'm sure they'll leave behind a crater large enough to bury quite a few bodies."

One finds it difficult not to form an impression that many Sinhalese feel that the tsunami has had a brighter side in that it has taught a lesson to the Tamils and the LTTE. Even Chandrika Kumaratunga and her colleagues seem to feel that the tsunami has brought the LTTE to its knees and this is the time to teach it a lesson.

The LTTE is a ruthless terrorist organisation, and Prabakaran is the most ruthless terrorist leader in the world. I have been repeatedly writing that the Sri Lankan Tamils need an LTTE minus Prabakaran and that if the LTTE throws him out and gives up terrorism, India and Sri Lanka should be prepared to do business with it. Without the protective role of the LTTE, the Tamils would be at the mercy of the Sinhalese chauvinists. Statesmanship demands that the Sri Lankan leaders should work for such a denouement through special gestures to the Tamils and the other leaders of the LTTE at this hour of tragedy. The signs of insensitivity in the attitude of President Kumaratunga are unwise and dangerous and could further aggravate the feelings of alienation of the Tamils.

(This article was published by the South Asia Analysis Group, New Delhi, Paper No. 1217, on 10 January 2005.)

Internal Dimensions To Sri Lanka's Peace Process

Kalpana Chittaranjan

The date, 22 February 2005 marks the completion of three years of a formal ceasefire between the Government of Sri Lanka (GOSL) led by Ranil Wickremesinghe and the Liberation Tigers of Tamil Eelam (LTTE). Despite this long ceasefire, real peace continues to be a distant dream, with solutions for an end to this long drawn ethnic strife remaining elusive to the island in the 47th year of an Independence. While it is important that the two warring sides come to some sort of an understanding before the suspended talks can be resumed, it is equally important that all the major political parties reach a united stand on this, the most urgent issue facing the country. Given the events that have occurred over the last three years, can it be said that the peace process is not in jeopardy, and that there is lesser threat of a resumption of the violent conflict – a conflict that has taken about 64,000 lives over the last two decades? It is difficult to answer this question with a straight 'Yes' or 'No'. But a Lanka-watcher, looking back at some of the major events, does reach certain conclusions as to where the peace-process is heading. Probably the most important indicator to the direction of this process is the politics of Lanka's (Sinhalese) South.

When the LTTE dropped its long-standing independence demand for Sri Lanka's northern and eastern regions in December 2002, the Wickremesinghe Government agreed to discuss the formulation of a new federal Constitution, providing the Tamil-majority areas with a high degree of autonomy within a unitary State. President Chandrika Kumaratunga was virtually excluded from the talks that ensued, arousing suspicions that a peace agreement was being brokered without her input or consent. This resulted in a power struggle between the President and the Prime Minister. The tussle became public when the letters exchanged between the two became a debate on defense strategy, and were published in the country's dailies.

The President fired the first salvo when on 12 September 2003 she wrote to Wickremesinghe about the LTTE threat to the Trincomalee naval base and harbour. Her letter stated that after receiving reports for several months about "the deteriorating security situation around the trincomalee base and harbour", she had requested of the army and navy commanders to make a presentation to her on the security situation there, "with special reference to the LTTE's armed presence in the form of camps, etc". According to her, the commanders had reported back that "there are 13 camps set up by the LTTE after the signing" of the ceasefire MoU. In his reply on 17 September, Wickremesinghe denied the remarks attributed to him in the *Lankadeepa* issue of 5 September, and made a pointed reference to the military operations against the LTTE when the Sri Lanka Freedom Party (SLFP) was in power and Kumaratunga was the President.

As the last missive in the 'letters episode' Kumaratunga, on 6 October, shot off a 11-page response to the Prime Minister. She said: "I find that your letter does not reply to the important security concerns that I have raised in my letter Your responses are evasive, and attempt to divert attention from the very serious threat to national security, by your acts of omissions and commissions in the name of the peace process". While the letter did not strictly confine itself to the "Trincomalee Naval Base and Harbour", the title of the letter, it did solidify her contention that the harbour and the base were in serious danger. She gave credence to her claim by basing it on the reports of the US PACOM Assessment Team, and of the army and navy Chiefs.

It is clear that only on the surface did the letters concern themselves with the serious matters of national security. They soon degenerated into conduits for the two rival leaders of the country to score points over each other, by exchanging allegations and counter-allegations. Earlier, in October, the World Bank Director for Sri Lanka, Peter Harrold, had noted firmly: "It is important we start to see some bi-partisan approach to peace now." In an interview (*Sunday Times*, 5 October 2003), he said that the biggest fear among donors was that the necessary situation of a bi-partisan governance could not be brought about when confronted with "chances of peace falling victim to the short-term dictates of politics". His fears soon became a reality. On 3 November Kumaratunga declared a two-day state of emergency when Wickremesinghe was on a tour of the US. She took over the three crucial portfolios of Defence, Interior, and Information, giving as reason the many concessions the Lankan Government had made during the preceding six rounds of talks with the LTTE.

The surprise move followed the LTTE's submission of an interim administration proposal on 31 October 2003, handed over to the Government by the Norwegian facilitators. The proposal called for the establishment of an Interim Self-Governing Authority (ISGA), in which the LTTE demanded political autonomy and administrative independence for eight Tamil majority districts of the North and East (Amparai, Batticaloa, Jaffna, Kilinochchi, Mannar, Mullaitivu, Trincomalee and Vavuniya), in which pro-LTTE Tamil Nationalist Alliance (TNA) holds a parliamentary majority of seats. It was to be followed by the right to self-determination, which, if a solution was not arrived at by then, could be through a plebiscite five years after the formation of ISGA. This, the LTTE proposal stated, would be the final settlement.

Peace talks, which was to resume in January 2004, had to be cancelled because the President's move deprived Wickremesinghe of control over security policy. To win a clear mandate from the electorate and consolidate her position, the President took recourse to an electoral pact with the Janatha Vimukthi Peramuna (JVP) on 20 January, dissolved Parliament on 2 February, and called for fresh elections on 2 April – nearly four years ahead of schedule.

The plan – what with its loose end – did not go according to the President's wishes. The United National Front (UNF) led by the Wickremesinghe Government was voted out of power when it managed to win only 82 of the 225 seats in the unicameral Parliament. Kumaratunga's United People's Freedom Alliance (UPFA), which is a coalition dominated by the Sri Lanka Freedom Party (SLFP) and the JVP – won 105 seats, eight short of a secure majority. The LTTE-backed Tamil National Alliance (TNA) won 22, thus becoming the third-largest party. The extremist Buddhist clergy party, the Jathika Hela Uramaya (JHU), contesting for the first time, won nine seats. The JVP boycotted the swearing-in ceremony of Prime Minister Mahinda Rajapakse, who had been a leader of the SLFP while in the Opposition, but later agreed to join the Government. The meeting point for these two parties was their opposition to Wickremesinge's stance in his talks with the LTTE which, they feared, would have led to a separate 'Eelam State'.

Norway, which had suspended its role as a facilitator in November 2003, saying it was not clear as to who was responsible for the peace talks on the Government side, was persuaded to resume its role by Kumaratunga on 23 April 2004. Earlier, in March 2003, 'Colonel' Karuna, the LTTE's Eastern Commander had risen in revolt, but was defeated in heavy fighting during April near the Verugal river, about 78 km. from Batticaloa.

It has been reported that Kumaratunga aims at abolishing the presidential form of government, now that her second and last tenure as President will soon be coming to an end. She wants to establish a parliamentary system, where the prime minister would be the sole in-charge. She does not at present have the required two-thirds majority in Parliament to amend the Constitution. The other controversy being debated furiously is the President's firm refusal to step down before November 2006, as against the UNF's vehement insistence that the presidential poll be held in November 2005.

The tsunami in December 2004 has also brought about new compulsions that the island-nation needs to solve before the question of peace talks can be taken up. Some of these include: a joint Government-LTTE mechanism to deal with relief and rehabilitation, the leader of the Sri Lanka Muslim Congress (SLMC), Rauff Hakeem's insistence that the international community deal with the Muslims at the national level as it does with the LTTE and the GOSL, the UNP's strong opposition to the ban on constructions within 100-

meters of the sea coast and; the SLFP-JVP infighting that threatens to tear the UPFA apart.

Given these conditions, one can conclude that a "no-war-no-peace" *status quo* is likely to continue, with little chance of a resumption of peace talks in the current scenario.

THE FUTURE BECKONS...

N. Sathiya Moorthy

"I feel Norway will come back to mediate between the Government and the LTTE. I only feel, Norway's suspension of their involvement was purely tactical. The President's attitude has gone through a lot of changes... and so has the Prime Minister's. All of this augurs well to work out a bipartisan approach, which is a crying need of the hour."

— Rauf Hakkeem, Sri Lankan Minister,
and President, Sri Lankan
Muslim Congress, *The Hindu,* 1 December 2003

A series of events, not all of them unexpected, since the ORF-Chennai seminar on "Sri Lanka: One Year After the Peace Accord", have refocused national, regional and global attention on the stalled peace process all over again. From the LTTE's much-awaited counter-proposals, to President Chandrika Kumaratunga's 'pre-emptive action', most of which she later denied, to Prime Minister Ranil Wickremesinghe's subsequent ice-breaking, if not path-breaking meetings with her, and to LTTE supreme Prabhakaran's much-anticipated "Heroes' Day" speech have all provided new insights into the evolving situation – again, not wholly unexpected.

To begin at the beginning, and without attributing motives to the LTTE's counter-proposals, it still beats comprehension why in the first place the organisation had to withdraw from the peace talks, particularly when it has since made its first-ever comprehensive written proposals. It would have made greater sense, and also served a greater purpose, had the LTTE let the peace process continue, as was the case, and then presented the counter-proposals to the Sri Lankan Government delegation across the table, rather than through the Norwegian facilitators. By withdrawing from the talks after going through what was considered a series of confidence-building meetings, if not measures, the LTTE has made the avoidable third-party involvement a continuing, and rather, a continual part of the peace process. After all, the Norwegians still would have had a place at the table, but the LTTE's repeated action, or inaction since President Chandrika first invited them to play a role, has made their presence central and pivotal to the peace process, at every turn. Worse still, such a course has also taken the peace process back to square one, so to say, whenever it was seen as making some progress.

The import of the situation would become clear when one considers the ground situation, between the time the LTTE pulled out of the talks and when it presented its counter-proposals, expressing an explicit willingness for reviving the peace process. Apart from LTTE political wing leader S.P. Tamilselvan, who said as much in his covering-letter for the counter-proposals, handed over to the Norwegian team, Prabhakaran has hinted at it in his annual "Heroes' Day" address on 27 November 2003. Foreign delegations that have met him during the period at Killinochchi too have reportedly returned with such a feeling. While it is a welcome sign, again questions remain. Having cited the demand for the Sri Lankan armed forces to withdraw from the 'High-Security Zones' (HSZ) in their possession in the Tamil-majority areas as the main reason for pulling out of the negotiations process, there is no guarantee now that the LTTE would not revive the same demand all over again, at a time of its choosing. This is particularly so because the ground situation on the HSZ has not changed since they withdrew from the peace talks. Not only has the Sri Lankan armed forces not withdrawn from the HSZ, no Sri Lankan Government leader, including anyone from the 'dovish' Prime Minister Ranil's camp, has said anything even remotely hinting at the possibility. By pulling out of the 'talks-on-talks' process when it did, the LTTE only revived fading suspicions about its recalcitrant attitude and motives from the past.

It is this underlying commonality of assessments between the two rival 'Sinhala majors', respectively headed by the President and that Prime Minister, that seems to have helped reconciliation between the two camps – a possibility in the days and weeks following the LTTE's counter-proposals. Both the Sinhala camps realise the futility and possibilities of going back to war. More importantly, President Chandrika and Prime Minister Ranil have been equally vociferous in 'marketing' the 'peace initiative', and the consequent 'peace dividend' in their respective times. They do not suffer from the 'Sinhala baggage' from the past, as of their predecessors did. If anything, the two decades of ethnic war has made both leaders realistic enough to accept the need for peace, and hence the peace negotiations. They also realise that they need to make amends for the mistakes made by their Sinhala predecessors *vis a vis* the Tamil minority population. While at the helm, they have taken the peace initiative in turn. Yet, in the Opposition, they have sounded the alarm, and not always for political reasons.

Shorn of personal egos, Ranil may have learnt in power what he did not know while in the Opposition, when his UNP stoutly shouted down President Chandrika's peace initiative with the LTTE. Conversely, President Chandrika's bugle-sounding in recent times may be born out of her experience at peace-making with the LTTE. It was her Government that had suffered the humiliation of Elephant Pass and Katunayake Air base, just as it had relished the re-capture of Jaffna town, earlier. The former events turned the tables not just on the Chandrika leadership but also on the Sri Lankan Establishment, when they were hopeful of negotiating with the LTTE from a position of strength since the recapture of Jaffna town.

The President's 'much-anticipated over-reaction' as witnessed by to the divestment of 'sensitive portfolios' of three Ministers, the proroguing of Parliament and the perceived imposition of emergency all came at a time when the Prime Minister was away, touring the US. Ranil reacted the way anyone would have done in his place. If Chandrika hurt the larger 'Sri Lankan sentiments' by initiating these steps when the Prime Minister was away in a foreign land, about to meet with the world's most important leader, namely, President George Bush of the US, Ranil too did not acquit himself, too well. He repeatedly asserted, at home and abroad, that "President Bush is with me, the US Congress is with me" – a fact that may not have gone down well with the average Sri Lankan, who loves his nation's sovereignty and territorial integrity as much as the LTTE would when it came to a separate 'Tamil Eelam'.

President Chandrika's 'failed blitzkrieg', if it needed be termed so, did serve more than one purpose. While making the political waters murkier, and constitutional positions even more confusing than already, it halted the run-away euphoria, or signs of paranoia, coming to attend on the LTTE's counter-proposals without any real cause or justification for either. Her actions shocked the nation into re-taking stock of the events from the previous fortnight, which meant no real change either way, on the ground. Two, it reflected the sentiments of a few constituencies that had begun feeling restless and uncomfortable at perceptions of the Ranil Government doing business with the LTTE, purportedly on the latter's terms. Included in this list were the 'southern Sinhala radicals', the demoralised sections of the armed forces, and even the minority Muslim community, which felt marginalised not only by the LTTE in their shared Tamil-speaking areas but also by the Government and the peace process. The subsequent events have since helped not only these segments, but also the Ranil leadership to halt, and then go, without over-reaching itself, or over-extending the peace process to accommodate the LTTE's whims, not wishes.

With this, some realism seems to be creeping back into the collective 'Sinhala consciousness', thus far missing since Chandrika-Bandaranaike Kumaratunga initiated the peace process after becoming Prime Minister first, and President later, in the mid-Nineties. While she did make efforts for a 'southern Sinhala consensus' in her days, it is only now that both leaders and the political parties that they represent are coming around to discussing the greater and lesser details of such an arrangement. In a way, it is a now-or-never situation for the Sri Lanka peace process as a whole, what with a series of elections culminating in the presidential polls of 2005 commencing their long journey in a couple of months. Electoral compulsions could still have the better of political realities, and this may become truer at every stage and at every turn, even if the President and the Prime Minister agree to agree on various aspects of the peace negotiations from now on.

For his part, Prabhakaran, in his "Heroes' Day" address has accused the southern 'Sinhala politics' for the prevalent and possible derailing of the peace process. He has particularly targeted President Chandrika, hoping for the Prime Minister's United National Party (UNP) and United National Front (UNF) to take it from there. Ironically, it is in the fortnight preceding Prabhakaran's complaint that the ruling UNP-UNF and the Opposition People's Alliance (PA), led by the President's Sri Lanka Freedom Party (SLFP), had ever spoken in any serious way about a possible 'southern patch-up', or consensus.

This becomes particularly relevant and all the more important, considering that any constitutional amendment for actualising a possible accord with the LTTE would require a two-thirds majority in Parliament, followed by a simple majority in a nation-wide referendum. This requires a 'southern consensus' at least in the present Parliament, with no guarantee of a 'clean sweep' for any party in the West. If the LTTE is serious about a peace accord, Prabhakaran should be welcoming the perceivable coming together of the two major Sinhala forces, not needle at the perceptible differences. Such differences also exist over the overall peace negotiations, particularly over the LTTE's counter-proposals. But the LTTE, if anything, feels hurt and wounded when any Sinhala party or leader voices concern.

LTTE's Proposals

It should be conceded that the LTTE's proposals on an Interim Self-Governing Authority (ISGA) have been crafted by the most committed of LTTE minds, and drafted by the most trained of legal brains. There are controversial elements that are bound to cause eyebrows to raise not only inside Sri Lanka, but also in international capitals, yet it is a good document to begin negotiations on. For one thing, the negotiations by the very process involve give-and-take, and the LTTE leadership is not unaware of it. Both Prabhakaran and Tamilselvan have repeatedly stressed on the revival of the peace negotiations, thereby hinting at the possibility of the LTTE's willingness to consider alterations, if not alternatives, to the document presented by it. To the extent, the LTTE document may represent the organisation's maximalist, and not a mandatory, position.

Significantly, there is no denying the need for an 'interim administration' in the Tamil-majority areas in the North and the East of Sri Lanka, pending a final settlement. But the very detailed nature of the LTTE's proposals also makes it a base-document for negotiating a final settlement, straightaway. In a nutshell, the LTTE has demanded all that is there to demand, short of a separate and independent 'Tamil Eelam'. That being the case, the revived negotiations in a way will be addressing issues that need tackling in a 'full and final settlement'. This could either be a boon or a bane for the peace process, based on how much of it the LTTE is willing to keep out of the agenda for negotiating an 'interim administration'.

These are also the elements that would make the difference between a federated or confederated Tamil Province – the LTTE document calls it (un-hyphenated) 'NorthEast' – under a united Sri Lanka, whose sovereignty and territorial integrity are not tampered with, on the one hand, and a separate 'Tamil Eelam', where the Sri Lankan State, as is known, would cease to exist, on the other. Obviously, the LTTE leadership is under no illusion that no Government in Colombo, Sinhala, Tamil or Muslim, could and would grant one. At the same time, none of them is also under any illusion any more that the LTTE, or the Tamil majority in the North and the East, would settle for anything less than provincial autonomy of a substantial nature. From that also flows further devolution.

In this context, an 'asymmetrical devolution' of powers, as applicable to Jammu and Kashmir under the Indian system, may be an option, but the LTTE needs to remember – and accept — that there would be similar scope and need for further devolution of an asymmetrical nature to address the apprehensions of the Muslim minority in what would become a 'Tamil-majority Province'. The role may have been reversed for the LTTE and the Tamils, but having given cause for such apprehensions in the Sri Lankan Muslim mind through the 'ethnic-cleansing' of the Nineties, and having followed it up with selective killings even during the current period of ceasefire, the LTTE cannot complain. After all, the Tamil grouse itself has its origins in such 'ethnic-cleansing' of the kind that they had charged the Sinhala majority with, since the Fifties and the Sixties. The tail, the LTTE should know, can wag either way.

Going by the Indian example, where the post-Independence euphoria attending on the integration of States has since given place to regional, sub-regional and linguistic aspirations, now distilled to communal and casteist anticipation and expectations, Sri Lanka should go in for wholesale devolution of a substantive and imaginative nature at one go. The LTTE should as much address the question as the Sinhala majority Government, as the interests of other Tamil-speaking segments like Muslims and 'plantation Tamils' are also involved in it. A war-weary nation waiting to limp back to normality and development cannot afford frequent and interruptive visitations by violence of the present kind.

A lot of apprehensions, real and imaginary, have been expressed over the LTTE's demand for policing powers in the integrated 'NorthEast'. While at least some of the causes for such apprehensions are real, the fact remains the LTTE is already in *de facto* control of the Tamil areas, and also has a parallel police force enjoying near-similar powers. What they are seeking thus is *de jure* status for their police force, just as they are seeking similar status for their 'civilian political administration' in the 'NorthEast'. Regularisation of a police force in a newly-formed Tamil Province could provide gainful and meaningful employment to the armed LTTE cadres, who could otherwise go astray if permanent peace were to return.

Similar arguments could also be put forward on the LTTE's demand for powers over Land, Revenue and Taxation, though, there are justifiable apprehensions about the use to which the LTTE would put them. It needs to be remembered that the Sri Lankan Government and the Sri Lankan Constitution would be conferring such powers not on the LTTE leadership, but on a new Province, as and when there is a peace accord. After all, in every civilised and democratic nation with a provincial set-up of the kind that is being thought about for Sri Lanka, Police, Land, Revenue and Taxation are subjects that come invariably under the jurisdiction of the regional government.

In the case of Sri Lanka, drawing upon the Indian experience with sub-regional development administrations like those for the Gorkhas in West Bengal and the Bodoland Territorial Council in Assam more recently, the Tamil Province should be ready to concede similar powers to the 'non-territorial' Muslim minority with a seven per cent population, most of them Tamil-speaking, and spread across the country, in pockets of varying sizes. For the same reason, the LTTE may have to re-look at the ISGA proposals wherein it has sought to include the Muslims, who feel insecure almost for the very same reason.

Yet, policing powers are vastly different from military powers, in form and content, and yet the LTTE has sought them in its proposals. While not mentioning land troops by name, the LTTE has clearly demanded *de jure* recognition of a left-handed nature, for the 'Sea Tigers'. Its demand to control 'access' to the seas along the 'Tamil Province' would mean precisely that, just as its demand for controlling the maritime resources off the shores of the Tamil areas mean this and more. With the Tamil areas abutting two-thirds of the sea-front in the island-nation, such a course as part of any interim arrangement, could only fuel southern Sinhala apprehensions. The Colombo Government and its armed forces definitely share the view that such access would help the LTTE arm itself even more, in preparation for a possible final war for 'external self-determination', which the LTTE has been fond of mentioning time and again, even after signing the Ceasefire Agreement on 22 February 2002. Conversely, as part of the final agreement, no sovereign State worth the name could ever grant such a demand. That would raise the question as to what the LTTE really has in its mind, even though it is possible that the militant organisation is using the maximalist position only to derive maximum benefit at the negotiating table.

Whither India?

Starting with the LTTE's demand for 'controlling the access' to the seas along the Tamil areas, there is enough in the evolving Sri Lankan situation that could be cause for anxiety to India. Such a course implies New Delhi recognising a 'third navy' in the Palk Straits, between India and Sri Lanka, rather the Tamil areas in the north of the island-nation. Yet, too much may have been made out of the situation. For now, India, as much as the Sri Lankan Government, seems to have conferred a *de facto* status on the 'Sea Tigers'. It cannot, and does not, interfere with the 'Sea Tigers' as long as the latter does not cross into the Indian seas.

At the other end, should a final settlement in Sri Lanka were to lead to the Colombo Government granting naval power to a component Province, there is nothing that India could do about it. The fact remains the LTTE already has a fleet of commercial vessels flying legitimate flags, and at times used for contraband-trade in weapons and the like. There also exists intelligence-sharing between the navies of India and Sri Lanka, and this could either continue, or be discontinued.

Long ago, it had become clear that the Sri Lankan State, nation and the people could not address the issues at stake, not to mention solving them. A third-party facilitator, if not a mediator, thus became a necessity. No nation or group could match India in this respect. It knows the place better than any other nation, including Norway and Japan – both of which are involved in peace-facilitation to different levels. It understands the language, culture, mood and perceptions of various segments of the Sri Lankan population as none other. What more, India has been closely associated with the various Tamil groups, first from the early years of Sri Lanka's independence on 4 February 1948, and later from the days of Tamil militancy in the early Eighties, and through the 'Thimpu Talks', the Rajiv-Jayewardene Accord and the 'IPKF fiasco'.

If New Delhi is still a hesitant observer to the ongoing peace process without taking the centre-stage, the 'IPKF fiasco' should take its share. That was when the Colombo Government under then President Ranasinghe Premadasa joined hands with the LTTE to ask for the withdrawal of the Indian Peace-Keeping Force (IPKF), sent there under the Rajiv-Jayewardene Accord. It is another matter that Premadasa became expendable for the LTTE once its purpose had been served and the IPKF was out of the way. For this reason, and also because the LTTE and Prabhakaran in particular were behind the suicide-bomber assassination of former Prime Minister Rajiv Gandhi, India has been playing hard to get, at least in public perception. Which again should be a lesson for others trying their hand at peace-making in Sri Lanka.

The Norwegian facilitators, and also the divided Sinhala leadership, they have been keeping the Indian Government abreast of the developments. It would flow from the reverse that India would not have been a patient listener alone. To the extent, there is reason to believe that New Delhi has been giving its wise counsel to the involved parties on the emerging situation from time to time. But the larger question would remain if India is ready to let nations like Norway and Japan, and organisations like the European Union and even the United Nations, not to leave out the US, to muddle the waters in its backyard. Apart from the strategic stakes in it for India, the likes of European Union Commissioner Chris Patten have also conferred part-legitimacy on the LTTE before it is due, by calling on Prabhakaran at Killinochchi. Even UN Secretary-General Kofi Annan was reported to have planned one such meeting in recent months, before cancelling his South Asia visit, including a New Delhi stop-over, citing the emerging Iraqi situation for his sudden pre-occupation. That way, while the presence of the Norwegian facilitators is understandable, the role of the Sri Lankan Monitoring Mission (SLMM) should cause as much concern to India, for its suggestion to confer *de jure* status on the 'Sea Tigers' as it is to the Sri Lankan Government, even otherwise.

It is in this context, Ranil Wickremesinghe's repeated assertions that the US was with him, and that the US Congress backed him need explaining. While India has been careful not to be seen as playing a useful role in seeking to narrow down the differences between the two Sinhala leaders occupying a cohabitational national leadership in turn lest it should be interpreted as an interference with the nation's sovereignty, Ranil's assertions of the kind may not help after a point. Yet, with its measured and matured approach since the 'IPKF fiasco', India has shown how a greater power in the neighbourhood could play diplomat in the internal affairs of a neighbour without being seen as a 'Big Brother'. Which is what the India-Sri Lanka Accord came to be seen as, not only by the pro-

LTTE Tamil groups in the island-nation but also by the Sinhala majority. What more, India is also believed to have influenced the LTTE to back out from the siege on the 40,000 Sri Lankan soldiers, holed up after the 'Elephant Pass fiasco', by sending out clear signals that they would not be allowed to be slaughtered, or starved to death.

So much so, Prime Minister Ranil now has the confidence to propose a land bridge between the two nations – and, repeat the suggestion at every opportunity. It would have been unthinkable for a Sri Lankan Prime Minister to propose one, even a couple of years back. A proposal of the kind, even coming from New Delhi, would have been interpreted as a sure-step towards India wanting to annexe Sri Lanka through social contacts and economic ties – and possibly military means, as well. Today, not only could a Sinhala Prime Minister wanting to become directly-elected President two years hence, make such a proposal, but there has also been no criticism, overt or covert, from any segment of the Sinhala politics or population, the JVP and the Buddhist monks, included. The opposition, instead, came from the LTTE.

Credibility Gap

While 9/11 may have contributed greatly to the LTTE's perceived perception that terrorism of the kind identified with it for close to two decades had become unacceptable to global powers, and that peace talks would be the best way out, the politico-military stalemate on the ground also had an unacknowledged role in setting the mood for the peace process. For, apart from the global watch on terrorist-funding and weaponisation attributed to 9/11, there was increasing awareness that the military position continued to be stalemated despite the demoralisation that had set in in the Sri Lankan armed forces. While the LTTE had *de facto* control of substantial areas in the Tamil-majority North and the East, legitimacy, and hence sovereignty, was lacking. After a time, the *de facto* status, which is at present a negotiating strength, could become a burden for the LTTE, what with comparative peace in the Tamil areas raising developmental expectations in the population, for which the leadership was ill-equipped, then as it is now.

The LTTE cannot project an image of 'injured innocence' and expect the world around to trust it. It carries the baggage from the past every time it moves towards the negotiations table, and it is for the LTTE and Prabhakaran to prove otherwise. This is also the baggage of the absence of legitimacy – and consequent need for responsible behaviour – that the LTTE has enjoyed as a terrorist organisation. While at a time the LTTE had a free run of weapons and terrorist bombings, suicide-killings and sea-smuggling, the legitimate Government in Colombo did not have such facilities. The Colombo Government was answerable to its people, global governments and international organisations like the UN and Amnesty International. Today when the tables are turned, and it's negotiations time, the Government is at an advantage unavailable to the LTTE. In turn, the LTTE cannot complain about the modes and methods of the civilised world, if it is really serious about a negotiated settlement. If anything, it should understand that this is only the first and easy step to democracy and domestication, which are both alien to the grain of the organisation.

Having chosen to take the hard path, and having used the confused global mood on the US war on Iraq to pull out of the peace talks when it did, the LTTE should know that the world is not as unexposed as before, to ignore its hit-and-run tactics. Suffice is to point out that the LTTE has justified the Indian decision to ignore its request to permit medical treatment for one-time ideologue Anton Balasingham, when he was named to head its team for the peace talks. Without notice, the LTTE overnight pulled him out of the peace negotiations, only to re-introduce him back again, once the revival of peace talks looked a possibility. Balasingham's revived call for India to "forget the past" and his declaration that "both sides have committed mistakes in the past" hints at equating the LTTE with the Indian Government in some way, and at the same time, cautioning New Delhi that the organisation could not be blamed if the peace process slipped out of India's hands at a later stage.

Obviously, the LTTE is playing the 'good-cop-bad-cop' game with the Sri Lankan Government and the rest of the world, including India, by using Balasingham and Tamilselvan in turn. It cannot complain now if peaceniks join critics to say that Prabhakaran has since surrounded himself with hawks. Not that many would have doubted such suggestions even earlier, but all along Balasingham has had made a difference. As with all autocratic and often dictatorial leaders, Prabhakaran would soon become a victim of his methods, the 'Stockholm syndrome' in the reverse, when his advisors would tell him only what he would like to hear – and not what Prabhakaran should hear. Or, is that the impression that Prabhakaran would want to create?

The LTTE on the one hand, and the 'southern Sinhala leadership' on the other, suffer from a credibility gap, not only against each other, but also within themselves. The LTTE and Prabhakaran may feel confident at having annihilated an alternative Tamil leadership. The more recent example is the sidelining of the 'anti-LTTE' Anandasangaree from the presidency of the near-non-existent Tamil United Liberation Front (TULF), once the dominant moderate Tamil political party, now pledged into the pro-LTTE, four-party Tamil Nationalist Alliance (TNA). The LTTE's invisible hand is clearly seen in Anandasangaree's controversial removal. But democratisation of whatever kind for the Tamil areas under a united Sri Lanka would come with options for the people.

What more, the LTTE needs to accept and appreciate that the attainment of a set political goal, diluted or otherwise, has the tendency to render the vehicle of the mission irrelevant and out-dated once that goal is achieved. The Congress movement of the Indian independence era, the Dravidian movement in Tamil Nadu, and the more recent disenchantment attending on the Asom Gana Parishad are all pointers. In the absence of an alternative focus, which now stands systematically eliminated, the currency and relevancy of the existing LTTE leadership could be prolonged, but only that much. Any final settlement should thus provide for this socio-political realism, which the 'Founding Fathers' of the Indian nation failed to apprehend and appreciate.

Ironically, it's in the absence of such 'trickle-down effect' and the post-Partition absorption of the Indian Muslim Leadership in the mainline Congress Party that new generations in the community have become direction-less. A study of the radicalised 'Muslim militancy' in Tamil Nadu may be a case in point, though it is also true of other parts of the country, to varying degrees. The over-bearing attitude of the LTTE can do precisely this to the Muslim youth in Sri Lanka, if the moderate political leadership is seen as failing the community. Current reports about the formation of a political party, 'Muslim Desam', in the Eastern Province may just be a warning signal. If, however, the LTTE leadership thinks that democractisation and the peace process are not for it, and it could go on and on with 'child soldiers', it also needs to take note of the increasing imbalance in the sex-ratio of the remnant Tamil population, even as the Sri Lankan Tamil Diaspora shows no signs or mood to re-emigrate to a 'Tamil homeland' to fight a never-ending war.

This does not absolve the divided Sinhala leadership of its failure to address the 'Tamil aspirations' far too long, or take note of the increasing disenchantment of its emerging youth population. While the Sinhalas among the youth population in an earlier generation took to the militant Janatha Vimukthi Peramuna (JVP), which could not sustain itself beyond a point, their Tamil counterparts, before long, took to militancy in the more purposeful and rather ruthless way of the LTTE. The Muslim youth now want to be heard, so does the Sinhala youth of a generation away from the JVP insurgency of 1971. Thus, politics and electoral majorities apart, the Sri Lankan Government has to really address issues that may have become non-issues for the monolith LTTE, which for the same reason would rather dismiss them as excuses. Even without this, President Chandrika and Prime Minister Ranil need to make the cohabitation of the kind work even better than they have done over the past couple of years, despite the against predictions.

Apart from the success of such cohabitations of a lesser kind in nations like India – N. Sanjiva Reddy as President and Indira Gandhi as Prime Minister was an example in the early Eighties, after the latter had 'ditched' the former once earlier in the 1969 presidential elections, leading also to the 'vertical split' in the ruling Congress – Chandrika has the example of her late mother to go by. Sirimavo Bandaranaike was a victim of the excessive concentration of Executive powers in the hands of the late J.R. Jayewardene when he became President. One can hope that Chandrika knows what it means to feel the hurt and insecurity of her mother's time. On the other hand, Prime Minister Ranil, who has been advocating constitutional amendments to dilute the presidency to 'manageable levels', may have other ideas as the next round of presidential elections approaches in 2005. He may be a credible candidate in the field, with Chandrika having run out her mandatory maximum of two terms in the high office.

All told, now is the time for a peace settlement in Sri Lanka, and earlier all the three sides – two of them Sinhala, and one Muslim – understand it, that much the better for the nation. The LTTE is in full control of the Tamil-speaking areas, and Prabhakaran is in full control of the LTTE. For now, the LTTE is also under the close-quarters observation of global nations, thus reducing the risks attending on the Sinhala political leadership, and maybe even those from the Muslim community. That has not prevented the LTTE from continuing to target low-level functionaries, including those from non-LTTE Tamil groups.

Prophesy and pontification apart, for the LTTE to be unrealistic in its expectations, and to push a tired nation to war all over again, could mean one too many things. For starters, the open seas surrounding the island-nation that has provided it with a sense of security and a reliable route for weapons and funds could well become an eternal trap, if and when global powers, including the US and India, move in, to put it out of business. That need not be the only way for the world to handle the LTTE. Instead, it could well be a part of the 'international safety-net' that Prime Minister Ranil is fond of talking all the time, without having to explain or describe what he has in mind, or what he has been promised.

ANNEXURE 1

AGREEMENT ON A CEASEFIRE BETWEEN THE GOVERNMENT OF THE DEMOCRATIC SOCIALIST REPUBLIC OF SRI LANKA AND THE LIBERATION TIGERS OF TAMIL ELLAM

PREAMBLE :

The overall objective of the Government of the Democratic Socialist Republic of Sri Lanka (hereinafter referred to as the GOSL) and the Liberation Tigers of Tamil Eelam (hereinafter referred to as the LTTE) is to find a negotiated solution to the ongoing ethnic conflict in Sri Lanka.

The GOSL and the LTTE (hereinafter referred to as the Parties) recognize the importance of bringing an end to the hostilities and improving the living conditions for all inhabitants affected by the conflict. Bringing an end to the hostilities is also seen by the Parties as a means of establishing a positive atmosphere in which further steps towards a lasting solution can be taken.

The Parties further recognize that groups that are not

directly party to the conflict are also suffering the consequences of it. This is particularly the case as regards the Muslim population. Therefore, the provisions of this Agreement regarding the security of civilians and their property apply to all inhabitants.

With reference to the above, the Parties have agreed to enter into a ceasefire, refrain from conduct that could undermine the good intentions or violate the spirit of this Agreement and implement confidence-building measures as indicated in the articles below.

Article 1 : Modalities of a ceasefire

The Parties have agreed to implement a ceasefire between their armed forces as follows :

1.1 A jointly agreed ceasefire between the GOSL and the LTTE shall enter into force on such date as is notified by the Norwegian Minister of Foreign Affairs in accordance with Article 4.2, hereinafter referred to as D-day.

Military Operations

1.2 Neither Party shall engage in any offensive military operation. This requires the total cessation of all military action and includes, but is not limited to, such acts as :

a) The firing of direct and indirect weapons, armed raids, ambushes, assassinations, abductions, destruction of civilian or military property, sabotage, suicide missions and activities by deep penetration units;

b) Aerial bombardment:

c) Offensive naval operations.

1.3 The Sri Lankan armed forces shall continue to perform their legitimate task of safeguarding the sovereignty and territorial integrity of Sri Lanka without engaging in offensive operations against the LTTE.

Separation of forces

1.4 Where forward defence localities have been established, the GOSL's armed forces and the LTTE's fighting formations shall hold their ground positions, maintaining a zone of separation of a minimum of six hundred (600) metres. However, each Party reserves the right of movement within one hundred (100) metres of its own defence localities, keeping an absolute minimum distance of four hundred (400) metres between them.

Where existing positions are closer than four hundred (400) metres, no such right of movement applies and the Parties agree to ensure the maximum possible distance between their personnel.

1.5 In areas where localities have not been clearly established, the status quo as regards the areas controlled by the GOSL and the LTTE, respectively, on 24 December 2001 shall continue to apply pending such demarcation as is provided in Article 1.6.

1.6 The Parties shall provide information to the Sri Lanka Monitoring Mission (SLMM) regarding defence localities in all areas of contention, cf. Article 3. The monitoring mission shall assist the Parties in drawing up demarcation lines at the latest by D-day + 30.

1.7 The Parties shall not move munitions, explosives or military equipment into the area controlled by the other Party.

1.8 Tamil paramilitary groups shall be disarmed by the GOSL by D-day + 30 days at the latest. The GOSL shall offer to integrate individuals in these units under the command and disciplinary structure of the GOSL armed forces for service away from the Northern and Eastern Province.

Freedom of movement

1.9 The Parties' forces shall initially stay in the areas under their respective control, as provided in Article 1.4 and Article 1.5

1.10 Unarmed GOSL troops shall, as of D-day +60 days, be permitted unlimited passage between Jaffna and Vavuniya using the Jaffna - Kandy road (A9). The modalities are to be worked out by the Parties with the assistance of the SLMM.

1.11 The Parties agree that individual combatants shall, on the recommendation of their area commander, be permitted, unarmed and in plain clothes, to visit family and friends residing in areas under the control of the other Party. Such visits shall be limited to six days every second month, not including the time of travel by the shortest applicable route. The LTTE shall facilitate the use of the Jaffna - Kandy road for this purpose. The Parties reserve the right to deny entry to specified military areas.

1.12 The Parties agree that as of D-day individual combatants shall, notwithstanding the two-month restriction, be permitted, unarmed and in plain clothes, to visit immediate family (i.e. spouses, children, grandparents, parents and siblings) in connection with weddings or funerals. The right to deny entry to specified military areas applies.

1.13 Fifty (50) unarmed LTTE members shall, as of D-day + 30, for the purpose of political work, be permitted freedom of movement in the areas of the North and the East dominated by the GOSL. Additional 100 unarmed LTTE members shall be permitted freedom of movement as of D-day + 6-. As of D-day + 90, all unarmed LTTE members shall be permitted freedom of movement in the North and East. The LTTE members shall carry identity papers. The right of the GOSL to deny entry to specified military areas applies.

Article 2 : Measures to restore normalcy

The Parties shall undertake the following confidence-building measures with the aim of restoring normalcy for the all inhabitants of Sri Lanka :

2.1 The Parties shall in accordance with international law abstain from hostile acts against the civilian population, including such acts as torture, intimidation, abduction, extortion and harassment.

2.2 The Parties shall refrain from engaging in activities or propagating ideas that could offend cultural or religious sensitivities. Places of worship (temples, churches, mosques & other holy sites etc) currently held by the forces of either of the Parties shall be vacated by D-day + 30 days and made accessible to the public. Places of worship which are situated in their respective "high security zones" shall be vacated by all armed personnel and maintained in good order by civilian workers, even when they are not made accessible to the public.

2.3 Beginning on the date on which this Agreement enters into force, school buildings occupied by either party shall be vacated and returned to their intended use. This activity shall be completed by D-day + 160 at the latest.

2.4 A schedule indicating the return of all other public buildings to their intended use shall be drawn up by the Parties and published at the latest by D-day + 30.

2.5 The Parties shall review the security measures and the set-up of checkpoints, particularly in densely populated cities and towns, in order to introduce systems that will prevent harassment of the civilian population. Such systems shall be in place from D-day + 60.

2.6 The Parties agree to ensure the unimpeded flow of non-military goods to and from the LTTE-controlled areas in accordance with Annex A. Quantities shall be determined by market demand. The GOSL shall regularly review the matter with the aim of gradually removing any remaining restrictions on non-military goods.

2.7 In order to facilitate the flow of goods and the movement of civilians, the Parties agree to establish checkpoints on their line of control at such locations as are specified in Annex B.

2.8 The Parties shall take steps to ensure that the Trincomalee - Habarana road remains open on a 24-hour basis for passenger traffic with effect from D-day + 10.

2.9 The Parties shall facilitate the extension of the rail service on the Batticaloa-line to Welikanda. Repairs and maintenance shall be carried out by the GOSL in order to extend the service up to Batticaloa.

2.10 The Parties shall open the Kandy - Jaffna road (A9) to non-military traffic of goods and passengers. Specific modalities shall be worked out by the Parties with the assistance of the Royal Norwegian Government by D-day + 30 at the latest.

2.11 A gradual easing of the fishing restrictions shall take place starting from D-day. As of D-day + 90, all restrictions on day and night fishing shall be removed, subject to the following exceptions : I) fishing will not be permitted within an area of 1 nautical mile on either side along the coast and 2 nautical miles seawards from all security forces camps on the coast; ii) fishing will not be permitted in harbours or approaches to harbours bays and estuaries along with coast.

2.12 The Parties agree that search operations and arrests under the Prevention of Terrorism Act shall not take place. Arrests shall be conducted under due process of law in accordance with the Criminal Procedure Code.

2.13 The Parties agree to provide family members of detainees access to the detainees within D-day + 30.

Article 3: The Monitoring Mission

The Parties have agreed to set up an international monitoring mission to enquire into any instance of violation of the terms and conditions of this agreement. Both Parties shall fully cooperate to rectify any matter of conflict caused by their respective sides. The mission shall conduct international verification through on-site monitoring of the fulfilment of the commitments entered into in this Agreement as follows

3.1 The name of the monitoring mission shall be the Sri Lankan Monitoring Mission, hereinafter referred to as the SLMM.

3.2 Subject to acceptance by the Parties, the Royal Norwegian Government (hereinafter referred to as the RNG) shall appoint the Head of the SLMM (hereinafter referred to as the HOM), who shall be the final authority regarding interpretation of this Agreement.

3.3 The SLMM shall liaise with the Parties and report to the R N G.

3.4 The HoM shall decide the date for the commencement of the SLMM's operations

3.5 The SLMM shall be composed of representatives from the Nordic countries

3.6. The SLMM shall establish a headquarters in such places as the HoM finds appropriate. An office shall be established in Colombo and in Wanni in order to liaise with the GOSL and the LTTE, respectively. The SLMM will maintain a presence in the distrcts of Jaffna, Mannar, Vavuniyua, Trincomalee, Batticaloa and Amparai.

3.7 A local monitoring committee shall be established in Jaffna, Mannar, Vavuniya, Trincomalee, Batticaloa and Amparai. Each committee shall consist of 5 members, two appointed by the GOSL, two by the LTTE and one international monitor appointed by the HoM. The international monitor shall chair the committee. The GOSL and the LTTE appointees may be selected from among retired judges, public servants, religious leaders or similar leading citizens.

3.8 The committees shall serve the SLMM in an advisory capacity and discuss issues relating to the implementation of this Agreement in their respective districts, with a view to establishing a common understanding of such issues. In particular, they will seek to resolve any dispute concerning the implementation of this Agreement at the lowest possible level.

3.9 The parties shall be responsible for the appropriate protection of and security arrangements for all SLMM members.

3.10 The Parties agree to ensure the freedom of movement of the SLMM members in performing their task. The members of the SLMM shall be given immediate access to areas where violations of the Agreement are alleged to have taken place. The Parties also agree to facilitate the widest possible access to such areas for the local members of the six above-mentioned committees, cf Article 3.7.

3.11 It shall be the responsibility of the SLMM to take immediate action on any complaints made by either Party to the Agreement, and to enquire into and assist the Parties in the settlement of any dispute that might arise in connection with such complaints.

3.12 With the aim of resolving disputes at the lowest possible level, communication shall be established between Commanders of the GOSL armed forces and the LTTE area leaders to enable them to resolve problems in the conflict zones.

3.13 Guidelines for the operations of the SLMM shall be established in a separate document.

Article 4: Entry into force, amendments and termination of the Agreement

4.1 Each Parties shall notify their consent to be bound by this Agreement through a letter to the Norwegian Minister of Foreign Affairs signed by Prime Minister Ranil Wickremasinghe on behalf of the GOSL and by leader Velupillai Pirabaharan on behalf of the LTTE, respectively. The agreement shall be initialed by each Party and enclosed in the above mentioned letter.

4.2 The Agreement shall enter into force on such date as is notified by the Norwegian Minister of Foreign Affairs.

4.3 This Agreement may be amended and modified by mutual agreement of both Parties. Such amendments shall be notified in writing to the RNG.

4.4 This Agreement shall remain in force until notice of termination is given by either Party to the RNG. Such notice shall be given fourteern (14) days in advance of the effective date of termination.

Annexes :
Annex A: List of goods Annex B: Checkpoints.

Annex - A.

The Parties agree to ensure the flow of non-military goods to and from LTTE dominated areas of the Northern and Eastern Province, as well as unimpeded flow of such goods to the civilian population in these areas. Non military goods not covered by article 2.6 in the Agreement are listed below :

Non military arms/ammunition
Explosives
Remote control devices
Barbed wire
Binoculars/Telescopes
Compasses
Penlight batteries

Diesel, petrol, cement and iron rods will be restricted in accordance with the following procedures and quantities :

Diesel and Petrol

The Government Agents (GA) will register available vehicles; tractors and motorcycles in the LTTE controlled areas. The GA will calculate the required weekly amount of diesel and petrol based on the following estimate :

Trucks/Buses - 250 litre/week
4 wheels tractor - 310 litre/week
2 wheel tractor - 40 litre/week
Petrol vehicle - 30 litre/week
Motorcycles - 7 litre/week
Fishing vessel - 400 litre/week

Cement

Cement required for rehabilitation and reconstruction of Government property; registered co-operatives; or approved housing projects implemented by the GOSL and international NGOs and more affluent members of the society; will be brought in directly by relevant institutions under licenses issued by Government Agents. The GA shall stipulate the monthly quantities permitted for such project based upon planned and reported progress.

Cement required for individual shops/construction/house owners/rehabilitation- initiatives will be made available through the co-operations on a commercial basis. The monthly import for this purpose will be limited to 5,000 bags during the first month and thereafter 10,000 bags/month. Individual sales by the co-operatives will be registered and limited to 25 bags per household.

Iron rods

Iron rods for building constructions will be brought in to the LTTE controlled areas under licenses issued by the GA.

A monthly re-assessment will be made to assess the possibilities of removal of the above restrictions.

Annex - B.

Checkpoints agreed in Ch.2.7 are as follows :
- Mandur
- Paddirupur
- Kaludaveli Ferry Point
- Anbalantivu Ferry Point
- Mamunai Ferry Point
- Vanvunateevu
- Santhiveli Boat Point
- Black Bridge
- Sitandy Boat Point
- Kiran bridge
- Kinniyadi Boat Point
- Valachenai
- Makerni
- Mahindapura
- Muttur
- Ugilankulam
- Omanthai.

http://www.peaceinsrilanka.org/insidepages/Agreement/agceasefire.asp#A2

The third session of peace talks between the Government of Sri Lanka (GOSL) and the Liberation Tigers of Tamil Eelam (LTTE) was held in Oslo, Norway on 2 to 5 December 2002. In a frank, open and constructive manner, the parties focused on three major areas:

- Consolidation of the ceasefire
- Humanitarian and rehabilitation action
- Political matters

The parties agreed on a working outline defining the objective as well as a number of substantive political issues for negotiation.

Responding to a proposal by the leadership of the LTTE, the parties agreed to explore a solution founded on the principle of internal self-determination in areas of historical habitation of the Tamil-speaking peoples, based on a federal structure within a united Sri Lanka. The parties acknowledged that the solution has to be acceptable to all communities.

Guided by this objective, the parties agreed to initiate discussions on substantive political issues such as, but not limited to:

- Power-sharing between the centre and the region, as well as within the centre
- Geographical region
- Human Rights protection
- Political and administrative mechanism
- Public finance
- Law and order

The parties recognised that progress on political issues must be supported by the continued consolidation of the Ceasefire Agreement. New concrete measures will be taken to facilitate further de-escalation and to improve normalcy:

- The GOSL will shortly return one of the hotels in Jaffna to its original use;

- The LTTE will ensure that all future transportation of area commanders will take place under the supervision of the Sri Lanka Monitoring Mission (SLMM);

- The LTTE will accept the right of political groups to carry out political work, including in the Jaffna peninsula and the islands, provided that they are unarmed, as stipulated by the Ceasefire Agreement;

- The GOSL will, in consultation with all relevant parties and groups, evolve a solution to the problems arising from recent developments in the Delft island;

- The parties will facilitate restoration and rehabilitation of places of worship in the north and the east belonging to all religious communities.

On the basis of their firm conviction that the maintenance of law and order in the north and east is of paramount importance, the parties agreed to request the Sub-Committee on De-escalation and Normalization to propose a common approach to settling cases involving the disputed use of private property, where such use has been impeded by the conflict. Furthermore, the LTTE will ensure that the activities of their law and order mechanisms will not be extended beyond the areas dominated by the LTTE.

The parties strongly underlined the need to move rapidly on humanitarian and rehabilitation efforts in the north and east. For this purpose, the early establishment of the North-East Reconstruction Fund will be critical. The parties agreed that the custodian of the fund should be selected and modalities for its operation agreed at the next meeting of the Sub-Committee on Immediate Humanitarian and Rehabilitation Needs. The parties expressed their appreciation of the strong support extended by several governments to the peace process at the Sri Lanka Support Meeting held in Oslo on 25 November, and urged these governments to rapidly release funds needed for humanitarian and rehabilitation efforts.

The parties acknowledged the need to ensure that the priorities and needs of women are taken into account in all aspects of the peace process. To this effect, they agreed to establish a permanent advisory committee which will, on a regular basis, submit proposals relating to women's interests to the sessions of negotiations and to the sub-committees of the peace process. The committee will consist of four representatives of each party.

As a priority area identified by the parties for humanitarian action, the parties stressed the need to improve the situation for children affected by armed conflict. Inspired by the international norms protecting the rights of the child, the parties underlined that children belong with their families or other custodians and not in the workplace, whether civilian or military. The LTTE will engage in a partnership with the United Nations Children's Fund (UNICEF) to draw up an action plan for restoring normalcy to the lives of children, and the parties called on the international community to provide financial support for such an action plan.

The GOSL will, in order to arrive at the broadest possible consensus, establish an appropriate mechanism for consultation with all segments of opinion as part of the ongoing peace process.

http://www.peaceinsrilanka.org/insidepages/Pressrelease/RNG/RNG5thDec.asp

ANNEXURE 2

Parties have decided to explore a political solution founded on internal self-determination based on a federal structure within a United Sri Lanka

Oslo, 5 December 2002

STATEMENT OF THE ROYAL NORWEGIAN GOVERNMENT

The third session of peace talks between the Government of Sri Lanka (GOSL) and the Liberation Tigers of Tamil Eelam (LTTE) was held in Oslo, Norway on 2 to 5 December 2002. In a frank, open and constructive manner, the parties focused on three major areas :

– Consolidation of the ceasefire
– Humanitarian and rehabilitation action
– Policical matters

The Parties agreed on a working outline defining the objective as well as a number of substantive political issues for negotiation.

Responding to a proposal by the leadership of the LTTE, the parties agreed to explore a solution founded on the principle of internal self-determination in areas of historical habitation of the Tamil-speaking peoples, based on a federal structure within a United Sri Lanka. The parties acknowledged that the solution has to be acceptable to all communities.

Guided by this objective, the parties agreed to initiate discussion on substantive political issues such as, but not limited to :

– Power-sharing between the centre and the region, as well as within the centre
– Geographical region
– Human Rights protection
– Political and administrative mechanism
– Public finance
– Law and order

The parties recognised that progress on political issues must be supported by the continued consolidation of the Ceasefire Agreement. Now concrete measures will be taken to facilitate further de escalation and to improve normalcy :

The GOSL will shortly return one of the hotels in Jaffna to its original use.

The LTTE will ensure that all future transportation of area commanders will take place under the supervision of the Sri Lanka Monitoring Mission (SLMM).

The LTTE will accept the right of political groups to carry out political work, including in the Jaffna peninsula and the islands, provided that they are unarmed, as stipulated by the Ceasefire Agreement.

The GOSL will, in consultation with all relevant parties and groups, evolve a solution to the problems arising from recent developments in the Delft Island.

The parties will facilitate restoration and rehabilitation of places of worship in the north and the east belonging to all religious communities.

On the basis of their firm conviction that the maintenance of law and order in the north and east is of paramount importance, the parties agreed to request the Sub-Committee on De-escalation and Normalization to propose a common approach to settle cases involving the disputed use of private property, where such use has been impeded by the conflict. Furthermore, the LTTE will ensure that the activities of their law and order mechanisms will nor be extended beyond the areas dominated by the LTTE.

The parties strongly underlined the need to move rapidly on humanitarian and rehabilitarion efforts in the north and east. For this purpose, the early establishment of the North-East Reconstruction Fund will be critical. The parties agreed that the custodian of the fund should be selected and modalities for its operation agreed at the next meeting of tyhe Sub-Committee on Immediate Humanitarian and Rehabilitation Needs. The parties expressed their appreciation of the strong support extended by several governments to the peace process at the Sri Lanka Support Meeting held in Oslo on 25th November, and urged these governments to rapidly release funds needed for humanitarian and rehabilitation efforts.

The parties acknowledged the need to ensure that the priorities and needs of wome4n are taken into account in all aspects of the peace process. To this effect, they agreed to establish a permanent advisory committee which will on a regular basis, submit proposals relating to women's interests to the sessions of negotiations and to the sub-committee of the peace process. The committee will consist of four representatives of each party.

As a priority area identified by the parties for humanitarian action, the parties stressed the need to improve the situation for children affected by armed conflict. Inspired by the international norms protecting the rights of the child, the parties underlined that children belong with their families or other custodians and not in the workplace, whether civilian or military. The LTTE will engage in a partnership with the United Nations Children's fund (UNICEF) to draw up an action plan for restoring normalcy to the lives of children, and the parties called on the international community to provide financial support for such an action plan.

The GOSL will, in order to arrive at the broadest possible consensus, establish an appropriate mechanism for consultation with all segments of opinion as part of the ongoing peace process.

ANNEXURE 3

TOKYO DECLARATION ON RECONSTRUCTION AND DEVELOPMENT OF SRI LANKA.

10 June 2003

OUTLINE OF THE CONFERENCE

1. The Tokyo Conference on Reconstruction and Development of Sri Lanka was held on June 9 and 10 in Tokyo with the participation of Ministers and representatives from 51 countries and 22 international organizations. The list of participating countries and international organizations is attached. The Prime Minister of Japan, Mr. Junichiro Koizumi, and the Prime Minister of Sri Lanka, Mr. Ranil Wickremesinghe made opening statements. The opening session was chaired by Mr. Yasushi Akashi, Representative of the Government of Japan.

2. Japan, Norway, the United States and the European Union (Presidency and Commission) functioned as co-chairs of the Conference. Representatives of the co-chairs, Minister

for Foreign Affairs of Japan, Ms. Yoriko Kawaguchi; State Secretary, the Ministry of Foreign Affairs of Norway, Mr. Olav Kjoerven; Deputy Secretary of State of the United States, Mr. Richard L. Armitage; Mr. Ioannis Theophanopoulos, representing the Presidency of the European Union; and Mr. Bernhard Zepter, representing the European Commission, delivered statements at the opening session. The President of the Asian Development Bank (ADB), Mr. Tadao Chino also delivered a statement at this session, followed by a video message from the President of the World Bank, Mr. James Wolfensohn.

3. In the operative session, the Governor of the Central Bank of Sri Lanka, Mr. A.S. Jayawardena reported on economic developments and prospects of Sri Lanka. The International Monetary Fund and the World Bank reported on Sri Lanka's macro-economic performance and the reconstruction and development agenda of Sri Lanka. The ADB and the United Nations (UN) system reviewed the "Needs Assessment" of the North and East prepared by the World Bank, the ADB and the UN system in full consultation with the Government of Sri Lanka and the Liberation Tigers of Tamil Eelam (LTTE). Civil society organizations were consulted during this process.

4. In the plenary session, participating countries and international organizations presented statements which identified their intention to provide economic assistance to Sri Lanka. Presentations were made on the contributions of civil society organizations and of private enterprise to the development objectives of the country.

History of the Sri Lankan Peace Process

5. The armed conflict in Sri Lanka in the last two decades has claimed more than 65,000 lives, and has resulted in more

than 800,000 internally displaced persons and a large number of refugees from the North and East. The current peace process commenced in 2000, when Sri Lankan President, Ms. Chandrika Bandaranaike Kumaratunga, and LTTE leader, Mr. Vellupillai Pirapaharan, asked Norway to serve as the impartial facilitator for peace negotiations. The Government of Sri Lanka and the LTTE entered into a mutual cease-fire agreement on February 23, 2002, with the able facilitation by Norway. Since September 2002, six sessions of talks have been conducted between the two parties and significant progress has been achieved. Participating countries and international organizations, which met in Oslo on November 25, 2002, committed themselves to providing immediate humanitarian assistance in support of the peace process. In April 2003, a pre-Tokyo Seminar was held in Washington DC chaired by the US Deputy Secretary of State with a view to building political momentum for the Tokyo Conference.

Objectives of the Conference

6. The objectives of the Conference are to provide the international community with an opportunity to demonstrate its strong and unified commitment to the reconstruction and development of Sri Lanka and to encourage the parties to redouble their efforts to make further progress in the peace process. While only one party to the peace process is present at the Conference, the international community takes the opportunity to demonstrate its commitment to support the establishment by the parties of the necessary administrative structure for the effective reconstruction and development of the North and East. A partnership between the Government of Sri Lanka and the LTTE will be necessary to rebuild these areas effectively. Adequate safeguards to secure the interests of all other communities should be included in this framework.

7. The Conference takes note of the economic challenges faced by the country and in this context endorsed the Government's "Regaining Sri Lanka" initiative, which is a comprehensive programme to develop Sri Lanka on a balanced and equitable basis.

8. Participants express their regret over the absence of the LTTE from the Tokyo Conference. The Conference provides the Government of Sri Lanka with an opportunity to reaffirm its determination to pursue the peace process, and focus on the reconstruction and development of Sri Lanka.

Importance of the Conference in Promoting the Peace Process

9. Participants express the view that a negotiated settlement in Sri Lanka will be a landmark achievement with regard to peaceful resolution of an armed conflict. The Conference commends both parties for their commitment to a lasting and negotiated peace based on a federal structure within a united Sri Lanka. Furthermore, the Conference stresses the importance of bringing tangible dividends of peace to all the people of Sri Lanka.

Balanced Humanitarian and Economic Assistance

10. The Conference notes the importance of urgent humanitarian assistance as well as medium to long-term assistance to rebuild the conflict-affected areas in the North and East, and to assist in the development of the entire country. The Conference emphasizes the importance of taking full account of the delicate ethnic and geographical balance in providing assistance. The Conference welcomes the "Needs Assessment" of the North and East, which identified needs in

the conflict-affected areas. The donor community expresses its willingness to extend assistance to Sri Lanka based on the source material provided for the Conference namely, "Regaining Sri Lanka", the "Needs Assessment" of the North and East, the "Needs Assessment" for the conflict-related districts adjacent to the North and East, and the Bridging Document, which links the "Needs Assessments" and "Regaining Sri Lanka".

Support Indicated by the Donors

11. The participating donor countries and international organizations have demonstrated their willingness to extend assistance to the entire country, to a cumulative estimated amount, in excess of US $ 4.5 billion over the four year period, 2003-2006. In addition, some countries and international organizations have offered technical support. Others have indicated that their commitments are based upon an assumption of a viable peace process.

12. Several countries and international organizations have specified significant part of their assistance to the North and East. A number of them have indicated that disbursement of such assistance will keep pace with satisfactory progress in the peace process; and others have indicated that, given such progress, they would be willing to consider making additional commitments.

Channels of Assistance to the North and East

13. The international community remains committed to supporting humanitarian relief and human rights protection, and takes the opportunity to encourage the parties to reach agreement on an innovative administrative structure for the

reconstruction and development of the North and East. The international community also reiterates its commitment to cooperate with the parties for this purpose. This structure will itself contribute to the process of reconciliation in Sri Lanka. The Conference recognizes with satisfaction that implementation of some humanitarian assistance projects is already taking place in the North and East through bilateral and multilateral channels in cooperation with local and international NGOs. The Conference also welcomes the establishment of the "North-East Reconstruction Fund (NERF)", which is to be administered by the World Bank, as an important channel for assistance to the North and East. The Conference also emphasizes the need for flexibility by the Government of Sri Lanka and the LTTE in accepting various forms of assistance from the donor community. The donor community also expresses its willingness to assist capacity building to enhance good governance so as to ensure accountable, transparent, speedy and efficient implementation of projects supported with its assistance.

Importance of Strong and Growth Oriented Macro-Economic Policy

14. The Conference notes that it is imperative for the Government of Sri Lanka to implement the sound macro-economic policy delineated in "Regaining Sri Lanka". The Conference stresses the need to adopt economic policies aimed at reducing poverty. Sustainable development also depends upon economic growth and job creation as well as encouragement of private enterprise.

Progress of the Peace Process

15. The Conference notes that during the past sessions of the peace talks, significant progress was achieved. Donors

remind the Government of Sri Lanka and the LTTE of the importance for both parties to make their utmost efforts to further promote the peace process founded upon the principles reflected in the Oslo Declaration. Donors recognize the urgent need to support the people in the conflict-affected areas of the North and East, and make allocations towards this purpose. With regard to the North and East, priority-setting and project-implementation will take place with the Government working in partnership with the LTTE, and with adequate safeguards for the interests of all communities. The Conference expects that the Government will ensure that the assistance pledged by the donor community to the reconstruction and development of the North and East is utilized specifically for that purpose.

16. The Conference also urges the parties to move expeditiously to a lasting and equitable political settlement. Such a settlement should be based upon respect for human rights, democracy and the rule of law. In this regard, the Conference looks forward to the parties reaching early agreement on a human rights declaration, as discussed at the sixth session of peace negotiations at Hakone.

17. The Conference welcomes the LTTE's commitment to the negotiated peace process, and urges the LTTE to return to the peace talks as soon as possible. The people in the conflict-affected areas of the North and East must be able to enjoy the dividends of peace immediately. Manifest commitment by both the Government of Sri Lanka and the LTTE to further the peace process will be necessary for the provision of international assistance to the reconstruction and development of the conflict-affected areas of the North and East.

Linkage between Donor Support and Progress in the Peace Process

18. Assistance by the donor community must be closely linked to substantial and parallel progress in the peace process towards fulfilment of the objectives agreed upon by the parties in Oslo. The Conference encourages the Government of Sri Lanka and the LTTE to enter into discussions as early as possible on a provisional administrative structure to manage the reconstruction and development aspects of the transition process. The process would need the expeditious development of a roadmap with clear milestones indicating the path towards a mutually acceptable final political solution. With this in view, the international community intends to review and monitor the progress of the peace process closely, with particular reference to objectives and milestones including:

a) Full compliance with the ceasefire agreement by both parties.
b) Effective delivery mechanisms relating to development activity in the North and East.
c) Participation of a Muslim delegation as agreed in the declaration of the fourth session of peace talks in Thailand
d) Parallel progress towards a final political settlement based on the principles of the Oslo Declaration.
e) Solutions for those displaced due to the armed conflict.
f) Effective promotion and protection of the human rights of all people.
g) Effective inclusion of gender equity and equality in the peace building, the conflict transformation and the reconstruction process, emphasizing an equitable representation of women in political fora and at other decision-making levels.

h) Implementation of effective measures in accordance with the UNICEF-supported Action Plan to stop underage recruitment and to facilitate the release of underage recruits and their rehabilitation and reintegration into society.

i) Rehabilitation of former combatants and civilians in the North and East, who have been disabled physically or psychologically due to the armed conflict.

j) Agreement by the Government of Sri Lanka and the LTTE on a phased, balanced, and verifiable de-escalation, de-militarization and normalization process at an appropriate time in the context of arriving at a political settlement.

Inputs from Civil Society Organizations and Private Enterprise

19. The Conference welcomes the inputs from the civil society meetings held in Colombo on 26-27 April 2003 and in Tokyo on 8 June 2003. The Conference is of the view that the intensity and continuity of involvement on the part of civil society organizations are essential to achieve success in the challenging task undertaken by the parties. The Conference is encouraged by the dynamic role played by private enterprise. The Conference also recognizes the contribution of academic communities, trade unions, professional groups, religious organizations and others.

Monitoring and Review

20. In view of the linkage between donor support and progress in the peace process, the international community will monitor and review the progress in the peace process. In

implementing its own assistance programmes, the donor community intends to take into careful consideration the results of these periodic reviews. With full regard to the position of Norway as the facilitator, Japan, in cooperation with the United States and the European Union, will undertake necessary consultations to establish the modalities for this purpose as early as possible.

Follow-up Action

21. The Conference requests the Government of Japan, as the host country, to convey the outcome of the Conference to the LTTE.

List of Participating Countries and International Organizations of Tokyo Conference on Reconstruction and Development of Sri Lanka 9 and 10 June 2003, Tokyo

Commonwealth of Australia
Republic of Austria
People's Republic of Bangladesh
Kingdom of Belgium
Federative Republic of Brazil
Brunei Darussalam
Kingdom of Cambodia
Canada
People's Republic of China
Kingdom of Denmark
Arab Republic of Egypt
Republic of Finland
French Republic
Federal Republic of Germany
Hellenic Greece
State of the City of Vatican
Republic of Iceland
India

Republic of Indonesia
Islamic Republic of Iran
Ireland
State of Israel
Republic of Italy
Japan
Republic of Korea
State of Kuwait
Lao People's Democratic Republic
Grand Duchy of Luxembourg
Malaysia
Kingdom of Nepal
Kingdom of the Netherlands
New Zealand
Kingdom of Norway
Sultanate of Oman
Islamic Republic of Pakistan
Republic of the Philippines
Portuguese Republic
Russian Federation
Kingdom of Saudi Arabia
Republic of Singapore
Republic of South Africa
Spain
Democratic Socialist Republic of Sri Lanka
Kingdom of Sweden
Swiss Confederation
Kingdom of Thailand
Ukraine
United Arab Emirates
United Kingdom of Great Britain and Northern Ireland
United States of America
Socialist Republic of Viet Nam

European Commission
Asian Development Bank
Asian Productivity Organization
Food and Agriculture Organization of the United Nations
International Committee of the Red Cross
International Federation of Red Cross and Red Crescent Societies
International Fund for Agricultural Development
International Labor Organization
International Monetary Fund
International Organization for Migration
Multilateral Investment Guarantee Agency
United Nations Secretariat
United Nations Human Settlement Programme
United Nations Development Programme
United Nations Population Fund
United Nations High Commissioner for Refugees
United Nations Children's Fund
United Nations Educational, Scientific and Cultural Organization
United Nations Office on Drugs and Crime
United Nations World Food Programme
World Health Organization
World Bank

http://www.mofa.go.jp/region/asia-paci/srilanka/conf0306/declaration.html

ANNEXURE 4

TAMIL NATIONAL LEADER HON. V. PRABHAKARAN'S HERO'S DAY SPEECH*

LTTE Headquarters
Killinochchi
Tamil Eelam
27 November 2004

'TAMIL TIGERS WILL LAUNCH FREEDOM STRUGGLE IF PEACE TALKS ARE FURTHER DELAYED' - LTTE LEADER

The leader of the Liberation Tigers of Tamil Eelam, Mr Velupillai Prabhakaran, in his annual statement marking Heroes' Day, cautioned the Sri Lanka government that his organisation would be compelled to launch the freedom struggle of the Tamil nation if peace talks were further delayed and the suffering of his people continued.

In an urgent appeal the LTTE leader called upon the Government of Sri Lanka to resume the peace talks, without conditions, on the basis of the Interim Self-Governing Authority as proposed by his organisation.

'If the government rejects our urgent appeal, adopts delaying tactics perpetuating the suffering of our people, we have no alternative other than to advance the freedom struggle of our nation,' Mr Prabhakaran declared.

The Tamil Tiger leader severely censored Sinhala political organisations for their lack of a clear, coherent policy or proper insight into the fundamental issues underlying the Tamil national question. While pointing out that 'there is division, discord, confusion and contradiction within the Sinhala political leadership on the Tamil issue,' Mr Prabhakaran urged the Sinhala political parties in the south to openly declare their official position on the core issues of the Tamils.

The LTTE leader further asserted that the Tamil people could not continue to live in a political vacuum without an interim solution or a permanent settlement. 'The Sinhala nation neither assimilates and integrates our people to live in co-existence nor does it allow our people to secede and lead a separate existence. We cannot continue to live in the darkness of political uncertainty, without freedom, without emancipation, without any prospects for the future,' he declared.

The following is the official translation of Mr Ppabhakaran's statement:

'Today we are faced with a critical and complex situation, unprecedented in the history of our liberation struggle. We are living in a political void, without war, without a stable peace, without the conditions of normalcy, without an interim or permanent solution to the ethnic conflict. Our liberation struggle will be seriously undermined if this political vacuum continues indefinitely.

'Three years have lapsed since we entered into a ceasefire agreement with the Government of Sri Lanka, after three decades of protracted armed struggle. You are fully aware that during this period of ceasefire we have been making every endeavour, with sincerity and commitment, to seek a negotiated settlement to the Tamil national question through peaceful means. In various capitals of foreign nations, with Norway as facilitators, we engaged in peace talks with the government. The six sessions of negotiations held over the duration of six months, turned out to be futile and meaningless. Sub-committees that were set up for the de-escalation of the conflict, for the restoration of normalcy, for the rehabilitation and resettlement of the displaced and for the reconstruction of the war damaged infrastructure, became non-functional. In the meantime, the Sri Lanka government, having excluded our liberation organization, participated in the donor conference held in Washington, thereby undermining our status as equal partners in the peace process. It was in these objective conditions that our organization decided to express our displeasure and disappointment by temporarily suspending the talks. Our intention was not to terminate the talks and put an end to the peace process. During the period of suspension we urged the government of Mr Ranil Wickremesinghe to formulate and submit a draft proposal for an interim administrative structure. We emphasized that the envisaged interim administrative mechanism should be invested with adequate authority to deal with the rehabilitation of the war affected people and to reconstruct the war devastated Tamil nation.

'We were not satisfied with the three successive draft proposals on an interim set-up submitted by Ranil's government. The draft frameworks lacked adequate administrative authority and they were unacceptable to us. Ultimately, we decided to formulate our own set of proposals. We discussed with our people at different levels and consulted political experts, legal specialists and constitutional scholars in the Tamil Diapsora and finalized our proposals for an Interim Self-Governing Authority. This is an original and pragmatic framework embodying necessary structures and mechanisms to address the urgent existential problems of our people. The proposed framework is invested with substantial authority to effectively and expeditiously undertake all tasks of resettlement, rehabilitation, reconstruction and development in the Tamil homeland. We submitted this proposal to establish an Interim Self-Governing Authority to Ranil Wickremesinghe's government on the 1 November last year and also released it to the media for public debate.

'Some international governments welcomed our proposal, because it was the first time the Liberation Tigers had clearly and explicitly spelt out their political ideas in writing. Ranil Wickremesinghe's government did not reject our proposal for an Interim Self-Governing Authority to deal with the rehabilitation of the war affected people and to reconstruct the war devastated Tamil nation. His government viewed our proposals as different from their drafts, yet it agreed to resume peace talks on that basis, whereas the Sri Lankan Freedom Party outrightly condemned our interim administrative framework as the foundation for a separate Tamil state. As the leader of the Sri Lanka Freedom Party and as the President, Chandrika Kumaratunga went a step further by taking punitive action that plunged the southern polity into a crisis. Ranil Wickremesinghe's regime was suddenly and seriously destabilised when President Kumaratunga took over three key Ministries, including Defence. Eventually, following the dissolution of Parliament by the President, Ranil's government collapsed.

'The ethnic contradiction between the Sinhala and Tamil nations became acute as a consequence of the general elections held at the beginning of the year. The elections paved the way for the hegemonic dominance of Sinhala-Buddhist chauvinistic forces in the southern political arena. The Janatha Vimukthi Peramuna (JVP), an anti-Tamil political party steeped in a muddled ideology of racism, religious fanaticism and orthodox communism, won a substantial number of seats and became the third largest Sinhala political organisation. President Chandrika has embraced this racist political party as the most important ally and partner in her coalition government. This government is constituted by an unholy alliance of incompatible parties articulating antagonistic and mutually contradictory views and policies on the Tamil national question.

'While the verdict of the general election helped to reinforce Sinhala-Buddhist hegemonism in the Sinhala south, Tamil nationalism arose as a unified collective force in the northeastern Tamil homeland. The political ideals of our liberation organisation received the overwhelming support of the Tamil people. Our organisation received the popular endorsement as the sole representative of our people. Our proposals to establish an Interim Self-Governing Authority received a mandate from our people. The Tamil National Alliance gained a sweeping victory by winning twenty-two seats, thereby becoming the political voice and the democratic force representing our liberation organisation. As never before, this general election has polarized the Sinhala and Tamil ethnic formations into two distinct nations, as two separate peoples with divergent and mutually incompatible ideologies, consciousness and political goals.

'Though there was a change of government in southern Sri Lanka and chauvinistic forces were able to gain political power, we continued to observe ceasefire and wanted to promote the peace process. We informed the Freedom Alliance government of Chandrika Kumaratunga, through the Norwegian facilitators, that we were prepared to resume peace talks based on our proposal to set-up an Interim Self-Governing Authority. It was at that time confusion and policy differences emerged within the ruling coalition.

'Politically, the most powerful partner in the Alliance, the JVP, vehemently opposed granting political rights or devolution of power to the Tamil people. It has severely criticised the Norwegian government, which plays the role of facilitator. It has also outrightly rejected our proposal for an Interim Self-Governing Authority. The JVP has warned that it would break away from the ruling coalition if peace talks resumed on the basis of our proposal. The extremist, hard-line attitude of the JVP towards peace and ethnic reconciliation has become a major challenge to Chandrika Kumaratunga.

'The government of Kumaratunga is facing a multi-dimensional crisis. On one side, the international community is exerting pressure on the government to resolve the ethnic conflict through peaceful means. On the other, the donor countries continue to insist that granting of the pledged aid package is conditional upon progress in the peace talks. Furthermore, the economy of the country is sliding into an abyss. With these multiple problems, the government is compelled to engage the LTTE in peace negotiations. But the internal contradictions and the fundamental policy differences in the ruling alliance have become a stumbling block to the resumption of peace negotiations. There is no clear, coherent policy orientation, or a consensus approach within the political parties of the coalition government. Since she has aligned herself with political parties drenched in anti-Tamil racism, militarism and Sinhala-Buddhist hegemonism, the President cannot advance the peace process based on a coherent, consistent strategy and policy. This is the authentic political reality prevailing in southern Sri Lanka. This political reality of the lack of consensus is skilfully covered up and concealed to the international community.

'We submitted our proposals for an interim administration at the final stage of our negotiations with Ranil Wickremesinghe's government. The leadership of the United National Party continues to insist that peace talks can be resumed based on our set of proposals, but the Kumaratunga government is imposing a condition for the resumption of talks. The government says that any form of interim administration should be an integral part of a permanent settlement. While we are demanding an interim administrative set-up, the Kumaratunga government is insisting on talks for a permanent settlement to the ethnic conflict.

'There are important reasons as to why we are insisting on the formation of an interim administrative set-up as early as possible. As a consequence of a brutal and protracted war our people are facing urgent existential needs and immense humanitarian problems. Hundreds of thousands of displaced Tamils continue to languish in refugee camps in appalling conditions. In the meantime, the donor governments have pledged a massive aid package for the relief and rehabilitation of the war affected people. Therefore, it is of critical necessity that an interim administrative mechanism should be instituted with adequate powers to undertake the task of providing relief and rehabilitation to the suffering Tamil population and to reconstruct the war devastated Tamil homeland.

'Though we have entered into a ceasefire agreement and observed peace for three years and participated in the peace talks for six months, our people have not yet received any peace dividends. The intolerable burden of the day-to-day life problems is suffocating our people. Our people are desperately anticipating relief and resolutions to their urgent existential problems. For these reasons we want the immediate resumption of peace talks, based on our proposal, so that an interim administrative authority can be established as early as possible to address the grievances of our people. If some elements of our proposals are deemed problematic or controversial, these issues can be resolved through discussions at the negotiating table. Once the interim administrative authority is institutionalised and becomes functional we are prepared to engage in negotiations for a permanent settlement to the ethnic problem. That is our position.

Our position is reasonable. We are advocating this position in relation to the actuality of the concrete conditions prevailing in the Tamil homeland. Nevertheless, President Kumaratunga is inviting us for talks on a permanent solution, advancing a position that even an interim administrative set-up should be worked out within the contours of a final settlement. We can point out different reasons as to why she gives primacy to talks on a permanent solution. One reason could be her strategy to satisfy extremist racist elements, particularly to placate the JVP, who are deadly opposed to our proposal for an interim administration. The second reason could be to impress upon the international community that she is genuinely committed to resolving the Tamil national question. The third reason could be to prolong the peace negotiations indefinitely by opting to talk on a most intractable and complex issue. We can come up with several other reasons. Whatever the real reason, we can clearly and confidently say one thing; it is apparent from the inconsistent and contradictory statements made by President Kumaratunga that her government is not going to offer the

Tamil people either an interim administration or a permanent solution.

'I do not wish to elaborate here the bitter historical experience of political negotiations we have engaged in with the Sinhala political leadership for more than fifty years to resolve the ethnic problem of the Tamil people. This is a political truth deeply buried in the collective psyche of the Tamil nation. Over a long period of time, we had talks on linguistic rights, on equal rights, on regional autonomy, on federal self-rule and entered into pacts and agreements, which were later torn apart and abrogated. Our liberation organisation is not prepared to walk the path of treachery and deception once again.

'The Sinhala political organizations and their leadership, which are deeply buried in the mud of Sinhala-Buddhist chauvinism, will never be able to comprehend the political aspirations of the people of Tamil Eelam. None of the major Sinhala political parties are prepared to recognize the fundamentals underlying the Tamil national question. None of the Sinhala political organizations is prepared to accept the northeastern region as the historical homeland of the Tamil-speaking people, that the Tamils constitute themselves as a distinct nationality and that they are entitled to the right to self-determination, including the right to secede.

The southern political movements do not have the maturity and magnanimity or the political sagacity to understand and accept the fundamentals of the Tamil national question, nor do they possess a consensus or a collective vision on the Tamil issue. What we can observe in the southern political spectrum is division, disunity and mutually divergent, contradictory notions and policies. We are surprised to note that President Kumaratunga is showing concern and interest in resolving the ethnic conflict when political parties aligned to her coalition government are advocating incoherent and irrational policies and articulating brazen forms of racism. We wish to make an open request to all the political parties constituting the governing Freedom Alliance, as well as to the opposition United National Party, to declare publicly their official policy on the fundamentals of the Tamil national question, particularly on the core demands of the Tamil's concerning homeland, nationality and the right to self-determination.

'It will be meaningful to talk about a permanent settlement if the Sinhala political organisations have a clear, coherent policy, a proper insight and a consensus approach towards the Tamil national question. If not, there is no meaning in engaging in talks about a permanent solution. There is division, discord, confusion and contradiction within the Sinhala political leadership on the Tamil issue. Having realized the truth that the Sinhala political leadership will not be able to offer a reasonable permanent solution to our people, we submitted an interim solution. We expressed our desire to resume negotiations, based on our proposals for an interim mechanism, to provide relief to our people's urgent existential needs. But the government of Kumaratunga is deliberately impeding the peace efforts by insisting that talks should be about a permanent settlement. Having covered up the serious policy differences and internal contradictions behind the curtain of a loose political alliance, President Kumaratunga is accusing the Tamil Tigers of intransigence. We are confident that the international community will soon be able to see the real face of Chandrika, who is acting with a deceptive mask of peace.

'We cannot continue to be entrapped in a political vacuum without an interim solution or a permanent settlement, without a stable peace and without peace of mind. The Sinhala nation neither assimilates and integrates our people to live in co-existence nor does it allow our people to secede and lead a separate existence. We cannot continue to live in the darkness of political uncertainty, without freedom, without emancipation, without any prospects for the future. There are borderlines to patience and expectations. We have now reached the borderline. At this critical moment we wish to make an urgent appeal to the Sri Lanka government. We urge the government to resume the peace negotiations without conditions, based on our proposal for an Interim Self-Governing Authority. If the Government of Sri Lanka rejects our urgent appeal and adopts delaying tactics, perpetuating the suffering of our people, we have no alternative other than to advance the freedom struggle of our nation. We call upon the concerned international governments to understand our predicament and prevail upon the Sri Lanka government to resume peace talks based on our fair and reasonable stand.'

27 November 2004

Annexure 5

Address by President Chandrika Bandaranaike Kumaratunga at the Inaugural Meeting of the National Advisory Council for Peace and Reconciliation

4th October 2004

On this important occasion, I would like to thank all of you present here for having accepted my invitation to participate in the National Advisory Council for Peace and Reconciliation (NACPR). We have here with us the Mahanayake Theros, as well as religious leaders from all the religious communities and leaders of important political parties represented in Parliament. We also have present here the leaders and representatives of major Non-Governmental Organizations that have played a role in bringing an end to the armed conflict and building Peace in Sri Lanka. I wish to welcome you all and express my gratitude and that of my Government for the willingness you have demonstrated to contribute to this great enterprise of collectively seeking solutions as a Nation to the most serious challenge posed to our motherland in its post independent history.

The setting up of the NACPR is yet another step along the path of my policy and that of my Government for Peace.

Our policy for the resolution of the conflict has been made clear and stated often. It has remained consistent and unwavering.

We continue to hold the view that the resolution of the problem lies mainly in negotiations between the Government and the main protagonist, the LTTE. To this end my Governments, for the past ten years; have engaged with the LTTE on four occasions (including the present one) in an attempt to arrive at a negotiated settlement that would be durable and acceptable to the majority of our peoples. In this context we are presently seeking through intense dialogue, to recommence the stalled negotiations process with the LTTE.

I wish to state firmly and clearly that the Government is committed to do all that is required to persuade the LTTE to return to the negotiating table. But of course, whatever we undertake as a Government, will be implemented within the framework of a united Sri Lanka, guaranteeing the sovereignty of the State and the security of the Nation and its peoples.

My Government also has a stated policy of conducting an open and inclusive process, in its endeavours towards Peace. We believe that no lasting Peace could be achieved without the involvement of all major players in this country. By this I mean, the people and their elected representatives as well as the religious and civil society leaders and others.

In the course of processes undertaken by my Governments for the resolution of the conflict, we have at most times, kept the country informed and obtained their participation in various ways, such as through the 'Sudu Nelum' movement, as well as through public briefings by the government. We have now arrived at the conclusion that a more structured forum for a wider and consistent consultation with the people is required.

You are aware of complaints made by leaders of some communities, such as some of the Opposition Parties, the Muslims and also religious leaders that they have not been consulted sufficiently, during various peace processes undertaken by some governments.

We have taken all these factors into consideration when we formulated the concept of a National Advisory Council, to undertake this much required national consultative process.

We have envisaged the NACPR on the following terms:-

- Firstly, as a national forum for consultation on the Peace Process between the Government and the citizenry, mainly through their elected representatives and also through their religious leaders, as well as leaders of civil society,

- This Council will serve as a forum, where the government will keep the country informed of the progress of the negotiations process, as well as measures undertaken for ethnic reconciliation and for reconstruction and development of the North and East.

- It will also serve as a forum for its members to inform the Government of their views and concerns, with regard to the Peace Process and also for them to suggest approaches to move the peace process forward. It will be a forum for every one of the varied communities that constitute our Nation, to have their voices heard on this most crucial issue.

- In addition, interested groups could be invited to express their views and concerns to this Council.

- I also hope that this council would serve as a forum for dialogue and advice to the government on measures that need to be adopted for national reconciliation, unity and ethnic harmony.

It is of great importance that I reiterate at this point, that the Government continues to posses the courage and singularity of purpose in executing its duty and responsibility to resolve the ethnic conflict that pertains in the country. We shall not waver in our commitment to seek solutions for a lasting Peace. We remain honestly, totally and forever committed to Peace. We are committed to the hilt to a non-violent, negotiated Peace; we are committed to end the war and armed conflict.

I must underline that we do not intend to deflect our responsibilities, as a government, which we know has to be total, in resolving the problems faced by the Sri Lankan State, whoever may have caused these problems. Let it be known clearly that the National Advisory Council for Peace and Reconciliation is not designed and created for such petty and self interested purposes.

My government shall continue to engage the LTTE, who we recognize as the primary actor, in the process of negotiating an end to the conflict and attaining Peace.

My Government's dialogue with the LTTE will be a separate and priority process. But as a democratic, people's government, we are under obligation to keep ourselves properly briefed of the views and concerns of all our peoples. We are aware that many peace efforts have stumbled due to the non-inclusion of the major players of our body politic in the process.

We believe that any peace process must be open, inclusive and obtain the participation of all the people at various levels. If everyone is not willing to participate, we must endeavour to obtain at least, the inclusion of the majority of our peoples. This is why we believe that a forum or institution such as the NACPR is essential for that part of the Peace Process which should include the participation of the country.

We see the two processes as moving parallel. The Government will engage the LTTE and continue the dialogue with it, through the facilitators, while the Government will separately consult with the country through the people's representatives, within the framework of the NACPR.

The first process is not dependent on the second; neither is the second on the first.

We, the government, have clearly stated views on the resolution of the present conflict. My Government has repeatedly undertaken numerous programmes for the purpose of implementing these policies. We are not looking for ways to move away from our commitment, nor to shove off our responsibilities on the Advisory Council as a pretext to run away from the challenges of the sacred responsibility which my Government undertook to shoulder for better or for worse, when we once again accepted the reigns of government in April this year.

Here I believe that it is important that I reiterate briefly my government's policy on the resolution of the Tamil people's problem.

My governments have attempted since 1994 to adopt a new strategy and radically different attitudes in the resolution of this problem.

We studied and attempted to understand the root-causes of the conflict and the particular form it has taken in Sri Lanka, in a scientific and objective manner.

We arrived at the view that our conflict was engendered by the inability of our nation at the moment of decolonization, 56 years ago, to weld together the separate sets of aspirations of the three main communities living in Sri Lanka, into one collective national vision, in which each community could live freely and in dignity within its own separate identity, in order to comprise one whole harmonious and united whole - a strong, stable and united state.

We recognized that we had to build a new, pluralist, multi-ethnic and multi-cultural state based on the cultural, religious and social identity of the majority Sinhala people who constitute around 75 per cent of our population, as much as the two main smaller communities, the Tamils and the Muslims and the tiny groups of Malays and Burghers, who constitute the rest of the country.

We believe that the solution lies in seeking alternatives to the concept of a monolithic, unitary State - to blend power with principle, to reconcile authority with freedom. We are looking at a form of power sharing with a high level of democratic participation in decision making, law making and governance by the regional authorities or the devolved units.

We do not believe that the dismemberment of the Sri Lankan State, demanded by the LTTE through the employment of terrorist means, would in anyway be a solution to the Tamil people's problems.

We are seeking a compromise that would satisfy the aspirations of all the communities of peoples living within our State - a compromise that would be democratic and pluralistic.

We believe that the State must resolve the contradictions that have arisen between the State and the nationalist consciousness of the Tamil community. We have to find means and procedures to accord expression of this consciousness and to give constitutional, legal and political authority.

I quote here from a recent speech I made in New York at the Asia Society; "We have and we shall - do all that is required of a democratic and responsible government, to ensure that we do not return to armed conflict."

But here I must reiterate - we believe that "Peace is more than the simple absence of war". It entails active engagement to identify and rectify the root-causes of conflict'.

On the one hand, we have to address the problems of socio-economic of all disadvantaged groups in the South as well as the North and East, marginalization through an effective programme for poverty alleviation and development. On the other, we have to formulate, in discussion with the adversaries on one hand and the representatives of our polity, new structures and systems to satisfactorily meet the shortcomings and problems faced by the Tamil community, whilst safeguarding the rights and interests of all other communities.

Whilst we believe that Peace has to be negotiated, we do not believe in "Peace at any cost". We believe that the sovereignty, the territorial integrity and security of the State must be safeguarded. We believe in a just Peace, which means not only the just rights of one community or one group within that community, but the just rights of all Tamil people, as much as all other citizens. We believe in a democratic and pluralist polity that rests on the bedrock of the Rule of Law and the guarantee of Human Rights in every corner of the country. We believe in a Just Peace with Democracy.

In our search for Peace and a lasting resolution of the conflict, we have chosen the path of a negotiated settlement because we believe that even the most unreasonable terrorist group may be persuaded without the use of coercion or arms.

My friends, we believe in Life, because we believe in humanity. We believe that even the most ruthless terrorist group must sometime reassume their humanity. We abhor terror and all forms of violence in the pursuit of political aims. We condemn the continuous killings and violence practiced against their opponents by the LTTE.

We do not believe that any problem could be resolved through the destruction of life, the protection of which in the last count, is the only moral justification for the existence of all human institutions, including the State.

We remain firmly committed to our concept of resolving conflict; based on the assertion that most socio-political conflicts (whether they be expressed in ethnic, religious or other forms) have their origins in some form of injustice and unequal treatment. In the Sri Lankan case, my government was the first to publicly accept that the Tamil people have undergone discriminatory and unjust treatment by consecutive governments, although we do not accept and cannot in anyway condone, the extreme responses of one group claiming to represent the Tamil people. If the government is to turn them away from this extremism, we believe that we must begin with finding solutions to the main causes that generated the conflict.

My government is making every attempt to persuade the LTTE to return to the negotiating table from which it withdrew 18 months ago. The LTTE insists that the government should agree to discuss at first only their ISGA proposals. The government's position has been that we accept the concept of setting up an Interim Administration in the interim period, whilst a permanent solution is negotiated and implemented. But, we require a commitment from the LTTE that the Interim Administration as well as the final solution would be based on the Oslo Declaration signed by the Government of Sri Lanka and the LTTE which declared that the Federal solution should be sought within the framework of a united Sri Lanka. The negotiations with the LTTE as well as the consultation within the NACPR could work out the level and extent of devolution and other details regarding this.

Let it be known clearly and without any doubt that the Government will continue to do all that is required of it to make Peace a reality. Through the consultations which we will engage in at the NACPR we are making an attempt to include, if not all, at least the majority of our nation in this great national endeavour.

We are all aware that the majority of our peoples expect the political parties to work together on this issue. They wish us to arrive at a consensus in dealing with peace negotiations and in reaching a lasting solution to the problem. I am aware that this view is held by a large majority of people irrespective of their political affiliations, which is also a strongly held view of all religious leaders. The International community has also consistently expressed this view.

The experience of other countries demonstrates that conflicts of this nature have been successfully resolved only when it has been approached as a national issue, which cuts across the limiting boundaries of party politics. The South African case is the best example of this. Also in the UK the main political parties have agreed to a common approach when dealing with the Northern Ireland problem.

Since 1994, for ten years, I have made numerous attempts at bringing together the two major political parties, the UNP and the Peoples Alliance (PA). Various proposals for arriving at a consensus and for working together were suggested to the UNP, having overcome many obstacles to obtain the agreement of my Party and our partners in Government. Every one of my attempts have been rejected or agreed to and then promises broken. The UNP and the Tamil National Alliance (TNA) have declined to participate in this initiative whilst, the Sri Lanka Muslim Congress (SLMC) and the Jathika Hela Urumaya (JHU) have requested some clarifications.

The leader of the UNP has informed me that he is of the view that consultation could take place after the government begins talks with the LTTE. The process we begin today is a separate exercise as I have stated earlier, which is designed for all of us here to engage in a free dialogue expressing specific views held by each group represented here, in order that the government be directly and clearly informed of your views. This would serve as an essential and most important input into the planning of the negotiations process and the policies and strategies adopted by the government. We, therefore, need your views not only once talks begin but even before talks can get started.

We are all aware that the LTTE too, has held a similar view for a long time. The LTTE leader Mr.Velupillai Prabhakaran has stated on numerous occasions that without the two major political forces of the South, arriving at a consensus on the resolution of the conflict, no effective solution could be implemented to the Tamil people's problem. I quote from his most recent statement in this regard in his speech in 26th November last year.

"Whenever the party in power attempts to resolve the Tamil issue, the party in opposition opposes it and derails the effort. This mode of conflict continues even when the opposition becomes the ruling party and attempts reconciliation. This Sinhala political drama with its typical historical pattern has been staged regularly for the last fifty years."

"As a negative consequence of this chess game, in which the Tamils are used as pawns, several peace efforts have failed; several peace negotiations collapsed, several peace agreements torn apart and several peace pacts became defunct. As such, the Tamil conflict continues without resolution. The tragic life of our people continues."

I would, therefore, like to urge the leader of the UNP as well as its members to reconsider their decision and to participate in this great national endeavour we commence today of arriving at a national consensus on the country's one single most important problem.

Finally, I would like to state in all sincerity that I truly believe that we are today engaged in a bold initiative that could lead to the much desired collective consensus of our Nation, hoped for by all our peoples. This should have occurred a long time ago, but even now let us attempt to put national interest before our own and dialogue honestly based on what is realistically possible and arrive at the essential elements to attain a lasting and durable Peace.

I have just been informed that the Government of USA has issued a statement two days ago endorsing our views with regard to the Oslo Declaration and calling upon the LTTE to end violence against political opponents and to cease the recruitment of child soldiers. The US Government has also commended me for the flexibility shown by the government in our efforts to arrive at an agreement with the LTTE to renew discussions.

What I am asking of ourselves may be a tall order. The stars are far away. Yet, I continue to hope and believe in this, our Nation's ability and strength to reach for those stars if we work together honestly.

I thank you.

Available at:

http://www.presidentsl.org/data/speech/2004/address_inaugural_meeting_NAC_peace_reconciliation.htm

CONTRIBUTORS

S..D. Muni, c Professor, South Asian Studies School Of International Studies, Jawaharlal Nehru University, New Delhi.

Paikiasothy Saravanamuttu Executive Director, Centre for Policy Alternatives, Colombo

N Ram Editor-in-Chief, The Hindu

Dr. Devanesan Nesiah Director, Marga Institute, Colombo

Dr. V. Suryanarayan Former Director, Centre for South and South-East Asian Studies, University of Madras, Chennai.

Dr. V. Suryanarayan Consultant Editor and Defence Correspondent, The Sunday Times, Colombo (Page : 119)

Col. R.Hariharan, VSM (retd)

Col General Staff (Intelligence), IPKF, Sri Lanka (1987-90)

Dr Gamini Samaranayake Department of Political Science, University of Peradeniya, Sri Lanka

K. Venkataramanan, Journalist and Sri Lanka analyst

M Rasgotra, IFS(retd), Ex-foreign Secretary, Govt of India, President, Institute of Asian Studies, ORF

B Raman, IPS(retd) Additional Secretary(retd), Cabinet Secretariat, Govt of India, Convenor, ORF-Chennai

N Sathiya Moorthy, Honorary Director, ORF-Chennai

Index